Democratic Responses
to Terrorism

Other titles in the Democracy and Terrorism Series,
Edited by Peter R. Neumann

DEMOCRACY AND TERRORISM
Leonard Weinberg

CONFRONTING TERRORISM
Peter R. Neumann

THE ROOTS OF TERRORISM
Louise Richardson

Democratic Responses to Terrorism

Edited by
Leonard Weinberg

Routledge
Taylor & Francis Group
NEW YORK AND LONDON

Routledge is an imprint of the
Taylor & Francis Group, an informa business

First published 2008
by Routledge
270 Madison Ave, New York, NY 10016

Simultaneously published in the UK
by Routledge
2 Park Square, Milton Park, Abingdon, Oxon OX14 4RN

Routledge is an imprint of the Taylor & Francis Group, an informa business

© 2008 Taylor & Francis

Typeset in 11/12½ Sabon by
Book Now Ltd, London
Printed and bound in the United States of America on acid-free paper by
Walsworth Publishing Company, Marceline, MO

All rights reserved. No part of this book may be reprinted or reproduced or utilized in any form or by any electronic, mechanical, or other means, now known or hereafter invented, including photocopying and recording, or in any information storage or retrieval system, without permission in writing from the publishers.

Trademark Notice: Product or corporate names may be trademarks or registered trademarks, and are used only for identification and explanation without intent to infringe.

Library of Congress Cataloging in Publication Data
Democratic responses to terrorism/edited by Leonard Weinberg.
    p. cm.—(Democracy and terrorism series)
 1. Terrorism—Government policy. 2. Democracy. I. Weinberg, Leonard, 1939–
HV6431.D463 2008
363.325'17—dc22   2007034645

ISBN10: 0–415–96490–3 (hbk)
ISBN10: 0–415–96491–1 (pbk)
ISBN10: 0–203–93319–2 (ebk)

ISBN13: 978–0–415–96490–6 (hbk)
ISBN13: 978–0–415–96491–3 (pbk)
ISBN13: 978–0–203–93319–0 (ebk)

Contents

Contributors	vii
Foreword *Fernando Henrique Cardoso* *President, Club de Madrid*	xi
1. Introduction: Democratic Responses to Terrorism *Leonard Weinberg*	1
2. Talking Sense: Guidelines for International Democracy Promotion *Theodore J. Piccone*	13
3. Strengthening Civil Society *Mary Kaldor*	27
4. Islam, Islamism and Democracy: The Case of the Arab World *Bassam Tibi*	41
5. Militant Muslims and Democracy: Knowns and Unknowns *Saad Eddin Ibrahim*	63

6. The United Nations and Terrorism 69
   Jeffrey Laurenti

7. Negotiating with Terrorists 91
   Peter R. Neumann

8. Anti-terrorism Legislation: Civil Liberty and Judicial Alteration 101
   Laura K. Donohue

9. Human Rights and the Challenge of Terror 157
   David Cole

Index 171

Contributors

David Cole is a professor at Georgetown University Law Center, the legal affairs correspondent for *The Nation*, a volunteer attorney with the Center for Constitutional Rights, and a contributor to the *New York Review of Books*. He is author, most recently, of *Less Safe, Less Free: The Failure of Preemption in the War on Terror* (2007) (with Jules Lobel), and *Enemy Aliens: Double Standards and Constitutional Freedoms in the War on Terrorism* (rev. ed. 2005), both published by The New Press.

Laura K. Donohue is a fellow at Stanford Law School's Center for Constitutional Law and at Stanford University's Center for International Security and Cooperation. Her research focuses on national security and counterterrorist law in the United States, United Kingdom, Republic of Ireland, Israel, and the Republic of Turkey. Prior to Stanford, Donohue was a fellow at Harvard University's John F. Kennedy School of Government, where she participated in the International Security Program, as well as the Executive Session for Domestic Preparedness. In 2001 the Carnegie Corporation named her to its Scholars Program, funding the project, "Security and Freedom in the Face of Terrorism." At Stanford, Donohue directed a project for the United States Departments of Justice and State and, later, Homeland Security, on mass-casualty terrorist incidents. She has taught at Stanford in the Departments of Political Science and History, and she has written numerous articles on counterterrorism in liberal, democratic states. Author of *Counter-terrorist Law and Emergency Powers in the United Kingdom 1922–2000*, she is completing a manuscript for Cambridge University Press analyzing the impact of British and American counterterrorist law on life, liberty, property, privacy, and free speech. Donohue obtained her A.B. (with honors, in philosophy) from Dartmouth College, her M.A. (with distinction, in war and peace studies) from University of Ulster, Northern Ireland, her J.D. from Stanford Law School, and her Ph.D. in history from the University of Cambridge.

Saad Eddin Ibrahim is Professor of Sociology at the American University in Cairo. He is founder and chairman of the Ibn Khaldoun Centre for Development in Egypt. A highly respected human rights activist, he has written extensively on Islam, civil society and democracy in the Arab world. He stood as a presidential candidate in the 2005 elections after being imprisoned for organizing pro-democracy protests during the previous elections.

Mary Kaldor is Professor of Global Governance at LSE and Co-Director of the Centre for the Study of Global Governance, LSE. She has written widely on security issues and on democracy and civil society. Her recent books include *New and Old Wars: Organised Violence in a Global Era* (Polity Press, 2nd ed. 2006), *A Human Security Doctrine for Europe: Project, Principles, Practicalities* (Co-editor with Marlies Glasius, Routledge 2005), *Global Civil Society: An Answer to War* (Polity Press 2003). As co-founder and editor in chief of the *Global Civil Society Yearbook*, she directs the research programme that underpins this innovative teaching, research and dissemination project.

Mary was a founder member of European Nuclear Disarmament (END), founder and Co-Chair on the Helsinki Citizen's Assembly, and a governor of the Westminster Foundation for Democracy. She is convenor of the Study Group on European Security Capabilities established at the request of Javier Solana.

Jeffrey Laurenti is Senior Fellow in International Affairs at The Century Foundation. The author of numerous monographs on subjects ranging from international peace and security; terrorism; U.N. reform and finance; and many other issues with multilateral dimensions. As a senior advisor to the United Nations Foundation, Laurenti served as Deputy Director of the United Nations and Global Security initiative, the foundation established to support the debate on international security of Secretary-General Kofi Annan's High-Level

Panel on Threats, Challenges, and Change. Laurenti was Executive Director of Policy Studies at the United Nations Association of the United States until 2003 and currently serves on the Association's Board of Directors. He was candidate for the U.S. House of Representatives in 1986, senior issues advisor to the Mondale/Ferraro campaign in 1984, and from 1978 to 1984 was Executive Director of the New Jersey Senate. He was graduated magna cum laude in government from Harvard College and earned his Masters in Public Affairs from Princeton University's Woodrow Wilson School of Public and International Affairs.

Peter R. Neumann is a research fellow in the War Studies Dept. at King's College London. His research on terrorism and intelligence has been published in distinguished academic journals, such as *Terrorism and Political Violence*, *Studies in Conflict and Terrorism*, and *Orbis*. Shorter pieces on international affairs have appeared, among others, in *The New York Times*, the *International Herald Tribune*, the *Baltimore Sun*, *La Nacion* (Buenos Aires), and the *Straits Times* (Singapore). Dr. Neumann comments on terrorism and international security for various media organisations in Britain, the U.S., and Germany.

Theodore J. Piccone is the Executive Director and Co-Founder of the Democracy Coalition Project, a policy research and advocacy organization working to promote international cooperation on democracy and human rights around the world. Mr. Piccone also serves as the Washington Office Director for the Club de Madrid, an association of former heads of state and government engaged in efforts to strengthen democracy. He served eight years as a senior foreign policy advisor in the Clinton Administration, as Associate Director of the Secretary of State's Policy Planning Staff (1998–2001), Director for Inter-American Affairs at the National Security Council (1996–98), and Policy Advisor in the Office of the Secretary of Defense (1993–96). Mr. Piccone also served as Counsel for the United Nations Truth Commission in El Salvador and as Press Secretary to U.S. Rep. Bob Edgar. His publications include *Strategies for Democratic Change: Assessing the Global Response* (co-editor with R. Youngs; FRIDE 2006); "International Mechanisms for Protecting Democracy," in *Protecting Democracy* (Halperin and Galic, eds., Lexington Books 2005); *Regime Change by the Book: Constitutional Tools to Preserve Democracy* (2004), and *Defending Democracy: A Global Survey of Foreign Policy Trends 1992–2002* (with R. Herman). He received a law degree from Columbia University and a B.A. from the University of Pennsylvania. He can be reached at tpiccone@demcoalition.org; 202-721-5630.

Bassam Tibi was born in Damascus and educated in Germany. He is Professor of International Relations at the University of Goettingen and White Professor-at-Large at Cornell University. Between 1980 and 2006, Professor Tibi had 17 visiting professorships and fellowships in four continents including Harvard, Princeton, Berkeley, and Ann Arbor in the U.S., Université de Youndé and University of Khartoum in Africa, the Islamic State University in Jakarta, and the National University of Singapore in Asia. Among his recent books are *The Challenge of Fundamentalism: Political Islam and the New World Disorder* (1998, updated 2002) and *Islam between Culture and Politics* (published in association with Harvard University 2001, updated and expanded 2005). His most recent article on Islamist jihadism as totalitarianism was published in the journal *Totalitarian Movements and Political Religion*.

Leonard Weinberg is Foundation Professor of Political Science at the University of Nevada and a senior fellow at the National Memorial Institute for the Prevention of Terrorism in Oklahoma City and at the National Security Studies Center at the University of Haifa (Israel). Over the course of his career he has been a Fulbright senior research fellow for Italy, a visiting scholar at UCLA, a guest professor at the University of Florence, and the recipient of an H. F. Guggenheim Foundation grant for the study of political violence. He has also served as a consultant to the United Nations' Office for the Prevention of Terrorism (Agency for Crime Control and Drug Prevention). For his work in promoting Christian–Jewish reconciliation Weinberg was a recipient of the 1999 Thornton Peace Prize. His books include *Global Terrorism* (2005), *Political Parties and Terrorist Groups* (2003, with Ami Pedahzur), *Right-Wing Extremism in the Twenty-First Century* (2003, eds. with Peter Merkl), *Religious Fundamentalism and Political Extremism* (2003, eds. with Ami Pedahzur), *The Democratic Experience and Political Violence* (2001, eds. with David Rapoport), *The Emergence of a Euro-American Radical Right* (1998, with Jeffrey Kaplan). His articles have appeared in such journals as *The British Journal of Political Science*, *Comparative Politics*, and *Party Politics*. He is the senior editor of the journal *Democracy and Security*.

Foreword

In March 2005, the Club de Madrid brought together more than a thousand policymakers, officials and experts for the International Summit on Democracy, Terrorism and Security. The event took place on the first anniversary of the Madrid train bombings in 2004. Those horrific attacks not only killed nearly 200 people—injuring thousands more—they also tested the Spanish democracy. It was both appropriate and necessary, therefore, that the Madrid Summit explore the twin issues of how democracies should confront terrorism, and how terrorism should be confronted by democratic means.

The final document of the Madrid Summit, the Madrid Agenda, emphasized the need to reconcile the imperatives of fighting terrorism and the preservation (and extension) of democracy and human rights. It resulted from an extensive—indeed unparalleled—process of consultation and research, which involved the contributions of more than 250 experts. Some of the thoughtful papers and comments, which informed the formulation of the Madrid Agenda, are reproduced in this book.

The book offers fascinating insights into how the challenge can be addressed. All the experts agreed that the threat from terrorism was real, but that it needed to be fought with full respect for human rights and the rule of law. This, they said, was not only a moral imperative, but also a practical one. If terrorism represents a form of psychological warfare aimed at provoking a repressive response, it is essential for democracies to maintain the moral high ground and deny the terrorists the legitimacy for which they long.

With terrorism as an increasingly global challenge, it has also become clear that all national institutions need to redouble their efforts to improve international cooperation. No nation can defeat terrorism alone, and more cooperation in this area would not only allow the sharing of political and financial costs, but also bring the international credibility that is needed to sustain national policies in the longer term.

Most important, perhaps, the Madrid Summit and the papers in this book have made it obvious that, ultimately, only democracy will defeat terrorism. In societies in which the people themselves determine their future, terrorists lack the growth medium of resentment on which they thrive. For democracy to become a societal immune system, however, it needs to be based on a vibrant civil society and full respect for the rights of ethnic and religious minorities.

In the short term, open societies may be more vulnerable to terrorism, because they allow extremists more space to operate, to recruit and advertise their misguided views than would be available in authoritarian regimes. In the longer term, though, terrorists will be less likely to succeed, because open societies allow people to express their grievances in ways other than through the use of violence. It is no accident, I believe, that no democratic government has ever been overthrown by terrorists or insurgents.

This book shows that the challenge is far more profound than often imagined. It lies in finding the terrorists and preventing them from doing harm, but it also entails responding with calm and constraint, and building vibrant democratic societies that will reject the terrorists and their message. I strongly recommend this book not just to scholars and policymakers concerned with the issue of terrorism, but also to citizens who also have a critical role to play in fighting this global threat.

Fernando Henrique Cardoso
President, Club de Madrid
Former President of Brazil

1

Introduction: Democratic Responses to Terrorism

Leonard Weinberg

This is a volume about how democracies respond or should respond to threats posed by terrorism. Its distinguished contributors focus on the efforts of states and international organizations to adjust their policies in order to curtail terrorist violence. In adopting this focus, the contributors pose and seek to answer a number of crucial questions. Does more democracy make for less terrorism in the Middle East, or elsewhere? Or, do the emergencies brought on by terrorist campaigns justify certain restrictions on the normal conduct of democratic law? Do these restrictions, in fact, play into the hands of terrorists? Is the terrorist threat overblown and are the restrictions on democratic rights imposed by governments simply a means of expanding their power at the expense of their citizens? Should democratic governments ever negotiate with terrorists?

These questions are at the heart of the current debate on the most appropriate relationship between democracy and terrorism. Unfortunately, there is a growing tendency for the discussion to take on a scholastic character, an exchange of abstractions among academics and lawyers. It seems helpful, then, to begin our own discussion with a few examples of what the democracies are up against. Here, for example, is Lawrence Wright's account of a pre-9/11 joint Taliban/al Qaeda operation in Afghanistan:

> Saudi Arabia reportedly sent four hundred . . . pickup trucks and other financial aid as a down payment for bin Laden . . .

> [T]he money and the trucks allowed the Taliban to retake Mazar-e-Sharif, a bastion of a Persian-speaking, Shiite minority, the Hazaras. Among the Taliban fighters were several hundred Arabs sent by bin Laden. Well-placed bribes left a force of only 1,500 Hazara soldiers guarding the city, and they were quickly killed. Once inside the defenseless city, the Taliban continued raping and killing for two days, indiscriminately shooting anything that moved, then slitting throats and shooting dead men in the testicles. The bodies of the dead were left to wild dogs for six days before survivors were allowed to bury them. Those citizens who fled the city on foot were bombed by the Taliban air force. Hundreds of others were loaded into shipping containers and baked alive in the desert sun.[1]

The United Nations estimated that somewhere between five and six thousand Hazaras were murdered in these attacks.[2]

Wright reports another example of a terrorist attack on tourists in Egypt:

> On November 17, 1997 . . . Six young men dressed in black police uniforms and carrying vinyl bags entered the temple precinct shortly before nine in the morning. One of them shot a guard, and then they all put on red headbands identifying themselves as members of the Islamic Group. Two of the attackers remained at the gate to await the shoot-out with the police, who never arrived. The other men crisscrossed the terrace temple grounds, mowing down tourists by shooting their legs, then methodically finishing them off with close shots to the head. They paused to mutilate some of the bodies with butcher knives. One elderly Japanese man was eviscerated. . . . The killing went on for forty-five minutes, until the floors streamed with blood. The dead included a five-year old British child and four Japanese couples on their honeymoons. The ornamented walls were splattered with brains and bits of hair.[3]

Below are two comments about the desirability of carrying out attacks on Westerners in their own countries. The first is a brief excerpt from the well-known February 1998 fatwa issued by Osama bin Laden. The second is a comment made by a British Islamist at a more recent public conference on Islamic ideals in Great Britain.

> The ruling to kill Americans and their allies—civilians and military—is an individual duty for every Muslim who can do it in any country in which it is possible to do it, in order to liberate the al-Aqsa Mosque and the holy mosque [Mecca] from their grip, and in order for their armies to move out of all the lands of Islam, defeated and unable to threaten any Muslim.[4]

> At a recent debate over the battle for Islamic ideals in England, a British-born Muslim stood before the crowd and said [the] Prophet Mohammed's message to nonbelievers is: "I come to slaughter all of you." . . . "We are Muslims," said Omar Brooks, an extremist also known as Abu Izzadeen. "We drink the blood of the enemy, and we can face them anywhere. That is Islam and that is Jihad."[5]

What is the relationship between those issuing such threats and those carrying out such deeds and the democracies? As the attacks on the World Trade Center and the Pentagon (September 11, 2001), commuter trains in Madrid (March 11, 2004) and the London Underground (July 7, 2005) suggest, rhetoric has been transformed into reality on more than one occasion. How then to respond to the question?

Certainly one way is suggested by the "Madrid Agenda", a set of principles developed in connection with an international summit conference sponsored by the Club de Madrid (an organization composed of former heads of democratic states) and held in March 2005 to commemorate the first anniversary of the terrorist bombings in that city. The Agenda identifies terrorism as an always unjustifiable attack on democracy and human rights. Further, the Agenda goes on, terrorism is now global in scope, affecting countries on a worldwide basis. Consequently, among the remedies suggested by the Agenda is heightened international cooperation, especially under the auspices of the United Nations.

The Agenda also stresses the importance of law enforcement agencies and, on occasion, the military as well. But it qualifies their roles in the struggle against terrorism by maintaining that the forces of order must never "sacrifice the principles they are meant to defend."[6] The rule of law comes first, no matter the severity of the threat or the act.

In the long run, according to the document, only democracy can defeat terrorism. "No other system of government can claim more legitimacy, and through no other system can political grievances be addressed more effectively."[7] Other measures, e.g. anti-terrorism legislation, enhanced cooperation among law enforcement agencies, are vital but intermediate steps in the fight against terrorist violence. Ultimately citizens can only be made safe from terrorism by the maintenance of democracy at home and its promotion abroad.

Whether true or not, the views expressed in the Madrid Agenda are not completely compatible with those expressed during the eighteenth and nineteenth centuries by two key figures in the evolution of the West's liberal democratic tradition. For example, in *On Liberty* John Stuart Mill writes, "Despotism is a legitimate mode of government in dealing with barbarians, provided the end be their improvement and the means justified by actually effecting that end. Liberty, as a principle, has no application to any state of things anterior to the time when mankind have become capable of being improved by free and equal discussion."[8] And in his enormously influential *Treatise of Civil Government* John Locke writes:

> For by the fundamental law of nature, man being to be preserved as much as possible, when all cannot be preserved, the safety of the innocent is to be preferred; and one may destroy a man who makes war upon him, or has discovered an enmity to his being, for the same reason that he may kill a wolf or a lion; because they are not under the ties of the common law of reason, have no other rule but that of force and violence, and so may be treated as a beast of prey, those dangerous . . . creatures that will be sure to destroy him whenever he falls into their power.[9]

For Mill and Locke a "barbarian" and a "beast of prey" (see the conduct described at the beginning of this introduction), are not under the "ties of the common law of reason" and need not be accorded the same status as members of civilized societies. Of course neither Mill nor Locke anticipated Guantanamo Bay, Abu Ghraib or, for that matter, the Geneva Conventions. Nonetheless, the current status of "enemy combatant" comes close to what they had in mind for individuals outside "the common law of reason". The question becomes, in this age of heightened democratic sensibilities, how do we best respond to such individuals today both as they operate within our own democratic societies and as they emerge in societies where despotism appears as a normal form of government? In other words, how do we protect ourselves from the barbarians?

The answers provided by the contributors to this volume come far closer to the principles expressed in the Madrid Agenda than they do to the views of Mill and Locke. Most of the contributors advocate democratic self-control and self-improvement. The democracies should not be provoked into compromising their own principles. Doing so simply plays into the terrorists' hands. By making the democracies better in various ways, terrorism will ultimately lose its appeal. And by promoting democracy in regions of the world presently denied its benefits, alienated young people will likely take to other means of political protest, at least in the long run.

In "Talking Sense: Guidelines for International Democracy Promotion" Theodore J. Piccone recognizes the sometimes counterproductive efforts of the Bush Administration to fight terrorism by spreading democracy in the Middle East, Central Asia and elsewhere. He calls our attention to the fact that both the United States and the European Union have embarked on long-term projects of democracy promotion. He recognizes though that these democracy promotion projects confront serious opposition frequently based on claims made by various jihadist organizations and religious figures that Western-style democracy is not a universal value at all but simply a type of intellectual imperialism.[10] Consequently, Piccone also recognizes the need for subtlety in promoting democratic change. If it appears, as it does in Iraq, that democracy is being imposed by outsiders, the chances of long-term success are meager because this imposition simply confirms the jihadists' views. Of course there are also problems when democracy emerges from within as, for example, when such organizations as Hezbollah and Hamas achieve success at the polls but decline to abandon the armed struggle and abide by the rules of a new and potentially constitutional order.

Other contributors stress the importance of democratic government as a barrier likely to inhibit terrorism, at least in the long run. Free elections though are simply one element of the democratic process. In her essay on "Strengthening Civil Society" Mary Kaldor emphasizes that establishing and then maintaining the rule of law should be the highest priority. International organizations, including non-governmental ones (NGOs), she stresses, can assist governments in its promotion inter alia through the training of law enforcement officials and judges to act in conformity with international standards. When rulers attempt to stand above the law and use it as a device to repress their opponents, law itself loses the public's respect and leaves the impression there is no meaningful difference between the government and its violent challengers. In fact, there is some evidence that countries governed in accordance with the rule of law experience fewer terrorist incidents than those where the rule of law does not prevail.[11] If democracy and the rule of law are to limit the appeals of terrorist organizations they, in turn, must rest on the foundation of a strong civil society, a network, Kaldor writes, of non-governmental and non-economic associations, organizations and movements that transform private concerns into the public sphere. In the absence of a strong civil society, one in which the rule of law prevails, democratic government is a fragile set of institutional arrangements or what Fareed Zakaria defines as "illiberal democracy".[12]

Both Bassam Tibi ("Islam, Islamism and Democracy") and Saad Eddin Ibrahim, ("Militant Muslims and Democracy") are concerned about the prospects for democracy in the Muslim world. Is there something fundamentally incompatible between Islam and democracy? The answer that has become virtually standard recently is "yes", because the idea of popular sovereignty cannot be reconciled with Muslim beliefs about the rule of God. As a result, Islamic militants repeatedly stress that Western-style democracy is a heresy and an appropriate target for violent confrontation wherever and whenever attempts are made to create it within the House of Islam.

On the surface, the militants seem to be right, at least in the sense that there are few democracies to be found inside this "House". But the Islamists and other observers fail to note, as Tibi does, that Indonesia, the world's largest Muslim country, underwent a successful transition to democracy in recent years. They also fail to recognize the fact that a moderate Islamic political party currently governs a still democratic Turkey and that a number of opinion polls suggest widespread public support for democracy throughout the Middle East.

This leads Tibi to make a crucial observation: Islamism, or what we in the West often describe as Islamic fundamentalism, may very well be incompatible with constitutional democracy, but that does not mean Islam itself is. In fact, Saad Eddin Ibrahim is among Islam's most passionate advocates of democratic change in Egypt and elsewhere in the Middle East. He, like Tibi, fails to see why democratic values cannot be applied in the Muslim world in general. For his part, Ibrahim claims that the jihadists are really the products of the oppressive anti-democratic regimes that dominate in much of the Middle East.

Not all that long ago arguments abounded in the West about the inability of countries dominated by Confucian values to transform themselves into democracies. Those arguments have largely been silenced as South Korea and Taiwan evolved into democracies. If these East Asian countries have been able to sustain democratic rule then why cannot the countries belonging to the Arab world?

In his "The United Nations and Terrorism" Jeffrey Laurenti provides a history of the U.N.'s response to the threat of terrorism. He points out that on various occasions the U.N. and its representatives have been the targets of terrorist violence. For example: the U.N. negotiator in the Israel/Palestine conflict Count Folke Bernadotte was assassinated by Zionist extremists in 1948, while some 55 years later the head of the U.N. mission in Baghdad, Sergio Vieira de Mello, was murdered by Sunni Muslim terrorists when they bombed that installation. Having called our attention to these and other episodes, Laurenti notes that the U.N. was organized in 1945 largely in order to maintain the peace, but the peace among states. Unlike its predecessor, the League of Nations, which was called upon to deal with the problem of terrorism following the 1934 assassinations of the Yugoslav king and French foreign minister by agents of a Croat group, the Ustasha, in its formative period the U.N. was not much concerned with the activities of clandestine terrorist bands. The issue of terrorism rose to international visibility, Laurenti reports, during the 1960s and early 1970s when anti-colonial sentiment and hostility to Israel at the U.N. had reached a high point. As a result, when called upon to respond to the 1972 Munich Olympic Games and other spectacular terrorist attacks from the era, the U.N. General Assembly reacted by suggesting the "underlying causes" of such attacks were the policies of "colonial, racist and alien regimes." The latter constituted the real problem. End colonialism, racism and alien domination and what the colonial powers called terrorism would end. This would occur because the violence was simply self-defense aimed at freeing Third World peoples from alien oppression. Laurenti devotes the balance of his contribution to describing how the U.N.—Security Council, General Assembly and Secretariat—moved from this low point to a position where it now is engaged in a serious struggle to repress terrorism, in all its various manifestations, and to punish member states that openly or secretly promote or sponsor it.

How do the democracies get the terrorists to stop what they are doing? Many have answered this question by referring to brute force. Peter R. Neumann, instead, considers the possibility of negotiations. He recognizes the difficulties involved and first considers the obvious objections. Negotiations confer legitimacy on violent criminals. Negotiating with one band of terrorists only encourages other bands of extremists to launch terrorist attacks out of the knowledge their efforts will eventually be rewarded too. Negotiations undermine the democratic principle by assigning political influence to small groups based upon their possession of bombs and guns rather large numbers and civilized persuasion.

On the other hand, Neumann points out that, rhetoric aside, many democracies in fact negotiate with terrorist organizations. He calls attention to the 1998 Good Friday Agreement and British negotiations with the IRA and others. He also notes that the Israeli government held secret negotiations with the Palestine Liberation Organization that led to the 1994 Oslo Accords. If it is a relatively common practice for democratic governments to pursue negotiated settlements with terrorists, Neumann considers the conditions likely to bring about their success. Success, according to Neumann, depends on who the terrorists are. How do they regard the utility of violence? How internally cohesive is the terrorist organization? Can its leaders really commit the membership to a peaceful course? When should democratic governments negotiate? Timing is important, Neumann argues. Governments need to wait until the terrorists express support for a permanent cease fire. Finally, he stresses how the negotiations should be conducted. On matters of substance, Neumann argues against discussions simply between government representatives and the erstwhile terrorist leaders. Rather, long-term success depends upon bringing all the interested parties into the negotiating process—as was the case of the negotiations over Northern Ireland. Neumann though is well aware there are more cases of failed than successful negotiations. And that on occasion, a failed negotiating process leads to a resumption of violence at a higher level than was the case before it began.

The authors of the last two essays in the collection are concerned with the price that the long-standing democracies in the West appear to be paying in their efforts to safeguard their citizens against terrorist violence. Both Laura K. Donohue ("Anti-terrorism Legislation: Civil Liberty and Judicial Alteration") and David Cole ("Human Rights and the Challenge of Terror") call attention to the danger that terrorism or the threat of terrorism causes governments in London and Washington to pursue policies which seriously erode civil liberties and personal freedoms. These governments have over-reacted to terrorism and, as a result, have jeopardized the quality of their own constitutional democracies.

Following 9/11 the European Union stipulated three guiding principles to govern the responses of democratic governments subject to terrorist campaigns:

1. "All aspects of the anti-terrorist policy and its implementation should be under the overall control of the civil authorities and hence democratically accountable."
2. "The government and security forces must conduct all anti-terrorist operations within the law. They should do all in their power to ensure that the normal legal processes are maintained and that those charged with terrorist offences are brought to trial before the courts of law."
3. "Special powers, which may become necessary to deal with a terrorist emergency, should be approved by the legislature only for a fixed and limited time, at the very minimum on an annual basis . . . "[13]

Donohue's primary concern is with the second of these principles. She notes the creation of "special courts" outside the normal judicial system to try cases involving the alleged commission of terrorist crimes. Donohue mentions the formation of such courts in the Republic of Ireland, Turkey, Israel and the United Kingdom (the United States has recently gone in a similar direction with the establishment of military tribunals to hear terrorism cases involving foreign nationals). Donohue's concerns are with the relaxation of evidentiary rules, burden of proof requirements, habeas corpus and attorney–client privilege. The British experience provides Donohue with the case study that dominates her contribution. In particular she traces the development of Diplock Courts in Northern Ireland from their establishment in 1976 to the present. The Diplock Courts were created originally in response to the threat of jury intimidation. The concern was that Northern Irish loyalists and republican "paramilitaries" were making the normal jury system untenable. Jurors (or potential jurors) and witnesses were threatened frequently if they heard or testified at cases involving terrorist violence. In the estimation of Lord Diplock normal trial procedures under these circumstances became impossible. As a result, trials involving terrorism were heard by single judges rather than juries and witnesses were permitted to testify anonymously to avoid the wrath of the defendants' confederates. Donohue's essay documents the abuses to which this system has been subject over the years.

David Cole's contribution to this volume is both more wide-ranging and scathing in its assessments of the current situation. Cole thinks that all three of the European Union principles (see above) have been seriously compromised by the American and British governments' responses to 9/11 and 7/7. In fact, he believes that the whole movement in the Western world towards the defense of human rights has been placed in jeopardy as the result of the American "war on terrorism" and similar British undertakings. To quote: "In the name of fighting terror, the United States has sought to redefine and water down the prohibitions on torture and cruel, inhuman and degrading treatment; engaged in forced disappearances and indefinite detention without trial . . . and run roughshod over rights of association." The British response, Cole claims, is hardly any better. He refers specifically to legislation providing for "control orders", i.e. house arrest, for both foreigners and British nationals suspected of terrorist activity based on secret evidence. Furthermore, Cole worries that the American and British actions are setting examples for other countries with shakier human rights records to emulate with even more serious consequences in terms of human rights violations.

The result, for Donohue, Cole and others who believe as they do, is clearly ironical. Democracy and the rule of law are promoted abroad as the best long-term means to erode the appeals of terrorism. On the other hand, those same governments encouraging the spread of democracy and the rule of law elsewhere are taking steps to evade their requirements at home and also in the name of fighting terrorism. Do as we say, not as we do.

Terrorist campaigns, in fact, have been defeated in various parts of the world, often without great difficulty. Latin America during the 1970s offered a number of success stories. Governments in Argentina and Uruguay were the targets of serious challenges by ruthless terrorist organizations. These challenges were brought to an abrupt end within a matter of a month or two after the military seized power in each. The price of the military's repression of terrorism was the end of democracy, in Uruguay for more than a decade. It is precisely this outcome that those who composed the Madrid Agenda hope to avoid. Democracy should not have to be sacrificed in order to defeat the terrorist threat. The price is too high.

With these thoughts in mind, we now turn our attention to the essays in this volume.

Endnotes

1. Lawrence Wright, *The Looming Tower* (New York: Alfred A. Knopf, 2006) p. 268. The Saudis believed the Taliban would be willing to exchange trucks for bin Laden.
2. For another account see, Vali Nasr, *The Shia Revival* (New York: W.W. Norton, 2006) pp. 157–58.

3. Wright, p. 257.
4. Quotation from Daniel Benjamin and Steven Simon, *The Age of Sacred Terror* (New York: Random House, 2003) pp. 149–50.
5. "Radicals vs. Moderates: British Muslims at crossroads", CNN.com, 1/18/2007.
6. *Addressing the Causes of Terrorism* (Madrid: Club de Madrid, 2005) p. 47.
7. P. 48.
8. John Stuart Mill, *On Liberty* (New York: Liberal Arts Press, 1956) p. 14.
9. John Locke, *Treatise of Civil Government* (New York: Appleton-Century-Crofts, 1937) p. 12.
10. For a recent discussion of this subject, see British Prime Minister Tony Blair's "A Battle for Global Values," *Foreign Affairs* (January/February 2007); "Their case is that democracy is a Western concept that is bring forced on an unwilling Islamic culture. . . . Some in the West even agree." P. 85.
11. See, for example, Alex Schmid "Prevention of Terrorism: Towards a Multi-pronged Approach" in Tore Bjorgo (ed.), *Root Causes of Terrorism* (New York: Routledge, 2005) pp. 209–32.
12. Fareed Zakaria, *The Future of Freedom* (New York: W.W. Norton, 2003) ad. passim.
13. Quoted in Paul Wilkinson, *Terrorism Versus Democracy* 2nd edition (London: Routledge, 2006) pp. 83–84.

2
Talking Sense: Guidelines for International Democracy Promotion

Theodore J. Piccone

A vigorous debate is underway among foreign policy experts and democracy and human rights advocates in the United States on the ends and means of democracy promotion, especially in the Muslim world. It is taking place at a time of growing doubts about the historically bipartisan consensus on the goal of spreading democracy as an important aim of U.S. foreign policy. The debate has intensified due in part to the counterproductive way in which the Bush administration has pursued its "freedom agenda," principally its decision to invade and occupy Iraq, as well as the alarming results of elections in Palestine, Lebanon and Egypt where parties not friendly to the United States performed well. For some, the U.S. government's approach has given democracy promotion a bad name and has made it even more difficult, practically speaking, for democratic reformers in the Arab world and elsewhere to work cooperatively with the United States government.

Given the controversial nature of the issue, it is worth reviewing some basic assumptions about the topic of international cooperation for democracy promotion in order to move beyond what should be non-controversial aspects of the subject. Then I will try to elaborate some guideposts that, given recent experience with democracy and human rights promotion, should inform the democracy promotion community as well as the larger national security establishment as the United States and its allies embrace the inherently difficult yet worthwhile task of promoting democracy around the world.

Assumptions and Clarifications

Democracy is Understood as a Universal Value. Despite having attended a few too many international conferences on democracy, it still surprises me that democracy promoters are so often asked (and ask themselves) what "democracy" means. Even a prominent institution like the International Institute for Democracy and Electoral Assistance (IDEA) in Sweden, on celebrating its tenth anniversary this year, felt it necessary to explain that "[d]efinitions of democracy differ and evolve."[1] I would argue, to the contrary, that there is widespread agreement at the political level, in countries of all different cultures and religions, about the definition of democracy. Its essential principles, as endorsed by the United Nations General Assembly and over 120 governments participating in the Community of Democracies, are: respect for fundamental civil and political rights including the rights to association and expression, periodic multiparty elections that are free and fair, universal and equal suffrage, an elected parliament, an independent judiciary, a free press, civilian and democratic control of the armed forces, and the rule of law.[2] As United Nations Secretary-General Kofi Annan wrote in his 2005 report *In Larger Freedom: Towards Development, Security and Human Rights for All*, democracy has been accepted around the world as a universal value. "Democracy does not belong to any country or region," wrote Annan, "but is a universal right."[3] This language was later echoed by all heads of state and government from every country of the world in the 2005 World Summit Outcome Document.[4]

Democracy, in Practice, Differs. An essential corollary to the point above is that, in practice, democracy does take different forms in specific national contexts. There is no model democracy or recipe for success. Democratic institutions are molded over time and in response to different historical circumstances. Legitimate democratic systems, for example, can be presidential, parliamentary or mixed. But the variety among these forms of democratic governance does not undermine the universality of democracy, as long as they allow for the expression of the essential elements set forth above. It is time for the international community to put to rest diversionary debates about the definition of democracy. Instead the bedrock principles of democracy already accepted at the intergovernmental level should be used as universal benchmarks for evaluating the *quality* of democracy in any given society, keeping in mind, of course, that there is no such thing as a "perfect" democracy.

Democracy Must Always be a Home-Grown Affair. It should be self-evident that a society's ability to adopt and sustain the basic elements of representative democracy rests in its own hands. A foreign formula imposed by military force, for instance, is tainted by its nature as a victor's demand over its defeated subjects. An occupying power, therefore, can never be genuinely democratic because it does not rule at the request or with the authority of the citizens of that society. Only after the occupying power leaves can a true democratic polity be formed, and it shall rise or fall depending on the freely expressed will of the people in accordance with a democratic constitution. In concrete terms, this means that democratic consolidation in Afghanistan and Iraq is at serious risk of failure due to the way in which these democratic transitions were triggered; they may yet succeed if and when the essential elements of democracy cited above are effectively functioning free from external military intervention or widespread internal conflict.

The International Community's Ability to Influence Political Events on the Ground is Limited but Real. In a globalized, interdependent world, in which communication flows rapidly across borders, there is a growing interplay between internal and external forces which directly affects the process of political change. As noted above, save cases of military invasion, it is always the domestic forces which hold the upper hand in determining the direction and pace of reform, or whether it happens at all. But history shows that external factors—political, social and economic—do play an important role in influencing events on the ground.[5]

At one level, international actors can create an environment that will help facilitate and encourage domestic democratic reforms. This is the long-term work of democracy promotion that, as shown in so many cases, can make a difference *when local conditions allow*. The international community's role in creating an enabling environment involves a variety of tools—direct assistance to civil society groups engaged in civic education and monitoring government activities; support to independent media; international and national election observers; economic and trade incentives; educational exchanges; training and technical assistance for parliamentarians, judges and police; projects to strengthen political parties and women's political leadership; professional military ties that reward military subordination to civilian authority; etc. These kinds of external support facilitate the building blocks necessary to consolidating democracy.

Sequencing of one over the other can play an important role in the democratic transition process, but in practice is usually limited by the lack of control of dynamic political events. In addition, there is growing recognition and urgency behind the need for facilitating economic, financial, trade and debt relief assistance to fragile democracies as a way to help them deliver tangible benefits to citizens who have put their faith in a democratic system.

On a second level, the international community can play a significant role in influencing events in the short- and medium-term by applying its leverage—political, economic, and diplomatic—to favor democratic change. To do so effectively, international actors must have in place the infrastructure necessary to act quickly to prevent democratic backsliding or to take advantage of new opportunities to move authoritarian leaders out of power. This infrastructure includes bilateral and multilateral agreements and mechanisms for deterring threats to democratic, constitutional rule and for rewarding steps toward democratic consolidation.[6] Absent the political will to implement them, however, such agreements are little more than paper tigers.

The Tide of Democracy Continues to Rise, but Erosion Persists. The evidence demonstrating the growth in the number of countries governed according to basic democratic principles is indisputable. In 1983, 36 governments could be categorized as democratic, according to the Polity IV index. In 2003, the number was 64. Comparable data from Freedom House shows a rise from 55 states categorized as "free" to 89 free states during the same 20-year period. Of course the pool of countries in the sample has grown due largely to the end of the Cold War and the dissolution of the former Soviet Union, which has spawned both democratizers and entrenched authoritarian regimes.

In the former group, a new surge of democratization appears to be underway as Georgia, Ukraine and Kyrgyzstan adopt some basic features of a democratic system. At the same time, there is clear evidence that many governments which embarked initially on a democratic path have moved backwards or fallen off completely. Countries such as Russia, Venezuela, Cote d'Ivoire, Zimbabwe, and Pakistan come to mind. There is not space here for getting engaged in a debate about whether, in fact, the end of history is near or rather the tide is turning against democratization. Let's assume for our purposes that there will always be a number of countries that fail to meet basic democratic standards, and that countries will move up and down a continuum between authoritarianism and liberal democracy. It should be the task of the democracy promotion community to devise strategies for creating an enabling environment for democratic reformers at the local, national and international levels.

The United States Has a Vital National Security Interest in the Spread of Democracy and the Rule of Law. The United States finds itself in a rare moment of bipartisan agreement that the extension of democracy, human rights and the rule of law around the world is a national security imperative. Prompted in part by the attacks of September 11 by criminal groups given refuge by authoritarian regimes, Washington has identified the absence of freedom and the rule of law as breeding grounds for terrorists and other criminals bent on harming the United States. More generally, the "democratic peace" theory and its corollaries (e.g., democracies with free press do not spawn famine—Sen; democracies do not generate refugees; democracies perform better on social and economic indicators—Halperin and Siegle) have become an article of high national security strategy, although a serious gap remains between its proponents and the traditional "realist" school of foreign policy. This melding of Wilsonian idealism and national security doctrine has taken off under the current Bush administration which, faced with the attacks of September 11, has articulated a new mission: the end of tyranny in the world. As President Bush proclaimed in his Second Inaugural Address, "We are led, by events and common sense, to one conclusion: The survival of liberty in our land increasingly depends on the success of liberty in other lands. The best hope for peace in our world is the expansion of freedom in all the world."[7] Secretary Rice, who is seeking to remold the foreign policy machinery to effect this strategy of "pragmatic idealism," seems determined to reorient U.S. policy to favor small "d" democrats in ways large and small.

The Bush team has set themselves a very high bar and one which, to date, has been carried out in ways that appear counterproductive to the mission at hand. Consideration of the administration's approach to democracy promotion, particularly in the context of radical Islamic terrorism, leads to a set of conclusions and recommendations for next steps.

Guidelines for Democracy Promotion

While many experts in the democracy promotion business are well schooled in the basic approaches to the field, others in the foreign policy establishment are not as well versed. In any event, the complexity of the task calls for a constant process of learning and relearning some fundamental lessons, some of which I try to lay out below.

1. *Be Prepared for a Fight.* The business of democracy promotion, while noble-minded, in fact can be quite messy and threatening to others, even in its non-violent manifestations. It seeks to upset a status quo which a lot of powerful groups have an interest in maintaining. Moreover, international democracy promoters seek to influence internal political change from the outside, which automatically sets up an us-versus-them dynamic that can often favor the entrenched ruling class. Witness, for example, the handiwork of Robert Mugabe in Zimbabwe, a former bread basket of southern Africa now mired in famine, repression and decay. Despite his authoritarian rule, Mugabe has shored up support at home and in the region by waging an incessant campaign of demonizing "Western neo-colonialist hegemons" seeking to hold his regime accountable to the very standards his government had pledged to uphold as a member of the Commonwealth and the Southern African Development Community. Another example is Venezuela, where President Chavez's regime, which has centralized control in the main governing institutions of the country and is trying to criminalize foreign funding of civil society organizations, has regularly rallied the faithful against the imperialist enemy to the north.

Among authoritarian regimes generally, the American and increasingly European push for democratization has also had the effect of reinforcing the North–South and East–West divisions which theoretically should have receded with the end of the Cold War. At the United Nations, the bloc of non-democracies, often led by China, Cuba, Saudi Arabia, Syria and Algeria, have sought to derail various initiatives to strengthen the U.N.'s ability to promote and protect human rights. Unfortunately, they have won over G-77 and Nonaligned Movement (NAM) democracies like India, Brazil, South Africa, Jamaica and Colombia which oppose external intervention in internal affairs and find common ground in seeking to hamstring a United States perceived as arrogant and too powerful.

This is not to say that the fight is not worth having. It is. But democracy promoters need to recalibrate their tactics so that our friends in other democracies can find common ground with us rather than with China, Venezuela and Cuba.

2. *The Means Should be Compatible with the Ends.* Given the inherently conflictual nature of the task, the United States and other governments sincerely committed to democracy promotion need to think very carefully about *how* they do it. Democracy promoters have the rhetorical upper hand in this business—it is hard to argue against the principle that all citizens of all nations have the right to govern themselves in accordance with basic principles of human rights, free and fair elections, the rule of law, etc. As cited previously, these principles are well grounded in international law. Similarly, international law and practice increasingly favor external intervention once democratic rule is in place and then reversed by unconstitutional fiat.[8] Nonetheless, perhaps more than in other areas of international relations, the ends cannot justify the means (absent some sort of international legitimacy for intervention). On the contrary, given democracy's essential characteristic as locally owned and driven, one must be especially careful to pursue means which are compatible with democratic standards and supported by democracy activists on the ground. We should, first and foremost, listen to the advocates of non-violent change in country and support *their* efforts in a way that will advance the day when tyrants lose their grip on power. The types of assistance, who should carry it out, at what time and in what degree will be different in every case.

It is in this area where the Bush administration has committed a cardinal sin. By turning to the democracy promotion rationale for the Iraq war, after all the others had proven indefensible, the White House has poisoned the well for both local and international democracy promoters. After all, we are not Denmark or Canada. We are the dominant military and economic power in the world. When we deploy the full arsenal of our powers to remove a serious but not direct threat to our national security, we poke a stick in many other eyes, both friends and enemies. And to justify invasion and occupation of Iraq as the launching pad for democracy promotion not only in that country but throughout the Arab world is only throwing fuel to the fire. This administration seems to have forgotten the first half of Teddy Roosevelt's famous dictum, "Walk softly and carry a big stick."

So our first priority when constructing a democracy promotion strategy should be to "do no harm" to the local advocates of reform. This requires a much more profound level of understanding of local cultures and power structures than previously demonstrated by U.S. embassies and aid agencies. It also means having an honest discussion with ourselves and our friends abroad about how high a profile the U.S. government should have when supporting democracy-building activities. There is no easy formula—in some places, dissidents want and need the protection of the U.S. embassy in warding off repressive measures by the state. In other environments, association with the United States can spell disaster for a political candidate trying to win office. In either scenario, understanding the local context is essential. A short two-year tour by U.S. embassy personnel or even shorter rotations by USAID experts and contractors cannot provide the kind of education and training our democracy promoters need in the field.

3. *Be Consistent and Lead by Example*. President Bush deserves credit for so boldly laying claim to the cause of democracy promotion as a principal aim of U.S. national security policy. The problem, when grounding the rhetorical appeal in the stark terms the president used in his second inaugural address, is the inevitable exposure to cries of hypocrisy about current and past American behavior which tells another story. I am not calling for a standard of perfection in the business of national security and democracy promotion. However, in the era of modern telecommunications, the reverberations of a bad decision or action, especially when done by U.S. military forces, are magnified and instantaneous and seriously undermine the U.S. government's efforts to be a vocal champion of democracy and human rights.

To make the point, one need go no further than the terrible damage caused by the human rights abuses committed by U.S. forces at the Abu Ghraib prison in Iraq and the Guantánamo Bay base in Cuba, actions facilitated by a policy approved at the highest levels of the government which condoned inhumane and degrading treatment. Several other examples more directly related to democracy promotion come to mind: Washington's continued official support of coup-leader Gen. Musharaff of Pakistan or of Islom Karimov, the dictator of Uzbekistan; the call for democratic change in Egypt followed by First Lady Laura Bush's endorsement of President Mubarak's cosmetic electoral reforms; the welcoming of the Vietnamese premier to the White House despite Hanoi's continued violations of democratic norms and human rights; the backing of a military-led coup against democratically elected Hugo Chavez of Venezuela, in direct contravention of the Inter-American Democratic Charter; and the maneuvering behind the anti-democratic ouster of Jean Bertrand Aristide of Haiti.

The problem is compounded by the administration's record on

democracy and civil rights at home. Its policy on detentions, enemy combatant status, warrantless electronic eavesdropping, electoral reforms, criminal justice, indeed the very way in which it came to power in 2000 all combine powerfully to cause both cynics and allies to question the sincerity of our leaders' rhetoric.

Policymakers should take another look at our foreign and domestic policies and consider how to put them in closer conformity with our self-proclaimed call to be a beacon of hope and freedom to mankind.

4. *It's the Process, Stupid.* One of the greatest conundrums facing democracy promoters is the "one man, one vote, one time" hypothesis—that, once elections are introduced in societies not prepared for true political pluralism, non-democratic forces will seize the opportunity to win office, claim a popular mandate and international legitimacy, and then proceed to shut down and repress opposition groups and genuine democratic debate. This phenomenon, also known as the "Algeria problem" for the way in which that country's military violently suppressed the Islamist parties poised to claim victory in 1991–92 elections, haunts the administration's current approach to the Middle East and other parts of the Muslim world. Political forces calling for fair political competition and other political rights in the Gulf states, Saudi Arabia, Jordan and Yemen, for example, are not only the most likely to win but also the most vocally opposed to the United States. A similar phenomenon is taking place in Latin America where populist leaders are winning office on a platform of opposition to U.S. policies of free trade, macroeconomic reform and military responses to drug trafficking and terrorism. When American policymakers try to influence the outcome, by voicing support for one candidate over another, it tends to have the opposite effect, as has been seen in Nicaragua and Bolivia. Putting aside the obvious problems associated with trying to impose democracy by military force in Iraq, the recent revelations that the United States covertly supported Iyad Allawi's campaign in order to diminish the victory of Shiite cleric Ali al-Sistani is another example of the United States' counterproductive use of its leverage in such situations.[9]

To reduce the chance of a "one man, one vote, one time" scenario, policymakers need to pull back on the rush to elections, particularly in places that have not laid the legal, civic education and political party infrastructure for a credible electoral process. This is particularly true in the Middle East where democratic forms of governance are largely untested. As noted in the recent Independent Task Force Report of the Council on Foreign Relations on Arab Democracy:

> the United States should promote the development of democratic institutions and practices over the long term, mindful that democracy cannot be imposed from the outside and that sudden, traumatic change is neither necessary nor desirable. America's goal in the Middle East should be to encourage democratic evolution, not revolution.[10]

The task force, co-chaired by Madeleine Albright, Chairman of the National Democratic Institute, and Vin Weber, Chairman of the International Republic Institute, has produced an excellent list of sensible policies the United States should follow when designing its strategy toward democracy promotion in the Arab world. Others which have studied the question have also come to the conclusion that U.S. support for democracy in the Arab world must include moderate Islamist parties which are committed to the democratic process, even if they are not entirely friendly to U.S. interests.[11]

5. *It's Better to Do it with Others.* Given its overwhelming economic, military and cultural power, the United States has a responsibility to lead with a very delicate hand. It should go without saying that our interests are best served when we work closely with our allies to pursue common interests.

In the democracy promotion field, the trend is toward greater cooperation as younger democracies, particularly in Eastern Europe, revise their foreign policies to favor more robust support for democratization.[12] This trend is happening both with the leadership of the United States, as in the case of the Organization of American States or the Community of Democracies (which also benefits from the active leadership of Chile, Poland, Korea, Mali, Portugal and others), as well as with the leadership of the European Union, especially through the E.U. enlargement process.[13] Other countries new to this field are coming on board as donors—India has contributed $10 million to a new United Nations Democracy Fund proposed by President Bush; Hungary has inaugurated a new International Center for Democracy Transition; Lithuania, Slovakia and Poland are taking the lead in advocating democratic change in Belarus. In one of the more recent examples of collaboration, both old and new democracies teamed up to support the transition to democracy in Ukraine, by funding the institutions and civic associations which made the Orange Revolution possible, and by coordinating diplomatic leverage to ease the antidemocratic elements out of power without bloodshed.[14] The African Union is developing a consistent if weak track record against unconstitutional seizures of power, most recently in Mauritania and Togo. Even the Association of South East Asian Nations (ASEAN), not exactly a club of democracies, has broken new ground by successfully pressuring Burma to desist from assuming chairmanship of the body.

Institutional arrangements to protect democracy against internal and external threats are well advanced, even if unevenly applied. The political will, however, to take the next step to establish mechanisms to prevent serious backsliding through good offices, mediation and early warning missions is still largely absent. Here again, fears of superpower hegemony are revived as autocrats rally against further erosion of state sovereignty.

"Doing it with others" also means that governments should continue and expand cooperation with nongovernmental forms of democracy assistance. A range of options are available—grants through quasi-governmental foundations like the National Endowment for Democracy or the German political party *stiftungs*; support to grassroots and international networks of civil society institutions; strengthening linkages among professional associations of lawyers, engineers and political scientists; greater cooperation with other nongovernmental donors, etc.

6. *Use Economic Incentives and Rewards.* The international community is increasingly moving away from punitive sanctions, which have been shown to hurt more than help the people intended to benefit from such a policy, and toward economic and trade incentives and rewards as a carrot for governance reform. In this regard, the European Union has led the way through its largely successful enlargement process. The Bush administration also deserves credit for launching the Millennium Challenge Account (MCA), which is designed to reward poor states with higher levels of development assistance if they can demonstrate a record of ruling justly, fighting corruption, opening their economies and investing in education and health. Unfortunately, implementation of the program has lagged way behind its promise, causing frustration amid potential beneficiaries and allies in Congress. Nonetheless, the approach is the right one from a democracy promotion and development point of view and appears to be gaining ground in Brussels.[15] The administration should seek ways to multilateralize it, in other words to seek agreement from other donors

to tie other grants, loans and trade privileges to a state's ability to govern in accordance with the rule of law. This can be done by building support for changing the rules at the World Bank, the International Monetary Fund and other multilateral institutions to allow for consideration of political issues in loan decisions.[16] Alternatively, a new global development fund could be created that is designed specifically to reward states that meet criteria like those used in the MCA program. This not only would advance U.S. interests in democracy and development, but also reduce the chances that terrorist groups would find fertile ground in weak or failed states unable to care for their people or secure their borders.

A Final Word

Assuming the trend of democratization continues around the world, the United States increasingly will face a major challenge in protecting its core interests as a global power. Its friends and allies who govern in democratic systems cannot ignore the opinion of large majorities of voters and expect to get re-elected on a similar platform of close cooperation with the United States. We must take into account the pressures our allies are under as they decide whether and how to work with us in addressing common security challenges. This is more than just a communications challenge, although that aspect alone deserves much greater attention and resources. We need to change our mindset and remember that, if we want cooperation from others, we need to help them keep their publics on board. We can do that by changing our policies and behaviors at home and abroad and by walking softly as we carry that big stick.

Endnotes

1. International IDEA, "Ten Years of Supporting Democracy Worldwide" p. 4 (International IDEA, Stockholm, Sweden 2005).
2. See, e.g., Resolution on Promoting and Consolidating Democracy, A/Res/55/96, adopted by U.N. General Assembly 4 December 2000: http://www.demcoalition.org/pdf/un_resolutionpromotindem.pdf; Warsaw Declaration of the Community of Democracies, 27 June 2000: http://www.demcoalition.org/2005_html/commu_cdm00.html
3. *In Larger Freedom: Towards Development, Security and Human Rights for All* (United Nations, New York 2005) p. 52. See also Universal Declaration of Human Rights.
4. "We recommit ourselves to actively protecting and promoting all human rights, the rule of law and democracy and recognize that they are inter-

linked and mutually reinforcing and that they belong to the universal and indivisible core values and principles of the United Nations, . . . The universal nature of these rights and freedoms is beyond question." United Nations General Assembly, World Summit Outcome, A/Res/60/1 (24 October 2005). See also Amartya Sen, "Why Democratization Is not the Same as Westernization: Democracy and Its Global Roots," *The New Republic Online*, (post date: 09.25.03; issue date: 10.06.03).

5. For an interesting discussion of the influence of a country's relationships to the West in its democratization process, see Steven Levitsky and Lucan A. Way, "International Linkage and Democratization," *Journal of Democracy*, vol. 16, no. 3 (July 2005) pp. 20–34. For a discussion on the challenges of democratizing authoritarian regimes, see Peter Burnell, "Democracy Promotion: The Elusive Quest for Grand Strategies," *International Politics and Society* 3/2004.
6. See Theodore J. Piccone, "International Mechanisms for Protecting Democracy," and Ken Gude, "Case Studies in Collective Response," in Morton H. Halperin and Mirna Galic (eds.) *Protecting Democracy: International Responses* (Lexington Books, Lanham, MD 2005).
7. President George W. Bush, Second Inaugural Address (Jan. 20, 2004).
8. For a comparison of "democracy clauses" of regional organizations' charters and protocols, see Theodore J. Piccone, "International Mechanisms for Protecting Democracy," in Morton H. Halperin and Mirna Galic (eds.) *Protecting Democracy: International Responses* (Lexington Books, Lanham, MD 2005).
9. Hersh, Seymour M., "Get Out the Vote: Did Washington Try to Manipulate Iraq's Election?" *The New Yorker* (July 25, 2005).
10. Council on Foreign Relations, "In Support of Arab Democracy: Why and How," Independent Task Force Report (June 2005) p. 4.
11. See, e.g., Amr Hamzawy, "The Key to Arab Reform: Moderate Islamists," Policy Brief, Carnegie Endowment for International Peace (August 2005).
12. For an evaluation of the ways in which forty different countries have sought to promote democracy internationally, see Robert Herman and Theodore Piccone (eds.) *Defending Democracy: A Global Survey of Foreign Policy Trends 1992–2002* (Democracy Coalition Project, Washington, DC 2002).
13. For a review of policies pursued by six established democracies, see Richard Youngs (ed.) *Survey of European Democracy Promotion Policies 2000–2006* (FRIDE, Madrid 2006).
14. See chapter on Ukraine in Theodore Piccone and Richard Youngs (eds.) *Strategies for Democratic Change: Assessing the Global Response* (Democracy Coalition Project and FRIDE, Washington, DC 2006) pp. 97–121; Robert Kagan, "Embraceable E.U.," *The Washington Post* (Oct. 4, 2004); Michael McFaul, "Transitions from Postcommunism," *Journal of Democracy*, vol. 16, no. 3 (July 2005).
15. The European Commission has recently announced creation of an incentive fund of 2.7 billion euro, in addition to its usual development

funding, to reward countries making tangible efforts to improve governance. "E.U. Seeks Greater Responsibility in Return for Development Aid," theparliament.com (August 30, 2006).
16. For a thoughtful and timely discussion on this subject see Morton H. Halperin, Joseph T. Siegle and Michael M. Weinstein, *The Democracy Advantage: How Democracies Promote Prosperity and Peace* (Council on Foreign Relations, Routledge, New York 2005) pp. 203–29.

3
Strengthening Civil Society
Mary Kaldor

Is al Qaeda part of civil society?

After all it is a non-state actor. It consists of a loose cross-border network of self-organised groups held together by a common sense of mission—in this case, a commitment to the violent struggle of Global Islam against the materialist decadent West. The main contact points are training camps or sympathetic mosques. Its funds[1] derive from voluntary contributions, either from rich individuals like Osama bin Laden himself,[2] or his supporters mainly in Saudi Arabia, or from the funding efforts of local groups both legal and illegal. It uses the electronic media—Internet, video cassettes, radio and television—to promote its message often in spectacular ways. In other word, its horizontal form of organisation is very similar to a non-governmental organisation (NGO).

Yet most people would consider the question ridiculous. Al Qaeda is surely the opposite of civil society. Even though civil society is usually defined as the space between the state, the market and the family, and often equated with NGOs, the term evidently has an underlying normative meaning. It has something to do with civility, with non-violent social relations, with a social contract and with the use of reason in debates about public affairs.

In developing strategies for civil society as a form of counter-terror, it is important to unpack this underlying normative understanding of the concept and to distinguish it from a more descriptive understanding, in which 'civil society' equals NGOs. This is crucial because there is a tendency for donors to believe they are strengthening civil society by funding NGOs. However, if we understand civil society in its more profound normative sense, then strengthening civil society has to involve a much broader programme of action and policy.

In what follows, I will start by analysing two different understandings of civil society. I will then discuss the ways in which civil society is antithetical to war and the so-called 'war on terror'. And in the final section, I will consider a strategy for strengthening civil society both 'from above' and 'from below'.

Two Understandings of Civil Society

In the United States and among the international donor community, civil society tends to be identified with the non-profit sector. Sometimes, the term 'social capital' pioneered by Robert Putnam is preferred. Although Alexis de Tocqueville did not use the term 'civil society', his influence has been very significant because his discovery, which was to inform so much of contemporary thinking, had to do with the importance of associationalism and self-organisation for democracy. In his study of democracy as practised in America, de Tocqueville argued that the guarantee of individual liberties was to be found in what he called 'democratic expedients'; these included local self-government, the separation of church and state, a free press, indirect elections, an independent judiciary, and, above all 'associational life.'[3] In America, he was greatly impressed by the extent of associations in civil life and put forward the argument those active associations were a condition for freedom and equality.

> As soon as several inhabitants of the United States have taken up an opinion or a feeling they wish to promote in the world, they look for mutual assistance; and as soon as they have found one another out, they combine. From that moment they are no longer isolated men, but a power seen from afar, whose actions serve for example and whose language is listened to . . . Among the laws that rule human societies, there is one which seems to be more precise and clear than all the others. If men are to remain civilised or to become so, the art of associating together must grow and improve in the same ratio as the equality of conditions is increased.[4]

The same argument has been made more recently by Robert

Putnam. In his monumental study of democracy in Italy, he found that differential development in the North and the South could be explained by social capital or the degree of social connectedness. People in the North had a long tradition of combining and forming self-help organisations and this contributed both to democracy and economic growth. More recently in his book *Bowling Alone* he identifies a disturbing decline in social connectedness in the United States, which he attributes largely to the influence of television.[5]

The growth of the non-profit sector worldwide, which has been documented by Helmut Anheier and Lester Salamon, is often viewed as a way in which more and more social functions can be self-organised, thereby reducing the intrusive role of the state.[6] A particularly significant phenomenon, which is traced in the annual *Global Civil Society* yearbooks,[7] is the dramatic growth of international NGOs.[8] But the growth of NGOs is not necessarily associated with a deepening of democracy or a more vibrant economy. On the contrary, it appears to be accompanied by growing political apathy, in terms of party membership or voter turnouts. Moreover, the growth of NGOs has been paralleled by the growth of religious and nationalist movements, many of which, like al Qaeda, are organised along the same lines as are what we tend to think of as NGOs. Thus the RSS, the social organisation that provides the basis for the Hindu nationalist Party in India, or the network of welfare groups that help to mobilise support for Hamas, have also expanded in recent decades. In his later work, Robert Putnam draws a distinction between 'bridging' and 'bonding' capital. 'Bonding social capital brings together people who are like one another in important respects (ethnicity, age, gender, social class, and so on), whereas bridging social capital refers to social networks that bring together people who are unlike one another.'[9] Thus the latter crosses social divides, tends to be horizontal in organisational form, and generally fills some needed social function. The former is vertical and can easily be a mechanism for extending patronage rather than for social problem-solving. But is al Qaeda bonding rather than bridging? And could one not imagine forms of bonding capital that contribute to civility? It is not at all clear that this new distinction can dispense with a more normative understanding of the concept of civil society.

The alternative understanding of civil society derives from its meaning in the late seventeenth and eighteenth centuries. At that time, civil society was a society characterised by the rule of law, based on certain fundamental individual rights, which was enforced by a political authority also subject to the rule of law. Indeed there was no clear distinction, at that time, between civil society and the state. Rather, 'civil society' was a generic term for a secular constitutional order.[10]

The term came to prominence during the transition from absolutist monarchies to the modern state, although it had a prehistory in ancient and medieval times. This was a period when earlier ties of blood, kinship and religion were breaking down. The growth of states and the establishment of a rule of law gradually eliminated private and often violent methods of settling disputes and created the conditions for these new forms of social interaction based on commonly accepted but impersonal means of communication, e.g. exchanges of money, newspapers, mail, etc.

The term was linked to the concept of 'civility'.[11] It meant respect for individual autonomy, based on security and trust among people who had perhaps never met. It required regularity of behaviour, rules of conduct, respect for law, and control of violence. Hence, a civil society was synonymous with polite society, a society in which strangers act in a civilised way towards each other, treating each other with mutual respect, tolerance and confidence, a society in which rational debate and discussion becomes possible. Norbert Elias referred to the 'civilising process' to describe the historical process whereby violence was removed from everyday life.[12] Emma Rothschild talks about the 'unfrightened mind'—the removal of fear, which provides the source of superstition.[13] This was the period that gave rise to debates about public affairs in the coffee houses of London or Paris, which Jürgen Habermas has described as the bourgeois public sphere.[14]

There is an interesting parallel here with the ideas of classical Islam. Classical Islam was both a religion and a political theory. The historian Ibn Khaldūn, writing at the end of the fourteenth century, argued that political authority was based on group feeling (*abassiya*).[15] Traditionally, *abassiya* derives from blood ties, e.g. tribalism. However with the development of cities, tribalism has to be replaced by a new kind of group feeling based on ethics and these are derived from Islam. Thus the term for civil society, *almujtamaa ammadani*, derives both from the word for city and from Medina, the city where Mohammed first established his Islamic society. It was a society characterised by the rule of law 'shari'a' and by a social contract between the rulers and the ruled *baya*. The interpretation of shari'a depended on wise judges, scholars trained in the fundamentals of Islamic thought, who debated their interpretations through the pulpit—the Islamic public sphere.

It was this meaning of civil society that was rediscovered in Latin

America and Eastern Europe in the last decades of the twentieth century as a tool for opening up military dictatorships and totalitarianism.[16] The dissident intellectuals in these regions tried to create independent spaces, in which individuals could act according to their consciences in the face of powerful influences from the state on culture and ideology. They were not trying to replace the state; rather they wanted a state based on a social contract rather than on coercion. For them, civil society was an arena of non-violence and public reasoning through which a social contract could be debated or negotiated. In constructing these new public spaces, they made use both of international law and of support from peace and human rights groups in other countries. At one and the same time, they were checking the power of the state and contributing to emergence of a set of rules and norms at a global level that we tend to call global governance.

The reason why we tend to identify civil society with NGOs is that public debate of this kind nowadays tends to take place outside the realm of formal politics, among NGOs and social movements, within universities or religious institutions. Instead of the bourgeois public sphere of the eighteenth century described by Habermas, we have a global public sphere that largely comprises these informal groups and organisations. According to Habermas:

> The expression 'civil society' has in the meantime taken on a meaning different from that of the 'bourgeois society' of the liberal tradition. . . . Rather, its institutional core comprises those non-governmental and non-economic connections and voluntary associations that anchor the communication structures of the public sphere in the society component of the life-world. Civil society is composed of those more or less spontaneously emergent associations, organisations, and movements that, attuned to how societal problems resonate in private life spheres, distil and transmit such reactions to the public sphere. The core of civil society comprises a network of associations that institutionalises problem-solving discourses of general interest inside the framework of organised public spheres. These 'discursive designs' have an egalitarian, open form of organisation that mirrors essential features of the kind of communication around which they crystallise and to which they lend continuity and permanence.[17]

Of course, classical concepts of civil society were exclusive. In de Tocqueville's America, slaves and native Americans were excluded—

a point that was not missed by de Tocqueville. In Western Europe, before the French revolution, civil society consisted of property owners, the bourgeoisie. And in the Middle East, in the period of classical Islam, it was Islamic society even though space was accorded to other religions. Moreover, civil society was territorially tied. It existed within the boundaries of the nation-state and the individual rights that formed the basis of civil society were suspended in wars against other nation-states. Many civil society thinkers believed that war was necessary to create the group feeling that held civil society together. But others, like Rousseau or Kant, argued that a true civil society could never be achieved except in the context of a universal civil society.

What is new about civil society today is its global character. By this I do not just mean that civil society is concerned about global issues or that civil society groups are linked with other groups in different parts of the world. I also mean that global rules and global connectedness provide the conditions for civil society even where the concerns are very local. The rediscovery of civil society in Latin America and Eastern Europe depended on the global framework and this is no less true today for civil society groups who promote democracy, poverty reduction or peace and human rights in particular countries or localities.

Terror and the War on Terror

Terror is profoundly inimical to civil society in this normative sense. It is both a cause and a consequence of a weak or absent civil society. Civil society in the normative sense only exists in atmosphere free of fear. Terror is an extreme form of fear.

Civil society is about the use of public reason. Many of the new nationalist and religious groups who engage in terror object to what they see as both the relativism of modernity and the claim that human reason is superior to other forms of human knowledge. They object to the doubt and questioning that characterises modern society. They insist that sacred knowledge is the superior form of knowledge, that there is a 'correct' interpretation of events that is given by God, which cannot be contradicted by human reason. Civil society is based on an assumption about the equality of human beings and respect for individual rights. The refusal of these nationalist and religious groups to accept the superiority of human reason also justifies the refusal to accept the fundamental equality of human beings. Even though al Qaeda embraces the global character of Islam and makes no distinction on the basis of ethnicity, non-believers are not counted as equals and the term 'non-believer' also applies to Islamic people who refuse to accept the al Qaeda ideology—for example, the Shi'as who are currently being attacked in Iraq.

The notion of 'us' and 'them' is deeply embedded in the ideologies of terror. Religious leaders see their struggle as a 'Cosmic War' against 'evil' and promote the idea that every follower has to participate in that struggle. By doing so, their political causes are given sacred legitimacy and their members are given a sense of participation in something larger than every day life. Likewise, nationalist groups that use terror as a technique often claim to be avenging historic injustices.

War implies certainty, the impossibility of compromise or co-existence—indeed the more blood that is shed, the more the cause is sanctified. According to Juergensmeyer:

> A warring attitude implies that its holder no longer thinks compromise is possible or—just as likely—did not want an accommodating solution to the conflict in the first place. In fact, if one's goal is not harmony but the empowerment that comes with using violence, it is in one's interest to be in a state of war.[18]

Civil society cannot be based on such absolute antagonisms. Argument and debate among adversaries as opposed to enemies, what Chantal Mouffe calls 'agonisms',[19] are what civil society is about. But antagonism and enmity close down debate; only two positions are allowed instead of many. If classical civil society refused antagonisms in the domestic arena, global civil society now runs counter to the notion of international antagonisms.

But if terrorism represents an attack on civil society, by the same token, it is the weakness of civil society that often gives rise to membership in a terrorist group. On the one hand, in an atmosphere of fear, people are attracted to extremist causes that seem to offer some form of protection, at least in the imagination or in the hereafter. On the other hand, it is the sense of exclusion, of not being heard, that contributes to the appeal of a violent spectacular message. 'Letters to Israel' were how Hamas described the suicide bombers. Thus terror and the absence of civil society reinforce each other.

But the war on terror is also inimical to civil society and that is perhaps why it does not work. Since President Bush announced the war on terror in response to the attacks of September 11, terrorist incidents have increased. There is a wave of terror in Iraq and

Afghanistan, the two countries where the war is being conducted—indeed these two countries are becoming new havens and training grounds for terror. The attacks in Madrid and London as well as in Indonesia, Saudi Arabia or Turkey do not seem to have been deterred by the war on terror. Videoed statements by bin Laden, interviews with al Qaeda spokesmen as well as arrested suspects, and reports from think tanks and intelligence agencies all suggest that the Hydra-headed monster, al Qaeda, has reorganised and restructured itself, feeding on widespread anger and resentment against the 'war' among young, usually male, Muslims.

The war on terror stems in part from the experience of policy-makers in the security field, whose main preoccupation has been the Cold War and the conflict with communism. In particular, the repertoire of means available for security policy largely consist of military means. A distinction is drawn between war, which is legitimate killing by agents of the state, and terrorism, which is criminal or illegal. The problem is that the terrorist themselves define what they are doing as war. Thus, the language of war and, above all, the destructiveness of war and military means perversely end up legitimating the actions of the terrorists. In both Palestine and Iraq, far more civilians have been killed by regular forces (Israeli or American) than by terrorist groups. This is not to justify the horrific character of terrorist violence but rather to explain how the war on terror feeds the terrorist rhetoric.

Moreover, the war on terror has the same polarising logic as terror. It magnifies the perceived power and reach of the terrorists; it gives them the respectable status of an enemy, it vests them with the role of an alternative pole to the United States. It narrows the space for dissent, for those who oppose the terrorists and yet remain critical of American policy. 'You are either with us or against us,' says Bush. It creates an atmosphere of fear in which dissent is unpatriotic and in which the erosion of civil liberties—the detention and torture of suspects, increased surveillance, etc.—weakens the legal basis for civil society.

Strengthening Civil Society

An alternative to war on terror is to strengthen civil society. Indeed the emergence of a global civil society is a necessary condition for countering global terrorism. It shows that neither the West nor Global Islam is monolithic. There are many in the West who oppose the War on Terror just as there are many Islamic communities in different parts of the world who understand Islam as a religion based on the use of public reason, as expounded by classical thinkers like Khaldūn, rather than absolutist dictates. And, indeed, 'today, the extent of Arab participation in global civic life is unprecedented.'[20]

Among governments and international organisations, there is a tendency to think that civil society can be strengthened through promoting associationalism. Democracy promotion programmes help to fund NGOs and offer 'capacity-building' assistance. Where civil society is strong such programmes can be beneficial. But where civil society is weak, such programmes can create artificial NGOs who know how to write proposals and reports but are more accountable to donors than the local beneficiaries they are supposed to represent or help and who may occupy the space for genuine public debate.

If we understand civil society in the normative sense described above, then the role of governments and international organisations is to provide enabling conditions. Civil society in the eighteenth-century bourgeois sense or in the classical Islamic sense depended on a legitimate constitutional order based on a social contract. The tasks of governments and international organisations is thus to guarantee that constitutional order. What would such a strategy of promoting enabling conditions mean in practice?

First of all, the job of governments is to uphold the rule of law so that citizens feel safe. It is their job to protect civilians and capture and arrest of criminals responsible for violence. And this applies to all forms of illegal violence, not just terrorism. Countering violence has to be treated as law enforcement not war. The latter just feeds into the terrorists' notions of perpetual struggle. It may be necessary to use military means, for example, in destroying terrorist camps but any military action must be viewed as law enforcement rather than war. This is not just a matter of procedure, that the use of military force should be approved through due process—for example the United Nations Security Council—it is also a matter of means. Law enforcement starts from the assumption of human equality. The lives of soldiers cannot be privileged over the lives of the civilians they are supposed to protect. Hence, military force must be used on the same principles as policing; soldiers are expected to risk their lives to save others.

The importance of means also applies to intelligence, policing and other legal procedures. The various counter-terrorist laws in Britain and the United States allow procedures to be adopted, such as detention without charges, that potentially contravene human rights. The term 'terrorist' has also been used to legitimise repressive behaviour in a number of countries; it is used, for example, in Australia against asylum-seekers, or against various secessionist movements in different countries.²¹ The risk is not just that this behaviour can further fuel anger and resentment among potential recruits to extremist causes, it is also the challenge to our own civil liberties and our claim to offer an alternative ideology. Governments have to balance the needs of counter-terrorism with civil liberties if they are to provide enabling conditions for civil society.

The second strand of such a policy is to provide political space for civil society. Exclusive and fundamentalist ideologies have to be countered by inclusive emancipatory dialogues. Even though these have to be conducted by citizens, governments and international organisations can stimulate such dialogues by genuinely engaging with the ideas and proposals that emerge. Indeed the belief that debates are heard and are being acted upon is probably the best way to stimulate civic activity. This is why, in my view, the potential of the so-called anti-globalisation or *alter mondialist* movement should be taken seriously; it does have an appeal, which at present no progressive political party or government can replicate. In particular, the World Social Forum, which has become the institutional expression of the movement, was responsible for coordinating the global popular mobilisation against the war in Iraq. This mobilisation involved both Europe and the Arab world and, for the first time, brought immigrant communities into the political process. This was particularly important in Britain, where Hindus and Sikhs as well as Muslims joined the demonstrations. What the demonstrations revealed was an enormous gap between the political class and civil society.

At the moment, these groups do not have serious formal political representation and there is a real need for progressive elected representatives to reach out to them. Indeed the London bombing can be in part explained, although not justified, in terms of the disappointment of the Muslim community that the public mobilisation against the Iraq war failed to influence the political process.

Reaching out to these new groups is not just a matter of dialogue, it also involves taking seriously and adopting or pressing for some of their demands, for example, a solution to the Israeli–Palestinian conflict, elimination of weapons of mass destruction through treaties and unilateral action rather than through 'counter-proliferation' and 'pre-emptive war', reform of global economic institutions.

Thirdly, such a strategy can help to provide the infrastructure for civil society. Particularly important is support for education and media. Universal primary education would be very important in reducing the incentive to send children to religious schools. In many countries, universities are the sites of civil society; hence support for research and teaching capacity can provide an environment for reasoned debate. There also needs to be much greater investment in global public (but not state) radio and TV. Independent community radio is especially important in countering extremist propaganda, as has been shown in Serbia and parts of Africa.

Finally, fear is not just about violence; it also results from the insecurity of poverty. The decline in social services, for example, as a result of neo-liberal policies has provided openings for humanitarian NGOs who also bring with them an extremist political message; this poverty reduction and the provision of social services could reduce dependence on this type of NGO. Likewise, unemployed or criminalised young men are the main breeding ground for these ideologies. Development needs to give priority to legitimate ways for these young people to make a living.

In the end, of course, the job of strengthening civil society has to be done by citizens themselves. At the Club de Madrid meeting in March 2005, it was agreed to establish a citizens' network against terror. The founding meeting of Citizens Against Terror (CAT) was held in Barcelona in March 2006, including a range of groups who are active in campaigning against terror—the families of 9/11; human rights activists from Iraq, Afghanistan, Sierra Leone, Palestine and Russia; the British campaign 'We are not Afraid', which was started after the July bombings. The agreed mission of CAT is contained in the box below.

Mission

To empower people across the globe to take non-violent action to bring an end to terror

We denounce terror, which we define as deliberate violence against civilians, by non-state or state actors, for the purpose of intimidation

Objectives

- To build a community of solidarity, to protect and support those challenging and those affected by terror, wherever they are
- To counteract terrorism and enhance human security through the frame work of international law, including human rights and humanitarian law
- To address the contexts which give rise to terrorism, through research, dialogue and the advocacy of non-violent alternatives

The most important way that CAT can be supported is through joining in. Governments and international organisations can help give such groups a public voice only by taking seriously the ideas and proposals that are put forward. In the final session of the Club de Madrid meeting, the U.N. Secretary-General Kofi Annan said:

> Not only political leaders, but *civil society and religious leaders* should clearly denounce terrorist tactics as criminal and inexcusable. Civil society has already conducted magnificent campaigns against landmines, against the recruitment of children as soldiers, and against allowing war crimes to go unpunished. I should like to see an equally strong global campaign against terrorism.

We must pay more attention to the victims of terrorism, and make sure their voices can be heard.[22]

Endnotes

1. The funds are estimated at $300 million. See Basil, Mark, 'Going on the Source: Why Al Qaeda's Financial Network Is Likely to Withstand the Current War on Terrorist Financing.' *Studies in Conflict and Terrorism*, 27 (2004) p.170.
2. Mark Basil points out that 'unlike the leaders of other terrorist organizations, [Osama bin Laden] did not rise to power primarily as a religious authority, military hero, or political figure' but as a wealthy financier. Quoted in ibid.
3. 'Americans of all ages, all conditions, and all dispositions constantly form associations. They have not only commercial and manufacturing companies, in which all take part, but associations of a thousand other kinds, religious, moral, serious, futile, general or restricted, enormous or diminutive. The Americans make associations to give entertainment, to found seminaries, to build inns, to construct churches, to diffuse books, to send missionaries to the antipodes; in this manner, they found hospitals, prisons and schools. If it is proposed to inculcate some truth or to foster some feeling by the encouragement of a great example, they form a society. Whenever at the head of some new undertaking you see the government in France or a man of rank in England, in the United States, you will be sure to find an association.' de Tocqueville, Alexis, *Democracy in America* (New York: Vintage Books, 1945; first published in 1835) p. 114.
4. Ibid. pp. 117–18.
5. Putnam, Robert, *Bowling Alone: The Collapse and Revival of American Community* (New York: Simon & Schuster, 2000).
6. Salamon, Lester M. and Helmut K. Anheier, *The Emerging Nonprofit Sector: An Overview* (Manchester: Manchester University Press, 1996).

7. The *Global Civil Society* yearbook is an annual publication by the Global Civil Society Programme at the Centre for the Study of Global Governance (LSE). The first yearbook was published in 2000. The latest edition is: Glasius, Marlies, Mary Kaldor and Helmut Anheier (eds.), *Global Civil Society 2005/6* (London: Sage, 2005). See also: www.lse.ac.uk/depts/global/yearbook.htm
8. The absolute growth of NGOs between 1993 and 2003 was 43 per cent. See Anheier, Helmut, Marlies Glasius and Mary Kaldor (eds.) *Global Civil Society 2004/5* (London: Sage, 2004) p. 302.
9. Putnam, Robert D. (ed.), *Democracies in Flux: The Evolution of Social Capital in Contemporary Society* (Oxford: Oxford University Press, 2002) p. 11.
10. See Anthony Black in Sudipta Kaviraj and Sunil Khilnani *Civil Society: History and Possibilities* (Cambridge: Cambridge University Press, 2001).
11. For a discussion of 'civility' see Keane, John, *Reflections on Violence* (New York: Verso, 1996).
12. Elias, Norbert, *The Civilising Process: State Formation and Civilisation* (Oxford: Blackwell, 1982; originally published in German in 1939).
13. According to Adam Smith, 'when law has established order and security, and subsistence ceases to be precarious, the curiosity of mankind is increased, and their fears diminished'. Rothschild, Emma, *Economic Sentiments: Adam Smith, Condorcet and the Enlightenment* (Cambridge: Harvard University Press, 2001) p. 12.
14. Habermas, Jürgen, *The Structural Transformation of the Public Sphere: An Inquiry into a Category of Bourgeois Society* (Cambridge: Polity Press, 1992).
15. Khaldūn, Ibn, *An Arab Philosophy of History: Selections from the Prolegomena of Ibn Khaldūn of Tunis*, trans. and arr. by Charles Issawi (London: Murray, 1950).
16. See Kaldor, Mary, *Global Civil Society: An Answer to War* (Cambridge: Polity Press, 2003) chapter 3.
17. Quoted in Ehrenberg, John, *Civil Society: The Critical History of an Idea* (New York: New York University Press, 1999) pp. 222–23.
18. Juergensmeyer, Mark, *Terror in the Mind of God: the Global Rise of Religious Violence* (Berkeley: University of California Press, 2000) p. 149.
19. See, for instance, Mouffe, Chantal, *The Democratic Paradox* (New York: Verso, 2000).
20. Said, Mohamed El-Sayed, 'Global Civil Society: An Arab Perspective.' In: Anheier, Helmut, Marlies Glasius and Mary Kaldor (eds.), *Global Civil Society 2004/5* (London: Sage, 2004) p. 71.
21. Human Rights watch (Opportunismwatch).
22. March 10, 2005.

4

Islam, Islamism and Democracy: The Case of the Arab World

Bassam Tibi

In response to the events of September 11, 2001, in the United States, and March 11, 2004, in Spain (E.U.), many have called for the institution of democracy, and for democratization, as the proper response to terrorism. Such calls for democracy and democratization, especially when directed to the Arab world, rely on unexamined assumptions about culture, law and political change in that world. They rely as well on unexamined presumptions about the notion of "democracy"; add to this the most consequential failure to distinguish between Islam and Islamism and the related historical and cultural blindspots in Western thinking about critical changes in the Arab world since 9/11.

The call for "regime change" in Iraq needs to be studied in this context. Summarized by the phrase "winds of change," the Bush administration's effort to democratize Iraq has been and is a strategic move aimed at restructuring the "greater Middle East" as a group of democracies. This policy, and this strategy, rest on the assumption that democratization in the Arab world will create sustainable stability in the region, and guarantee to the United States reliable and accountable allies.

Yet the outcome to date of the invasion of Iraq (March 2003), and events elsewhere in the region (since 9/11) do not support the assumptions on which the policy was based, and most certainly have not produced stable democratic processes or institutions. In both Iraq and Palestine genuine democratic elections have taken place—and have brought Islamists to power. Islamists in power have not enacted democratic institutions to match the democratic electoral processes which brought them to power. Multi-party, culturally diverse and complex democracies have not come into being. In fact, democracy as a concept of a political culture is at odds with the purposes, intellectual and cultural foundations of Islamist regimes. We must therefore distinguish between "democracy" viewed as electoral process, and "democracy" viewed as political culture. And we must ask a series of critical questions: Is the political culture of democracy compatible with the political ideology of Islamism? Do democratic electoral processes in Iraq and Palestine evidence a shift within Islamism toward an acceptance of democracy as a value? Do free elections produce the democratization of the Arab world long anticipated/advocated in the West? Is praise of democratic electoral processes in Iraq and Palestine mere naivety, mere ignorance about the realities of political Islam (Islamism)? Is the shari'a-oriented[1] political Islam in Iraq and elsewhere compatible with the culture of democracy after all—or at all? Is democratization in the European or American sense feasible in the age of Islamism?

These are large questions. I intend to address them systematically, based on 30 years' intensive study of political assumptions and behavior in the Arab world.

In this project we must take into account key moments in the development of Islamism; distinguish among American, European and Islamic understandings of democracy and democratization; and analyze in depth relationships among Islam, Islamism and democracy in order to establish proper grounds for assessing the ongoing electoral victories of Islamists and determining whether Islamism is consonant with the culture of democracy.

The Inquiry and its Assumptions: Historical Notes

The terms "Islamism" and "political Islam" are used here interchangeably. Historically, the beginning of Islamism in the world of Islam can be traced to the formation of the Society of Muslim Brotherhood[2] in Egypt in 1928. In general, Islamism (political Islam) is an Islamic variety of religious fundamentalism.[3] Beginning as an indigenous movement in Egypt, the Muslim Brotherhood has become transnational in scope, extending in the following decades to the rest of the Arab world. Two branches of the movement have developed over time, embracing highly divergent strategies. One branch, functioning primarily in Egypt, has become moderate, deciding to participate in a variety of ways in the game of democracy. Followers of the moderate branch of the Muslim Brotherhood in Egypt are part of the elected Parliament, despite electoral tampering which sought to exclude them. The other branch has drifted to jihadism, embracing terrorism as a strategy and a value. Hamas of Palestine and Hizb al-Tahrir of Jordan grew from this process.

From the very outset, the movement of the Muslim Brothers has been opposed to democracy in the Western sense. Its goal has been the formation of an "Islamic State" based on divine shari'a law. In its program the Movement aspires to a *nizam Islami*/Islamic system of government based on *hakimiyyat Allah*/God's rule. It considers popular sovereignty an example of infidel thinking, and rejects it. Only God, not man, rules the world. The Islamic state envisioned by the Muslim Brotherhood and its transnational progeny is based on a constructed and politicized shari'a, which in fact heralds a new totalitarianism.[4]

In Iraq, the costly liberation of the country from the Sunni-based dictatorship of Saddam Hussein and his "republic of fear"[5] has brought to power an alliance of three Shi'i Islamist parties. The Iraqi election in December 2005 ended with an electoral victory for the Shi'i Islamists. In principle, they seem to accept making a choice between ballots and the bullets. These Islamists are therefore identified as *institutional Islamists*, in contrast to the *jihadists* who insist on resorting to jihad enacted as an irregular war of terrorism. Nevertheless, even though the Islamist Da'wa party reflects a variety of institutional Islamism in Iraq, its practice blurs the line between institutional Islamism and jihad. It is allied with two jihadist movements, namely the Supreme Council for the Islamic Revolution in Iraq/SCIRI (its military wing is the Badr Brigades/Failaq Badr) and the bloc of Muqtada al-Sadr and his equally jihadist al-Mahdi army composed of fighting irregulars. It can be argued that Iraq, ruled by this alliance, has become a tyranny of the Shi'i majority[6] over the Sunni minority. If so, this is no democratization.

Confusion between institutional Islamism and jihadism is also at issue in Palestine, where the Palestinian Hamas[7] movement advanced to the status of ruling party after it won an absolute majority in the election of February 2006. Hamas ousted from power the secular Fatah of the Palestinian National Authority/PNA, which had negotiated the peace accords with Israel. But the U.S. and the E.U. have both listed Hamas, on the basis of its terrorist assaults undertaken against civilians and acknowledged by the movement itself, as a "terrorist" movement. Hamas has obviously pursued jihad in its own sense of the term. Even though the Islamism of the AKP in Turkey is a case of its own[8] and will therefore not be included in the focus of the present inquiry, it is worth noting that the Islamist AKP government of Turkey was the first to receive a Hamas delegation, followed by Iran. None of the other Arab states has done so. The Europeans have been uncertain about how to deal with Hamas' rise to power because Hamas rose to power as the result of a voting procedure, but it has failed to reject terror and therefore is denied E.U. funding.

These recent electoral outcomes in Iraq and Palestine highlight issues in the E.U., especially E.U. neighborhood policies.[9] E.U. countries face the rise of political Islam within their own borders as Islamism spills over to Europe via global migration. Not only the United States and the Bush administration promote democratization in the Arab world. The E.U. views the Mediterranean states as "the enlargement-related sphere"; it considers itself a promoter of democracy in the neighboring regions in a process of democratic transition. On these grounds, the E.U. legitimates its involvement in the affairs of Arab states by defining them as "non-candidate neighboring states" and views their democratization as a matter that touches upon European politics and its stability. This interest has its roots in two European sources of fear: terrorism and migration. Politicians and theorists suggest that democracy in the Arab world is part of the solution to both fears.

At issue in the Middle East itself, and among those who study and seek to restructure it, is the politicization of religion and the religionization of politics. The result is a culturization of conflict in the Middle East. The hallmark of the age of the "cultural turn," post bi-polarity, is, therefore, for Islamists, the return of the sacred in political-religious disguise. Can democracy grow from this context of the shari'atization[10] and jihadization of Islam? Can there be a specific Arab or Islamic democracy based on shari'a? To be sure, one is here reminded of the fact that the term "shari'a" occurs only once in the *Qur'an*, where it has a very different meaning from that one used by the Islamists.

Islam, Freedom and Democracy

In the Arab world democracy and democratization[11] are not recent issues. Arab understanding of these terms is closely related to the civilizational interaction of Arabs with Europe in the context of European expansion, both with respect to its negative (colonialism) and positive (cultural borrowing) meanings. In the classical age Greek philosophy became an essential part of the heritage of Islam.[12] But today the fact that democracy has ancient Greek origins is used by Islamists to reject it, placing it among the despised "*hulul mustawradah*/imported solutions"[13] (from the West). These Islamists overlook the historical fact that Islamic civilization not only encountered and adopted Hellenism long before Europe itself did, but also acted as a mediator in passing the Greek legacy in an Islamic version to the West. The historian of civilizations Leslie Lipson tells us in his seminal work: "Aristotle crept back into Europe by the side door. His return was due to the Arabs, who had become acquainted with Greek thinkers."[14]

In view of these historical records it has to be asked why the Arabs of our present could not embrace, in a historical continuity, democracy as an outcome of cultural modernity, as their ancestors embraced the accomplishments of Hellenism. Can the claim of democracy to universality be acceptable to Muslims? Is a civil Islam paired with democracy, as found in Indonesia,[15] also possible for the Arab world? Can the alliance of civilizations be based on a shared commitment to democracy? These questions determine the scope of the ensuing analysis of Islam and Islamism. The consonance both of Islam and Islamism with democracy, understood as a component of cultural modernity, as well as a political culture, is the core issue addressed in the present inquiry. Hypothetically, this paper claims that religious and cultural reforms in Islam could potentially contribute to an embracing of democracy. It puts forward the hypothesis recognizing that early twenty-first century Islamism[16] rests on the idea that "*hakimiyyat Allah*/God's rule" stands by definition in contradiction to democracy (to the degree that democracy is based on popular sovereignty) and that powerful constraints therefore inhibit enactment of this claim.

The Present Moment

In addressing contemporary problems related to the introduction of democracy to the world of Islam in general and to the Arab world in particular, the well-known pro-democracy activist and scholar Saad Eddin Ibrahim noted at the European meeting of the Club de Madrid on "Safe Democracy, Terrorism and Security" that Arab societies are squeezed "between autocrats and theocrats". This succinct and precise phrase touches upon the "Arab predicament" which followed the repercussions of the war in 1967 and which was exacerbated through the rise of political Islam. Shari'atization of the state by Islamism presents itself as an alternative to the rule of the existing autocracy.

Contemporary Islamists are ideologically, and in their practice, not democrats but theocrats, and basically outspoken fundamentalists. The problem for those interested in democratization lies not with an alleged essential Arab culture nor with Islam, but with the use of Islam and pan-Arabism for legitimating neo-patriarchy in the Arab world in a time of crisis of legitimacy.[17] In response, political Islam propagates the formula: "*al-hall huwa al-Islam*/Islam is the solution". For Islamists this solution is the Islamic shari'a state. In general, Islamists reject cultural modernity,[18] in particular its components of secular democracy and civil society, altogether.

Based on the reality that public choices in the Arab-Islamic world are at present dominated by anti-Western sentiments, are at present pro-Islamist, and that Islamism is the only existing well-organized opposition (e.g. Egypt),[19] it can be assumed that any free election in the Islamic Middle East—the Arab world plus Turkey and Iran—would cede political power to the Islamists. The situation is ironic in view of the 2002 report[20] of the United Nations Development Program (UNDP) which finds that a lack of democracy is among the major explanations for present misery in the Middle East. Would Islamists alter this? Is it a sign of open-mindedness to share the views of the Swedish Minister of Foreign Affairs, Carl Bildt, who along with the former Spanish Foreign Minister Anna Palacio has in a *Financial Times* commentary applauded the electoral victory of Hamas—overlooking its anti-Semitic charter—stating that Hamas' success was an exemplary victory for democracy in the entire Middle East? Or do Bildt and Palacio's responses simply indicate naivety and ignorance about political Islam and the Middle East as well?

The degree to which audiences in the West are confused about the nature and effects of an effort to democratize the Arab world are evident in recent comments by Western journalists. In "The Americans and Arab Democracy" *The Economist* (February 25, 2006) bashed the U.S. after the democratic seizure of power by the Islamist-jihadist movement Hamas: "Americans cannot preach democracy in Palestine, then chastise the winners". An editorial in *The Financial Times* (May 28/29, 2005), asks the West to accept the "uncomfortable reality [that] Islamist groups . . . may be the greatest beneficiaries of its policy [of democratization]." The author concludes that "America should open a dialogue with the Islamists." Another *Financial Times* editorial, written six months later (December 28, 2005) argued that a "promoting of democracy" would bring Islamists to power because "Islamist movements remain the only potent opposition to existing rulers. . . . Their participation in the political process remains the best hope of moderating their often radical views". Finally, Steve Erlanger, editor at *The New York Times*, writing in *The International Herald Tribune* on March 17, 2006, compared the landslide 2006 victory of Hamas in Palestine with Iranian Islamic Revolution of 1979. Is the West to cooperate with the political Islam and its various movements, hoping to mitigate their inclination to jihad (as Graham Fuller, CIA/Rand analyst, suggests)? Are we to emphasize polemical defamation and bashing of the West throughout the Middle East today, which claims that the West only admits democracy and democratization on its own terms, and only when its outcome is favorable to Western interests (a view heard among some postmodern Westerners as well)?

If democracy were restricted to a voting procedure, and democratization to accepting the outcome of a voting procedure, then the seizure of power by Hitler's NSDAP in 1933 would have to be accepted as a democratic process. It most certainly was not. Democracy is not merely a technique for holding an election (ballot), but a political culture and lifestyle based on acceptance of pluralism. To be sure there can be no democracy without voting. But voting alone does not define democracy. This paper asserts that there can be no democracy devoid of a fundamental type of political culture and way of life attached to it. Despite all variations, democracy exhibits universal features and rests on universal human aspirations/values. Given these assertions we can ask specific questions: Does democracy exist when Hamas abolishes the Constitutional Court established by the PNA? Can Iraq be called democratic when the al-Mahdi army prohibits posting pictures of other candidates competing with Muqtada al-Sadr? Is the reluctance of the AKP in Turkey to constitutionally establish the freedom of faith a sign of democracy? Is the totalitarian ideology of *hakimiyyat Allah*/God's rule in a shari'a state as envisioned by the Muslim Brotherhood in Egypt consonant with democracy?

What is the Relation between Religious Fundamentalism and Islamism?

In affirming the idea that democracy is not simply a voting procedure, but primarily a political culture of pluralism, civil society, individual human rights, of contestation and of secular tolerance, we have to ask how democratic a constitution is that provides the following: "No laws may contradict the fixed principles of Islam and create a supreme court composed of experts in Islamic law that will have the power to strike laws down as unconstitutional"(*Wall Street Journal*, September 19, 2005, p. A15). This language, cited by the *Wall Street Journal*, refers to a clause of the Iraqi constitution. A similar provision exists in the Afghan constitution. Clearly, such provisions are not models for democratization, but rather for the shari'atization of the state (see note 10).

Democracy and Democratization in the Arab World: Their Failure as Ground for the Rise of Political Islam

The UNDP report on the Arab world, written in 2002 by Arab experts, states that the core problems of the region, underlying its backwardness, are related to the absence of democracy and human rights (see note 20). The report acknowledges the failure to introduce democracy, in the modern sense, at home.

The failure of Arab leaders to deliver democratic rule in their encounter with modernity has led, in fact, to the rise of political Islam. It is wrong to blame outside powers and their influences for this state of affairs. And it is inappropriate to ask why India, despite its colonial past, is a democratic state while Arab countries are not.

References to colonial rule fail to provide a sufficient explanation for the difference. We must ask instead why attempts to introduce democracy in the Arab world have failed while non-Western countries have succeeded—why Middle Eastern countries remain outside the third wave of democratization.

The following periodization of modern Arab history needs to be kept in mind as we answer the questions:

1. A period of Arab liberal thought prevailed in the region from Tahtawi in the early 19th century until the early 1930s. During this period early post-colonial experiments with democratic rule took place—in Egypt, Syria, and Iraq, for instance—and systems of parliamentarian democracy were accepted and implemented. The period represented an encounter with Europe—a positive encounter as the Arab world confronted the challenge of modernity, and a negative encounter in the post-colonial context. Corruption and clientelism were evident and they are clearly homemade obstacles to democracy.
2. The failure of democratic rule by multi-party systems 1920–52 smoothed the way for various coups d'etat, coups d'etat that established populist rule by the military. Clientelism and corruption were identified with the democratic multi-party system of the first period. That system was replaced by authoritarian single-party systems, Nasserism and Baathism. The

secular ideology of pan-Arab populism replaced liberal thought and pluralism as a theoretical base for the change. Pan-Arab populism viewed pluralism, expressed in multi-party democratic structures, as divisive, resulting in the fragmentation of Arab nations. Some Pan-Arab thinkers argued for a specific Arab "democracy" based on unity—an argumentative strategy which concealed the fact that dictatorships were at work in the name of Arab authenticity.

3. The defeat of the Arab secular-populist regimes in the Six Days War[21] of 1967 opened the way for a kind of "enlightenment" instigated by disillusioned Arab intellectuals, who asked for "self-criticism". The desire for self-criticism did not last long. Instead, the rise of "The Islamic solution/*al hall al-Islami*" (see note 13) has produced a truly populist, mobilizing, ideology, pushing away the seeds of "enlightenment". Political Islam offers its own ideology and system of rule called "*hakimiyyat Allah*/God's rule." In Volume I of his trilogy *al-hall al-Islami/ The Islamic Solution* (see the reference in note 13) the most influential Muslim Brother and global TV mufti of our present time, Yusuf Qaradawi (he appears regularly as "global mufti" in al-Jazeera television) coined the formula "imported solutions". In Volume I as well Qaradawi rejects "democratic rule" as a failed, imported solution. For Qaradawi, an authentic "Islamic solution" stands in opposition and contrast to democracy. This writing is the true face of political Islam, a fact most Westerners do not understand. Its reality is evident in Iraq, Palestine, Lebanon and Turkey.

Two lessons are to be learned from the Iraq case. First, democracy cannot be introduced from the outside. Second, if democracy is to be established in the Arab world, its needs to be rooted domestically. Therefore, consideration of local givens and constraints, and a honoring of cultural peculiarities, needs to be undertaken, and on the agenda, of any party or interest seeking to introduce democracy and democratization to a particular region. Such efforts must not fall into the trap of legitimating particularism as an expression of Arab authenticity.

A balanced assessment of these claims considers Islam even as it also considers cultural peculiarities in the Arab world, and a return of the sacred during a crisis of secularism. Restraints must be put on the application of cultural relativism in any attempt to found democracies in the Arab world. I therefore opt for, and argue for, recognizing limits on diversity as democratic enactment takes place, in favor of establishing cross-cultural international standards as an alternate ground for democratization. Above all, I argue against the reintroduction of the shari'a in the name of democracy (see note 10), and also against what Islamists term the "*dawla Islamiyya*/Islamic state."²² In my view, the Islamic state is not consonant with democracy, but amounts to a new totalitarianism. I view the institution of democracy and human rights as an alternative to Islamic fundamentalism.

I need to make clear that this rejection of Islamism is not a rejection of Islam.

Islam itself is a cultural underpinning for democracy in the Arab world; indeed democracy in the Arab world must rest on Islam. However, the reference to Islam must be restricted to an Islamic ethics (note 31) of democracy, never elevated to an Islamist shari'a-based rule. I therefore reject the approach of Esposito and Voll[23] to Islam and democracy—an approach widely disseminated but utterly wrong. More promising are efforts by enlightened Muslims to rethink Islam and recommend an Islamic reformation. I cite especially the works of M. Arkoun and M.A. al-Jabri in this regard.[24] By contrast with Esposito and Voll, new thinking needs to distinguish between Islam and Islamism, and then draw differences *within political Islam* between institutional and jihadist Islamism. Unless analysts take these substantial distinctions into account, no useful analysis is in sight. The present paper views the contemporary debate on democracy in the Arab world as a proper response to terrorism, and considers the distinctions given above under conditions of bipolarity in general, and the repercussions of the Iraq war in particular.

Long before the promotion of liberal democracy became the catchword of the 1990s in the West, Arab opinion leaders themselves and other Muslims as well[25] engaged in discussing the problems of Islam, freedom and democracy. They focused on Islamic civilization in its present position at the crossroads. Having dealt with Arab dictators in a benign manner for decades, Western politicians began at the same time to consider the need for democratization in the Middle East as a 21st-century initiative. In particular after September 11, the West started to seriously consider a promoting of democracy in the Arab world as a new strategy. Their thinking was not new.

As early as November 1983, pro-democracy Arab opinion leaders met to address this pertinent issue. Having been denied the right to hold their meeting in an Arab city (Cairo), they had to resort to a foreign Mediterranean city, Limassol in Cyprus. The title of this historical meeting was "The Crisis of Democracy/*Azmat al-*

democratiyya"²⁶ in the Arab world. The Arab presenters and facilitators attending the conference were aware of the fact that democracy would be a cultural novelty with respect to the Arab-Islamic *turath/* cultural legacy. Therefore, they were conscious of existing structural and cultural obstacles standing in the way of democratization, thus creating impediments to its implementation. They recognized that "culture matters"²⁷ for democratization.

The 2002 UNDP report on "Arab Human Development" prepared by Arab experts (see note 20) does not refer to the proceedings of the Arab congress of 1983 mentioned above (note 26), nevertheless highlights the fact that the intensifying misery of the region is primarily home-grown and is due to the absence of democracy. I agree with the report, and argue that although we must not overlook structural and political impediments to democracy in the Middle East, both internal and external, we must argue that the absence of democracy is also related to cultural factors as constraints. The absence of democracy and human rights in the Arab world is therefore to be discussed under the formula cited above, "culture matters". At issue is the absence of democracy as a political culture and, of course, of absence of institutions intended to safeguard such a culture. To alter this state of affairs, cultural change is needed.

Post Saddam Hussein Iraq is a critical case in this discussion. The Iraq war,²⁸ waged in the name of democracy, did not contribute to, or promote, democratization as imagined by those who started the war, but has instead exacerbated the issues under consideration in this paper. First, since March 2003, tensions between the Arab-Muslim world and the West have intensified. Second, tensions within the West with regard to understanding democracy, have deepened the transatlantic rift between European and American opinion leaders. Third, the status of political Islam (Islamism), including the position of Iran in the region, has been strengthened. The repercussions of the Iraq war seem to reverse the formula "from global jihad to democratic peace"²⁹ coined to express the hope of including the Arab world in a new wave of global democratization. Instead, the region is moving from comparative stability toward global jihad. The battlefield for this trend is Iraq, where it has become abundantly clear that public understandings of "democracy" and "the rule of law" differ markedly from understandings of these concepts in other cultures, especially the West. The Islamists especially understand "democracy" in their own way.

Europeans clearly positioned themselves when they chose to commemorate the victims of the Madrid attacks of 11 March 2004 during the Madrid meeting in March 2005. The Madrid meeting focused on "security" within the formula of "safe democracy",[30] a formulation viewed as an alternative to the American "war on terrorism". These transatlantic differences are not the concern of this paper. Nevertheless I refer to this split in Western attitudes in the spirit of demonstrating that three different (i.e. American, European and Arab-Muslim) understandings of the concept of democracy are currently in play. All of them are pertinent to the present analysis. The very existence of these differences challenges claims about the universality of democracy and the rule of law. The existing fault lines are related to cultural constraints which are responsible for the failure of contemporary efforts to introduce democracy to the Arab world. Of course, the absence of structural requirements and needed institutions is equally important. Given the politicization and shari'atization of Islam pursued by Islamists—the only effective opposition to autocracy in the Arab states—the potential consonance of Islamism with democracy is the critical issue to be assessed. From my standpoint, once rethinking of Islamic political thought takes place and religious reforms are enacted, democracy can be harmonized with Islam.[31] I have grave doubts about whether democracy can be harmonized with Islamism.

The Call of Political Islam for the Shari'a as a Constitutional Law[32] in an "Islamic State" and the Shari'atization of Islamic Politics

When Western politicians and commentators define democracy and essential steps toward achieving it, they consistently speak about the rule of law. Postmodern and universalist thinkers in the West seem not to know that there is no common understanding of law. For Muslims, law is the shari'a, a view evident in Iraq among both Shi'a and Sunna. Shari'a law is in direct conflict with international legal standards.[33] For jihadists, shari'a is an absolute; for institutional Islamists, shari'a can be institutionalized in constitutions, as happened in Iraq.

Democratization in our age of Islamism proves to be a most uneasy task. The shari'a is not a constitutional law and its use to legitimate an Islamic state cannot be considered an alternative to the existing malaise. Yet, there is a need for change. In talking about change, mere descriptions of a sad situation cannot be satisfactory. Change requires, first, an explanation of the social malady underlying the need for change in order to determine where we are and where to go. Second, it requires freedom among critics of the present situation to analyze the situation itself and present it in public forums. Such freedoms do not exist for Muslim reformers, who are committed to establishment of democracy and who point at tensions between the shari'a and international law. Arab intellectuals, who are committed to the cause of liberty, are unable to speak freely, unable to act freely to establish an authentic framework for democracy in their own countries. Either they fear imprisonment if they reveal their political commitments, or, if they are allowed to speak of those commitments, lack access to the means of cultural and political expression. The means of cultural and political expression are under the complete control and surveillance of the state, reserved for mercenary intellectuals willing to subject themselves to state ideologies and propagate them. Given the fact that at present Islamism is the only visible opponent to such repression, a shari'a-inspired order, i.e. the Islamist option for an Islamist state, comes to seem natural to some.

The repression of intellectuals who advocate democracy, and who analyze contemporary political realities, was noted as early as October 1980, when Arab scholars and thinkers assembled in Tunis to address the future of their region, including the option for democracy. They easily reached consensus during the 1980 meeting, concluding that the option of democracy. In this context they easily reached a consensus. There is (was) no political freedom in the majority of Arab countries, and there is a need for change for the Arabs *"face à leur destin"*.[34] Arab advocates of political change and democratic reform face another obstacle as well: the "orientalist" bias that guides perception of the Arab world in the West (whether in Europe or the United States). Some in the West cite incompatibility between democracy and Islam. Others continue the thinking of Edward Said, whose work is described by a prominent Arab writer, Sadiq Jalal al-Azm, as an example of "Orientalism in reverse".[35]

The need of the moment is to accept the fact that post bipolarity is an age of cultural turn. I place (and read) the varying explanations for the absence of democracy in the Middle East in this larger context. It is not enough for reformers inside (or outside) the Arab world to blame imperialism and other external factors as the only causes for the failure to institute democracy. Blame games referencing "conspiracies/ *mu'amarah*"[36] lead nowhere. Better to recover and enact the approach of Sadiq Jalal al-Azm, who advocated an approach of self-criticism committed to the ideals and rationality of the Enlightenment.[37] In medieval Islam, the standard of reason-based knowledge prevailed, in the context of Hellenization, but not so today. It is not shari'a, declared "constitutional law," but rather Islamic rationalism that needs to be revived, accepted and enacted. In order to establish political freedom, Arab societies need as well to establish the structural and institutional underpinnings of democracy. Such underpinnings are not only ideas but practices, including the practices of human rights, freedom of expression and freedom of assembly. All members of Arab society must participate, at every level. The culture of democratic pluralism, practiced within structural and institutional frameworks, is the essence of democracy. Let it be stated in candor: unreformed Islam has a predicament with the political culture of pluralism[38] and only a reform Islam is in position to come to terms with it.

Conclusions: Is Democracy Alien to the Arabs?

As stated earlier, democracy as a cultural concept is a novelty introduced into the world of Islam. In an age of identity politics,[39] and in the context of the cultural turn, we must discuss whether democracy as a cultural concept comports with the claimed authenticity of Islam. The spirit of socially emerging "gated communities" is culturalized, negatively affecting democratization. At this historical moment, the universality of democracy remains at issue for many, if not most, Arab thinkers.

There is an established tradition in Islam of the Imam in power as a personalized authority.[40] Writing from this perspective, Majid Khadduri has published many books in which Arab politics is reduced to the study of the biographies of Arab politicians.[41] This approach could be methodologically viewed as flawed and smacks of Orientalism. Power in Arab politics is in fact personalized, that is, not subject to institutional limitations. This does not mean, of course, that no institutions or structures underlie personalized politics in Arab societies. In Islamic history, the traditional question was: "Who is the *Imam fadil*/right Imam?" (see note 40) not "what are proper and just institutions?" (see note 48).

Among the very few exceptions in Islamic tradition, one finds al-Farabi's classical work on *al-Madina al-fadila*[42] in which he discusses the proper order for continuing the ancient Greek legacy within the Islamic tradition of rationalism. This reference to Islamic intellectual history shows that universal standards are possible without fully rejecting the notion of authenticity. The point is that institutions matter.

It is also worthwhile to look at Barrington Moore's *Social Origins of Dictatorship and Democracy*.[43] Moore provides a comparative analysis of Western and non-Western historical types of political development. He demonstrates that those European societies which were able to develop a pattern of democracy had had certain comparatively autonomous medieval institutions. The unfolding of these institutions contributed to strengthening the society vis-à-vis the state. Practices and institutions during the medieval period undergird much later developments in Europe. A working democracy presupposes the existence of institutions of a civil state and a civil society, not only a concept of a civil Islam such as the one that exists, founded on indigenous cultural grounds, in Indonesia. In the Arab world, civil society is weak, as are all the participatory institutions of the state. The only working institution is the one of *mukhabarat*, the secret police guaranteeing oppressive surveillance of the population.

Under these conditions the *asalah*/authenticy debate is no more than ideological talk, whether by political Islam speaking against the existing order, by the Islamic rulers seeking to undermine any democratization. Therefore, too often references to the historical origins of democracy in Europe serve to undergird arguments for the claim that democracy does not apply to Islam. Nevertheless there are courageous Arab intellectuals and their organizations, such as Saad Eddin Ibrahim and his Ibn Khaldūn Center for Civil Society, who define and promote the conditions necessary for the institution of democracy.[44] These efforts are, as it is well known, oppressed by the state and deprived of their necessary impact. Ibrahim told his story at the summit of Madrid in March 2005 after he was released from his jail in Cairo.

I conclude that learning from others as cultural borrowing is not alien to the history of Arab-Islamic heritage. Democracy has Greek origins, but Hellenism was also a part of the Islamic legacy. Varieties of democracy have adjusted to diverse local conditions in various parts of the world. The local/global duality should, however, never serve as an argument for rejecting universality: i.e. commonalities which define democracy trump civilizational differences. Authenticity, identity politics and the need for cross-cultural commonalities can be harmonized; they need not rival one another. To date, the Islamists have not understood or met this standard. Therefore, the success of their political organizations in achieving power and even the vote—such as Hamas (Palestine), SCIRI (Iraq), the Wasat Party (Egypt), Muslim Brothers (Egypt), Hizbollah (Lebanon), al-Nahda (Tunisia), the Islamic Action Front (Jordan), FIS (Algeria) among others—is not a sign of victorious democracy, nor of a democratization.

This critical assessment is not meant to rebuke the contemporary Islamic revival, but to assert that the adoption of democracy requires many different steps and strategies. We need to distinguish once again between Islam in general, and varieties of political Islam, those calling for a shari'a state in particular. Long before political Islam became a popular public choice, the Lebanese political scientist Hassan Saab, one of the true proponents of liberal democracy in the Arab world, published a book in which he argued for a "pro-democracy Islam" as opposed to an "Islam of despotism". Saab argued for a "comprehensive spiritual revolution in the soul of the man and in his life too".[45] This was (and is) a plea for an attitudinal cultural change required in order to achieve democracy in the Arab world (see note 27). Saab supports the argument that culture matters if democratic traditions are to be introduced. This kind of liberal Islamic thinking, committed to democracy, is rare among the Islamists of our present.

In short, it can be concluded that the return of the sacred via Islamism does not signal a renaissance of religion,[46] nor is it an expression of a spiritual Islam. If Islamists honestly—i.e. not tactically—accept democracy, then it would be wrong to address them as Islamists, because the term "Islamism" would no longer apply to them. The ideology of political Islam is based on the very belief "*din-wa-daula*/unity of state and religion". Both of its current directions, i.e. institutional Islamism on the one hand and jihadism on the other, share this mindset even though institutional Islamists accept to play the game of voting under "democratic" procedures. Institutional Islamists do this for tactical reasons and therefore dispense with jihadist violent actions. However, they do not share the political culture of democratic pluralism. By contrast, Islamist jihadists believe in global jihad, that is in an Islamic world revolution as the only means of restoring the global *siyadat al-Islam*/Islamic supremacy.

In combating terrorism we need to deal with Islamism democratically via an inclusive not an exclusive strategy. It is a democratic attitude to include the institutional Islamists in the game of democracy, while watching their actions to ensure that no undermining of democratization is at stake in the name of democracy. When it comes to jihadists the only reasonable approach for dealing with their violence is a security strategy. For jihadists it is only the *action directe* of violence that counts. This double strategy requires simultaneously dialogue with Islam and a security approach vis-à-vis Islamism.[47]

The final statement in these conclusions is that the views of contemporary political Islam, as expressed by Yusuf al-Qaradawi who rejects democracy as an "*hall mustawrad*/imported solution," can only be countered by widespread public education in democracy.[48] The latter is urgently needed in the Arab core of Islamic civilization. While engaging in this venture it will be necessary to contradict those who see in Hamas and similar movements contributors to democracy. The bottom line is this: the Islamism of the new Islamists is not an "Islam without fear".[49] For me, as a liberal Muslim, it causes "fears" to be taken seriously. The "democracy" of political Islam is not the light at the end of the tunnel freedom-loving Arabs are yearning for.

Endnotes

1. See the commentaries by Bassam Tibi, "The Clash of Shari'a and Democracy," *International Herald Tribune*, September 17/18 (2005) p. 6; and "So wird der Irak nicht demokratisch," *Die Zeit* (March 9, 2006) p. 10.
2. On the history of this movement and its ideology see the classic by Richard Mitchell, *The Society of the Muslim Brothers* (London: Oxford University Press, 1969).
3. See Bassam Tibi, *The Challenge of Fundamentalism. Political Islam and the New World Disorder* (Berkeley, CA: University of California Press, 1998; updated 2002).
4. See Bassam Tibi, "The Totalitarianism of Jihadist Islamism and its Challenge to Islam and to Europe," in: *Totalitarian Movements and Political Religion*, vol. 8, 1 (March 2007) pp. 35–54.
5. Samir al-Khalil, *Republic of Fear. The Politics of Modern Iraq* (Berkeley, CA: University of California Press, 1994).
6. On the Shi'a of Iraq, see Yitzhak Nakash, *The Shi'is of Iraq* (Princeton, NJ: Princeton University Press, 1994); more recent, but more biased: Faleh A. Jabar, *The Shi'ite Movements in Iraq* (London: Saqi, 2003). See also the recent book by Nakash, *Reaching for Power. The Shi'a in the Modern Arab World* (Princeton, NJ: Princeton University Press, 2006).
7. See Shaul Mishal and Avraham Sela, *The Palestinian Hamas* (New York: Columbia University Press, 2000); and the most recent study by Matthew Levitt, *Hamas. Politics, Charity and Terrorism in the Service of Jihad* (New Haven, CT: Yale University Press, 2006) and on the overall context Beverley Milton-Edwards, *Islamic Politics in Palestine* (London: Tauris, 1996) is still worth being read.
8. On the Turkish AKP as an Islamist party see Bassam Tibi, *Mit dem Kopftuch nach Europa? Europa auf dem Weg in die E.U.* (Darmstadt: Primus-Verlag, 2005; updated and expanded 2007), chapter one; and M. Howe, *Turkey Today—A Nation Divided over Islam's Renewal* (Boulder, CO: Westview Press, 2000), chapter 15 and also pp. 243–63.
9. See Michael Emerson (ed.), *Democratization in the Neighborhood* (Brussels: Centre of European Policy Studies/CEPS, 2005), which includes a chapter by Bassam Tibi, "Islam, Freedom and Democracy," pp. 93–116.
10. The Islamist use of *Shari'a* is different from traditional *Shari'a*. See

Bassam Tibi, *Islam between Culture and Politics* (New York: Palgrave, 2001; expanded 2nd edition 2005), chapter 7, pp. 148–66.

11. See the chapter on "Democratization" old and new in Beverley Milton-Edwards, *Contemporary Politics in the Middle East* (Cambridge: Polity, 2000), pp. 145–72.
12. See Franz Rosenthal, *The Classical Heritage of Islam. Arab Thought and Culture* (London: Routledge, 1994). On the two waves of the Hellenization of Islam see W.M. Watt, *Islamic Philosophy and Theology* (Edinburgh: Edinburgh University Press, 1962, reprint 1979), part two and three.
13. Yusuf al-Qaradawi, *al-hall al-Islami*, 3 volumes, vol. 1: *al-hulul al-mustawradah*/The Imported Solutions (Cairo: al-Risalah, 1970; reprint 1980). This al-Qaradawi speaks weekly in Jazeera TV and is therefore viewed as "global mufti".
14. Leslie Lipson, *The Ethical Crises of Civilization* (London: Sage, 1993), p. 62.
15. See Robert Hefner, *Civil Islam. Muslims and Democratization in Indonesia* (Princeton, NJ: Princeton University Press, 2000).
16. See the references in notes 3 and 4 and the early study by Nazih Ayubi, *Political Islam* (London: Routledge, 1991). See also the entry chapter by this author on "Fundamentalism," in Mary Hawkesworth and Maurice Kogan (eds.), *Routledge Encyclopedia of Government and Politics*, 2 vols. (London: Routledge, 2004), here vol. 1, pp. 184–204. See also note 3 above.
17. See Hisham Sharabi, *Arab Neo-Patriarchy. A Theory of Distorted Change in Arab Society* (New York: Oxford University Press, 1992; first 1988) and see Michael Hudson, *Arab Politics. The Search for Legitimacy* (New Haven, CT: Yale University Press, 1977), in particular pp. 1–30.
18. This concept is used in line with Jürgen Habermas, *The Philosophical Discourse of Modernity* (Cambridge, MA: MIT Press, 1987).
19. On political Islam in Egypt see Barry Rubin, *Islamic Fundamentalism in Egyptian Politics* (London: Macmillan, 1990); and more recently, Carrie Rosefsky-Wickham, *Mobilizing Islam. Religion, Activism and Political Change in Egypt* (New York: Columbia University Press, 2002).
20. UNDP, *Arab Human Development Report. Creating Opportunities for Future Generations* (New York: United Nations, 2002).
21. On the repercussions of the Six Days War see Fouad Ajami, *The Arab Predicament. Arab Political Thought and Practice since 1967* (Cambridge: Cambridge University Press, 1981), in particular on political Islam pp. 50–75. See also Bassam Tibi, *Conflict and War in the Middle East*, 2nd ed. (New York: St. Martin's Press, 1998), chapters 3 and 4, and on political Islam chapter 12.
22. On the ideological concept of an Islamic state see Bassam Tibi, *The Challenge of Fundamentalism* (referenced in note 3), chapters 7 and 8.
23. John Eposito and John Voll, *Islam and Democracy* (New York: Oxford University Press, 1996). These authors not only explicitly fail to distinguish between Islam and Islamism, but also implicitly equate the democ-

ratization of Islam with the Islamization of democracy and go for the latter; see my critical review in *Journal of Religion*, vol. 78, no. 4 (October 1998) pp. 667–69.
24. Mohammed Arkoun, *Rethinking Islam* (Boulder, CO: Westview, 1994) and Mohammed Abed al-Jabri, *Arab-Islamic Philosophy* (Austin, TX: CMES at the University, 1999).
25. In particular worth mentioning is the work of Hamid Enayat, *Modern Islamic Political Thought* (Austin, TX: University of Texas Press, 1982), here pp. 125ff.
26. Center for Arab Unity Studies (ed.), *Azmat al-democratiyya fi al-watan al-Arabi*/The Crisis of Democracy in the Arab World (Beirut: CAUS Press, 1984). This volume includes the papers presented at the historical Limassol meeting. I was there among the speakers and addressed the requirements for democracy in my paper on cultural and structural obstacles. The paper completed in Arabic is included on pp. 73–87 of the cited volume.
27. "The Culture Matters Research Project/CMP" was chaired by Lawrence Harrison at Fletcher School/Tufts University (2003–5). The papers of the project were published 2006 in two volumes (the first, a general one and "Essays on Cultural Change," the second volume "Case Studies" under the title: *Developing Cultures*, edited by L. Harrison and published by Routledge. I am the author of a study on Islam in vol. 1 and of a case study on Egypt in vol. 2).
28. See Liam Anderson and Gareth Stansfield, *The Future of Iraq. Dictatorship, Democracy or Decision?* (New York: Palgrave, 2004).
29. Toby Dodge, *Iraq's Future: The Aftermath of the Regime Change* (London: IISS/Adelphi Papers 372, 2005). See Bassam Tibi, "From Islamist Jihadism to Democratic Peace? Islam at the Crossroads in Post-Bipolar International Politics," *Ankara Papers 16* (London: Taylor & Francis, 2005), pp. 1–41 with a reference to the debate launched by Bruce Russet, *Grasping the Democratic Peace. Principles for a Post-Cold War World* (Princeton, NJ: Princeton University Press, 1993).
30. See the brochure of the Club de Madrid: *Democracy, Terrorism and Security* (International Summit in Madrid, March 8–11 2005) documenting the Madrid Summit on a European democratic response to the challenge of the jihadist terrorism of March 11 2004 as the European variety of September 11 2001.
31. See the references in note 24 and also Bassam Tibi, "Democracy and Democratization in Islam," in: Michèle Schmiegelow (ed.), *Democracy in Asia* (New York: Campus 1997), pp. 127–46.
32. See the reference in note 10 and the seminal work by Joseph Schacht, *An Introduction to Islamic Law* (Oxford: Clarendon Press, 1964; reprint 1979). The third "International Conference on Comparative Constitutional Law," held in Tokyo, September 2–4 2005 added shari'a to its work. See Bassam Tibi, "Islamic Shari'a as Constitutional Law?," in: The Japanese Association of Comparative Law (ed.), *Church and State. Proceedings of the International Conference on Comparative Constitutional Law* (Tokyo: Nihon University, 2006), pp. 126–70.

33. See Abdullahi A. An-Na'im, *Toward an Islamic Reformation. Civil Liberties, Human Rights and International Law* (Syracuse: Syracuse University Press, 1990); and Bassam Tibi, "Islamic Law/Shari'a, Human Rights, Universal Morality and International Relations," *Human Rights Quarterly*, vol. 16, no. 2 (1994), pp. 277–99.
34. See Centre d'Etudes et de Récherches Economiques et Sociales/CERES (ed.), *Les Arabes face à leur destin* (Tunis: CERES, 1980), my chapter on pp. 177–216.
35. The Arab-Muslim Yale-educated Enlightenment philosopher Sadiq Jalal al-Azm speaks in his book *Dhihniyyat al-tahrim*/The Mentality of Taboos (London: Riad el-Rayyes Books, 1992), pp. 17–128 of an "Orientalism in reverse/*al-istishraq ma'kusan*" and addresses this as a conspiracy-driven thinking; see the next note.
36. On conspiracy-driven Arab political thought see Bassam Tibi, *Die Verschwörung/al-Mu'amarah. Das Trauma arabischer Politik* (Hamburg: Hoffmann & Campe, 1993); and the Spanish edition, *La conspiracion. El Trauma de la Politica Arab* (Barcelona: Editorial Herder, 1996).
37. Sadiq Jalal al-Azm, *Al-naqd al-dhati ba'd al-hazima*/Self-Critique after the Defeat (Beirut: al-Tali'a, 1968); see also note 44 above; and on al-Azm see Fouad Ajami, *The Arab Predicament* (referenced in note 21), pp. 30–37.
38. See Bassam Tibi, "The Pertinence of Islam's Predicament with Democratic Pluralism for Democratization," *Religion-Staat-Gesellschaft*, vol. 7, 1 (2006), pp. 83–117.
39. See Gary Lehring, "Identity Politics," in: Mary Hawkesworth and Maurice Kogan (eds), *Routledge Encyclopedia of Government and Politics*, new edition (London: Routledge, 2004) pp. 576–86; and my chapter "Fundamentalism" on pp. 184–204. On Islamic identity politics see Bassam Tibi, Islam: "Between Religious-Cultural Practice and Identity Politics," in: Helmut Anheier and Raj Isar (eds.), *Culture, Globalization and Conflict* (London: Sage, 2007).
40. On this see Bassam Tibi, *Der wahre Imam. Der Islam von Mohammed bis zur Gegenwart* (Munich: Piper, 1996; reprinted several times, last 2002). See also Fouad Khuri, *Imams and Emirs. State, Religion and Sects in Islam* (London: Saqi, 1990).
41. The books by Majid Khadduri, *Arab Contemporaries. The Role of Personalities in Politics* (Baltimore, MD: The John Hopkins University Press, 1973); and *Arab Personalities in Politics* (Washington, DC: Middle East Institute, 1981) read like an illustration of this tradition of Imam personalizing political authority.
42. Abu Nasr al-Farabi, *al-Madina al-Fadila*/On the Perfect State, translated and edited by Richard Walzer (New York: Oxford University Press, 1985).
43. Barrington Moore, *Social Origins of Dictatorship and Democracy* (Boston, MA: Beacon Press, 1966).
44. Saad Eddin Ibrahim (ed.), *al-Mujtama'al-Madani*/Civil Society, Annual

Yearbook (Cairo: Markaz Ibn Khaldūn, 1993). On the ideas of Saad Eddin Ibrahim see his book *Egypt. Islam and Democracy* (Cairo: AUC Press, 1996), in particular chapter 12 on civil society and the prospects of democratization in the Arab world, pp. 245–66.
45. Hassan Saab, *al-Islam tijah tahidiyat al-hayat al-'asriyya* (Beirut: Dar al-Ilm, 1965), p. 123.
46. On this issue see Bassam Tibi, "Habermas and the Return of the Sacred. Is it a Religious Renaissance or the Emergence of Political Religion as a New Totalitarianism?," *Religion-Staat-Gesellschaft. Journal for the Study of Beliefs and Worldviews*, vol. 3, no. 2 (2002), pp. 205–96.
47. On the needed double-track strategy see Bassam Tibi, "Between Islam and Islamism. A Dialogue with Islam as a Pattern of Conflict Resolution and a Security Approach vis-à-vis Islamism," in: Tami A. Jacoby and Brent E. Sasley (eds.), *Redefining Security in the Middle East* (Manchester: Manchester University Press, 2002), pp. 62–82.
48. See Bassam Tibi, "Education and Democratization in an Age of Islamism," in Alan M. Olson, David M. Steiner and Irina S. Tuuli (eds.), *Education for Democracy: Paideia in an Age of Uncertainty* (Lanham, MD: Rowman & Littlefield, 2004), pp. 203–19. This publication grew from the Paideia Project run at Boston University, where the papers were presented and discussed ahead. See also the publication of the CEPS project referenced in note 16 above.
49. There I strongly reject the argument of Raymond W. Baker, *Islam without Fear. Egypt and the New Islamists* (Cambridge, MA: Harvard University Press, 2003), see also the references to Egypt and Islamism in notes 19 and 27 above.

5

Militant Muslims and Democracy: Knowns and Unknowns

Saad Eddin Ibrahim

What Do We Know about Militant Muslims?

1. *Religious Narrative.* The militants' reading of Islam as enunciated in its Holy Book, the *Qur'an*, and the *Sunna* or traditions of the Prophet Mohammed, is that it is the perfect religion, culminating and subsuming all other monotheistic religions—i.e. Judaism and Christianity. Its uniqueness lies in its simplicity and lucidity, as it needs no clergy to mediate between the Creator God Almighty and the believers. Islam's claim to superiority draws from its comprehensiveness as a belief system, a worship system, and a transactional system of rules and regulations to guide Muslims in everyday life. The militants further believe that strict adherence to its precepts and rules (the shari'a), ensures a perfect community (*Umma*) in this world, and access to Heavenly Paradise in the Hereafter.

2. *Historical Narrative.* For the militants, the history of Islam and Muslims is broadly divided into two stages. There was the Golden Age of the Prophet Mohammed and his four Guided Successors (*al-Kholafa al-Rashideen*) in which the *Umma* was pious, virtuous, just, and strong. Muslims were the masters of the world in all respects—from culture and science to commerce and military. They had an empire that extended from the Great Wall of China in the East to the Iberian Peninsula in the Atlantic West. The second stage was one of steady decline and decay, as Muslims increasingly strayed away from "The Straight Path" (*al-Sirat al-Mustaqim*) of Islam, resulting in the

disintegration of their empire. Ultimately, Muslims were encroached upon by non-Muslims, and the "Abode of Islam" (*Dar al-Islam*) was colonized by the heathens and infidels, who have not ceased their humiliation of the believers.

3. *Moral Narrative.* To restore their souls, dignity, land and power (*ezza*), Muslims must rid themselves of all repugnant thoughts, beliefs, and behaviors, and go back to *al-Sirat al-Mustaqim*. In so doing, Muslims will be rightfully repenting to Allah Almighty, emulating the Prophet and his blessed companions. They will obtain the same results: a virtuous, just, powerful community on earth and eternal Heaven in the Hereafter. As in most ideologies, these purified narratives are internalized in the would-be Islamic "activist," and with a dose of passion turn "militant." With additional doses he (or she) would be a deployable "martyr" (*shaheed*). Martyrdom is the ultimate sacrifice for the *Umma*, Service to the Faith, and a shortcut to Eternal Heavenly Paradise.

4. *Membership Profile.* As in most radical movements, most Islamic activists are young, educated, and idealistic. They seek individual salvation and more collective self-fulfillment. After a few years, the movement becomes their life and career. As they invariably engage in violent actions, the movement becomes their only refuge from "hostile authorities" at home or abroad. Membership commitment to the movement strengthens it until it becomes total immersion, submergence, and submission. At this point, deployment of members becomes all the easier for the leadership.

5. *Evolutionary Trajectory.* Though most Islamic movements start as local affairs, they quickly discover or contrive kinship affinities with the like-minded across national boundaries. This is often facilitated by common articles of faith, such as that all Muslims are brothers. Religious solidarity supersedes all other loyalties such as to race, class, or nation. It is also facilitated by common narratives and a shared perception of a real or imagined common enemy, be it atheist Soviets or decadent Westerners. As it becomes transnational, and with a few successful exploits against the enemy, such movements acquire an aura of their own and attract broader support from Muslim youth worldwide. The likes of Osama bin Laden become folk heroes, as Ché Guevarra was to millions around the world in the 1960s. As movements globalize in membership, resources, and action, they also begin to broaden their ideological reframing of issues and

strategic outreach. Thus, the plight of Palestinians, Iraqis, and Muslims in the Philippines, Bosnia, Kashmir, and Chechnya has become a common cause for all Islamic militants, regardless of birthplace or current nationality.

6. *Reasons for Outrage.* Other than the perceived reasons for discontent with protracted autocracy at home, the militants' reading of the world situation adds to their outrage. The non-Muslim "Other" who is currently at the root of the domination and exploitation of *Dar al-Islam* is Western hegemony in general and the United States in particular. The earlier struggle to bring down the godless rulers at home may have failed or been made more difficult because of their unholy alliance with or subservience to the sinister West. Therefore, the dual jihad is justifiably directed against both the "near" and "far" enemy. The battlefront becomes worldwide, i.e. from the Philippines to the United States, and from Turkey to Morocco.

7. *The Mobilizing Power of the Islamic Metaphor.* Causes have been staunchly fought under the banner of Islam: from the anti-Shah struggle in the 1970s, to the Soviet occupation of Afghanistan in the 1980s, to the Israeli occupation of southern Lebanon (1982–2000), to the Palestinian resistance in Gaza and the West Bank, to that of Chechnya against the Russian Federation. While these and similar fights may have local triggers, different beginnings, and only slight organizational links to one another, they have all discovered the potent mobilizing power of "Islam." Some 40 years ago, Clifford Geertz discovered this potential as he observed Islam in practice at both ends of the Muslim world, Indonesia and Morocco. Despite vast differences in interpretations, rituals, and religiosity, at both ends it was the Islamic metaphor that exuded an ambiguous but powerful sense of purpose and collective identity. It is this metaphor that militant Islamists have appropriated and are exploiting to the hilt.

What do We Need to Know about Islamists?

1. Militants are not the only spokespeople for Islam or for the 1.4 billion Muslims. In fact, indisputable evidence indicates that militants are a tiny portion of Islamic activists, who are themselves a minority among today's adult Muslims. There has been a lively debate among competing Islamic groups in nearly every Muslim country and across national borders about the "proper understanding" of Islam and the "proper conduct" of Muslims

in the contemporary world. As in all debates, there are shades and nuances along both ideational and organizational lines. The debate has become more passionate since 9/11. An expanding Muslim public is alarmed by the "hijacking" of Islam by extreme militants like bin Laden and those implicated in the 9/11 attacks and similar violent episodes. Identifying major interlocutors and mapping out the contours of this ongoing debate is only a beginning; we need to refine and sharpen our understanding of this raging discourse.

2. Competing Islamic activists are targeting several constituencies at home and abroad for engagement, spreading their messages, pleading for sympathetic understanding, for civilized dialogue or for constructive partnerships. At home such constituencies include the government in power, the public at large, women, and non-Muslim communities. Abroad, they include expatriate Muslim communities living in the West, and Western governments, especially the United States. At one extreme of this sought-out engagement is an open war, al Qaeda versus the United States and its perceived allies. At the other extreme end is a quest for partnership and inclusion. The Turkish Islamic Party of Justice and Development (AKP) has made hundreds of reforms in order to gain the accession of Turkey into the European Union. How much support does each of these competing Islamic variants command in its respective society, and the Islamic world at large, and specifically within each of the targeted constituencies? The University of Michigan's World Value Survey produces raw data on this and other related questions. But rigorous analysis and further research are still needed. What are the shifts underway, if any, in the relative weight, influence, and language of discourse among competing and rival Islamic groups, as well as between their joint camp and the "secularists" or non-Islamists?

3. Several Islamic groups have recently disavowed violence, declared their commitment to democracy, and engagement in politics. Wherever and whenever opportunities have permitted, some of them have in fact acted accordingly, such as in Indonesia, Morocco, Turkey, Yemen, Jordan, Kuwait, and Bahrain. More recently, the Muslim Brotherhood in Egypt and its Palestinian offshoot Hamas have opted for electoral politics, and shown better-than-expected voter approval. Many observers at home and abroad are casting doubt on the sincerity of the Islamists' commitments to democracy. Since social actors

are neither born "extremists" nor "moderates," it is reasonable to search and test hypotheses bearing on conditions —structural, situational, or international—of processes that lead to either. It may very well turn out that research on the issue at hand could be framed on rules and conditions of inclusion and exclusion vis-à-vis the societal and global mainstream.
4. In October of 1996, Istanbul's Swedish Institute hosted a conference on Islam, Democracy, and Civil Society. The Taliban had just seized power through military force in Afghanistan, and the Islamist Necmettin Erbakan had just been democratically voted Prime Minister in Turkey. A conference paper noting these contrasting events in the name of Islam was titled "From Taliban to Erbakan: The case of Islam, Civil Society and Democracy." Today, neither is in power, but their successors and remnants are still around, albeit metamorphosed. The Taliban were bombarded out of power and became fugitives in the mountains. After his ousting by the Turkish military, Erbakan's Fadhila Party was reconstituted as Tayyip Erdogan's AKP. Between the Afghani and Turkish variants there is the Muslim Brotherhood, which has been evolving and devolving since its inception in 1928. The tapestry of Islamic movements across the world from Indonesia to Morocco provides ample opportunity for both theoretical and policy research in social sciences.
5. When the Istanbul conference was held in the mid-1990s, barely one-third of the world's Muslims were living under democratically elected governments. Ten years later, the percentage has doubled to two-thirds. Does the regional neighborhood have much to do with this transition from non-democratic to democratic governance? Is it socio-political pressures, or is it globalization?

What Kind of War Is Winnable with Islamists?

If war begins as an idea in the human mind, so does peace. Terrorism and counterterrorism are no exceptions, if we factor out what particular parties to a conflict use in the way of terminology—e.g. jihad, martyrdom, suicide, or terrorism. The question, however, is whether that kind of war is winnable by force of arms, or whether it must be fought and settled by other means. If so, what are these means? These and related questions would be at the core of policy-oriented research on Islamic movements in the twenty-first century.

Much of contemporary Islamic-related militancy is a mirror image of enduring autocracy in many of the majority Muslim countries. Between autocracy and theocracy, democratic governance represents the most viable alternative. It should be given an opportunity.

6

The United Nations and Terrorism

Jeffrey Laurenti

That the United Nations itself should be singled out for terrorist attack would inevitably come as a shock to the organization and the public. Its charter mission of peace—with the mandate to address the sources of conflict as well as the symptoms—and its claim to impartiality should have insulated it from even the cauldron of Middle East strife. But a spectacular attack taking the life of the head of a U.N. mission would make clear that even the United Nations could be the target of violent extremists for whom an honest broker represents a dangerous obstacle to fervently held political objectives.

This grim reality was brought home in the U.N.'s earliest years, with the assassination of Folke Bernadotte in September 1948 by Jewish terrorists intent on sabotaging his effort to end the four-month Arab-Israeli war with a compromise settlement falling far short of Zionist aspirations. Almost precisely 55 years later, a savage attack on the United Nations headquarters in Baghdad killed the head of the U.N. mission, Sérgio Vieira de Mello, and 16 others—and with them the faint hope that the United Nations could nurture a post Saddam political order broadly acceptable to Iraqis, independent of the Americans. In both cases, shadowy extremists' use of terrorism against the peacemakers succeeded in wrecking a process toward a peaceful solution and underscored the U.N.'s own vulnerability and apparent ineffectuality.

Terrorist violence is even more problematical for the United Nations than for the states that constitute it. The paradigm of political violence against which the international security institutions of the post war era were organized was of classic armed conflict organized by states. The U.N. was chartered—like the North Atlantic Treaty Organization and subsequent alliances and regional pacts—to thwart aggression and breaches of the peace by *states*. The international legislation limiting warfare to armed combatants and barring the targeting of civilians—inspired by revulsion at how ground troops and aerial bombing had terrorized civilian populations in the Second World War—were obligations on *states*. The experience of the wartime Partisan resistance to foreign or home-grown fascism gave people little cause to believe the international community needed to concern itself with violence by non-state groups.[1]

In the decades that followed, armed insurgencies against colonial rule frequently attacked police stations, markets, schools, and local officials to destabilize the colonial regime, and inevitably the embattled imperial power would label the rebels opposing it as "terrorists"—inuring an entire generation of Asians and Africans against Western denunciations of terrorism. European governments beset by terrorist attacks against their authority in Indochina, Algeria, or Angola pointedly preferred to keep the U.N. at arms length, aware that most member states would diagnose colonial rule as the underlying political cause of the violence.[2] Though they might seek support from their allies, NATO too stayed aloof; the United States in particular stoutly resisted being drawn into its allies' misbegotten colonial conflicts. Indeed, for half a century nations would tend to view terrorism not as a challenge to all, but as a symptom of a besieged government's own missteps.

The seizure of Israeli hostages by the Black September Palestinian terrorist group at the Munich Olympic Games in 1972, which resulted in the death of 11 athletes and five hostage-takers, transformed the landscape. Spectacular acts of terrorism became a substitute for an on-the-ground insurgency, exported to third countries with no connection to the political conflict—a pattern that would be repeated in Palestinian attacks in Rome, Vienna, and on Italian cruise ships. A week after the Munich attack Secretary-General Kurt Waldheim insisted the General Assembly should "take adequate measures to prevent acts of violence against innocent people in the future."[3] The Assembly's response became a template for its approach to the issue for more than three decades. It tied its expressed "concern over increasing acts of violence which endanger or take innocent human lives" to "finding just and peaceful solutions to the underlying causes which give rise to such acts of violence."[4] Only gradually would it tilt the focus of its concern from implicitly exculpatory "causes" to the effective elimination of the violence.

A General Assembly Odyssey

Useful as attention to "underlying causes" might be, the General Assembly's 1972 focus on hectoring "colonial, racist and alien régimes" for their "repressive and terrorist acts" that "give rise to" attacks on innocents outraged Israelis and many Westerners. Over time, this optic would seem increasingly out of focus from even developing country realities, as Sikh terrorism against Indian passenger aircraft, Tamil terrorism against Sri Lankan civilians, and ultimately Islamist terrorism against Algeria's once-revolutionary government discredited the Assembly's simplistic analysis of root causes. As a result, the political balance began to shift between those for whom a liberation struggle legitimized terrorism, and those for whom terrorism delegitimized a liberation struggle.

In 1985—the year that a bomb in the luggage of an Air India jumbo jet exploded off the coast of Ireland and killed all 329 persons aboard—the Assembly revised its now perennial resolution on terrorism to declare that it "unequivocally condemns, as criminal, all acts, methods, and practices of terrorism wherever and by whomever committed," to call on all states to adhere to the growing corpus of antiterrorism conventions, and to demand "the speedy and final elimination of the problem of international terrorism."[5] Still, the Assembly pointed to the purported political roots of terrorism arising from the outrages of racist and alien regimes. With apartheid still the rule in southern Africa and with Israel not yet recognizing the Palestinian Liberation Organization, the majorities in the Assembly clung insistently to their diagnosis of political root causes.

A turning point came in 1993—the year when South Africa abandoned apartheid, the Oslo accords opened the way to Israeli–Palestinian mutual recognition, and jihadists made their first attempt to destroy the World Trade Center (and threatened the United Nations itself). The Assembly's resolution on terrorism that December, for the first time since Munich, made no mention of "colonial, racist and alien régimes" and "foreign occupation," and instead cast terrorism as a threat to human rights.[6] The Assembly crystallized the new consensus in the Declaration on Measures to Eliminate International Terrorism that it promulgated in 1994, wasting no words on "underlying causes" of terrorist violence and instead lamenting the rise in "terrorism based on intolerance and extremism."

The Declaration hinted at a definition of terrorism—"criminal acts intended or calculated to provoke a state of terror in the general public, a group or persons or particular persons for political purposes"—and declared them "in any circumstance unjustifiable, whatever the considerations of a political, philosophical, ideological, racial, ethnic, religious or any other nature that may be invoked to justify them."[7]

The Declaration exhorted governments to ratify the extant corpus of antiterrorism conventions, warned them not to sponsor or tolerate terrorist activities and training camps, and insisted that they not grant asylum to anyone engaged in terrorist activities. Still, the Assembly did not envision an active U.N. operational role. Indeed, when U.S. President Bill Clinton devoted his entire address to the General Assembly in September 1998—a month after al Qaeda's deadly attacks on American embassies in East Africa—to the urgency of international action against a rising tide of global terrorism, he did not suggest measures the United Nations could usefully take.

The shock of September 11 led the United States and other member states to find ways that the U.N. could operationally complement their national and bilateral efforts against terrorism. In 2002 the General Assembly—playing catch-up with a Security Council that was moving energetically (by U.N. standards) on the issue—approved establishment of a Terrorism Prevention Branch in the U.N. Office on Drugs and Crime to provide the technical assistance that many member states asserted they needed from the U.N. in order to counter terrorist networks. Yet the same Assembly, still locked in a bitter test of wills over U.N. budgetary levels between a United States that wanted to continue a zero-growth policy and developing countries that demanded increases, allocated only three new professional posts to the terrorism branch to fulfill its capacity-building mandate.[8]

Still, by the early 21st century, the General Assembly had completed a three-decade odyssey on terrorism, after the deeply divisive days of decolonization and national liberation struggles, to reflect a hardening consensus of governments worldwide against terrorist violence and their mobilization to suppress terrorist groups, within the bounds of international human rights law. In the Assembly debate, if not in Assembly resolutions after 1994, "root causes" would not be completely forgotten, and international opinion could still be mobilized to pressure hardline governments to address political and social issues that violent oppositionists might invoke to seek new recruits into terrorist campaigns. But the normative priority was now tilted irreversibly toward suppression of the killers.

To be sure, the United Nations is well known for words rather than action. Iran's president Ali Khamenei famously told the General Assembly in 1987 that the U.N. was just "a paper factory for issuing worthless and ineffective orders"[9]—a view in which many in the capital of the "Great Satan," which Ayatollah Khamenei denounced even more fiercely, knowingly concurred. But the Assembly has also been the negotiating forum for a number of international conventions proscribing a wide range of terrorist acts—a cumulative package of legal obligations that became the scaffolding for enforcement action by the U.N. Security Council after the leveling of the World Trade Center in 2001. Even amid the Third World apologetics for terrorism in the name of national liberation in the 1970s, East–West and North–South agreement to prohibit particular acts, regardless of political motivation, proved possible when severe or multiple incidents exasperated a critical mass of governments: proscriptions against airline hijacking (1970), hostage-taking (1979), and attacks at airports and seizure of ships (1988); requirements for detectable markers on plastic explosives (1991) and the suppression of terrorist bombings (1998) and financing of terrorism (2000). What has continued to elude Assembly negotiators is agreement on a comprehensive definition of terrorism to subsume all those criminalizing specific acts.

Even before the September 11 attacks, as adherence to the 12 antiterrorism conventions widened, their provisions were "increasingly seen as creating a norm of universal jurisdiction that applies to all states,"[10] enforceable in courts of countries that chose to exercise it even if the acts were not committed within their borders. But the action of the Security Council in copying major provisions from key antiterrorism conventions and pasting them into Security Council Resolution 1373, adopted unanimously, stunningly raised the U.N.'s antiterrorism profile in a single instant. Citing "any act of international terrorism" as "a threat to international peace and security," the Security Council made these provisions legally binding on all states, whether they had ratified a particular convention or not. In the mood of crisis that followed the unprecedented lethality of the September 11 attack in New York, member states accepted the Council's right to "legislate" obligations for them in the al Qaeda emergency, reassured by the fact that they had already been privy to the original negotiations that produced the conventions. The legislation had been hammered out in a universally inclusive political process; the Council was simply taking extraordinary measures to apply them when international peace and security were under unprecedented attack.

Security Council Resoluteness

On terrorism as on security more generally, the Security Council had been discredited for decades by the larger paralysis caused by the Cold War cleavage among its permanent members. It was characteristically unable to agree on any response to the Munich attack in 1972, with permanent members blocking competing West European and "non-aligned" draft resolutions. But the unremitting antagonism among the permanent members quickly disappeared with the Soviets' liberalization in the late 1980s, freeing the Council to act with increasing resoluteness against international terrorist violence.

As late as 1986, the response by U.S. President Ronald Reagan to a Libyan-directed terrorist attack on a nightclub frequented by American servicemen in West Berlin was simply to bomb Libya—it would scarcely occur to U.S. policymakers then to find redress in the Security Council. The Libyan retaliation two years later—planting the bomb that blew up Pan Am flight 103 over Lockerbie, Scotland, in December 1988—opened the way to dramatic innovations in Security Council activism. American and British investigators eventually established Libyan officials' responsibility; the French likewise traced culpability for the mid-air explosion of Union de Transports Aériens (UTA) flight 772 to Libya; and in 1992 these three permanent members demanded Council action to compel Libya to turn over for trial the officials accused of responsibility for the attacks—backed up by sanctions on air travel to Libya. In the heady days of great-power comity following Iraq's expulsion from Kuwait, the Council adopted the enforcement resolution they proposed on a vote of 10 to 0; all the Council's African and Asian members except Japan abstained, including China and India.[11] The sanctions proved effective. By 1996 the U.S. State Department acknowledged that Libya had curtailed its previous active support for terrorist cells, and by 1999 Tripoli had handed over the suspects for trial in The Hague, at which point the Council lifted the sanctions.

When a 1995 assassination attempt on the life of Egyptian president Hosni Mubarak was traced to Sudan-based conspirators, the Security Council again turned to the sanctions tool to compel a government to cease its support and protection for terrorist groups operating on its soil.[12] The Sudanese subsequently expelled a number of notorious terrorist figures (including a Saudi, Osama bin Laden, who headed for Afghanistan); by pledging cooperation against al Qaeda after the World Trade Center attack, the Sudanese satisfied the Council and won the revocation of the sanctions.

In both cases, the Council's diplomatic and economic instruments of coercion ultimately succeeded because the targets were states. (Similarly, the Council's application of pressures against Syria after its security services organized the 2005 assassination of Lebanon's former prime minister, Rafik Hariri, would also show results, even without the application of sanctions.) The Council has, in short, had apparent success in enforcing the norm—recognized declaratively by the General Assembly—that states must not sponsor terrorism. Before the end of the cold war, it was not uncommon for states' security services—and not just in the Arab world—to sponsor assassinations and other terrorist attacks; since the advent of the Security Council's antiterrorist enforcement measures, the incidence of official culpability in terrorism appears to be sharply reduced.

But the Council's efforts to deploy the same instruments to suffocate the increasingly audacious al Qaeda network, by pressuring the Taliban government in Afghanistan that gave it sanctuary, proved unavailing. Resolution 1267, adopted in 1999, imposed the sanctions on "the Afghan faction known as the Taliban, which also calls itself the Islamic Emirate of Afghanistan"—a regime that was already shunned by the international community (it had diplomatic relations with only three governments, all in the Muslim world, and its foes still clung to Afghanistan's seat in the U.N.), and the war-ravaged country was one of the most destitute and economically hermetic in the world. The air sanctions imposed by the Council, it is true, proved a burden on the easy movement of the swelling ranks of al Qaeda operatives into Afghanistan, but this was hardly an insuperable obstacle since travel was possible overland from Pakistan. Moreover, the air sanctions did not, of course, prevent al Qaeda operatives from learning to pilot planes.

The Taliban–Qaeda network seemed clearly impervious to the tools of statecraft that states, either individually or collectively, could use as leverage to press a recalcitrant leadership to change course. Kabul's ruling authorities ignored the Council's core demand, that "the Taliban turn over Osama bin Laden without further delay," not only in the face of Council sanctions, but even when an aroused United States reiterated it as an ultimatum before decisive military action in late September 2001. And once al Qaeda had been deprived of its unique territorial sanctuary by the joint military effort of U.S. air power and the Afghan Northern Alliance, policymakers had to devise a far more problematical strategy for dealing collectively with international terrorist networks not connected to states—where there is no territory and no government apparatus to wear down by sanctions or attack by force. In effect, the Security Council faced the same quandary as that confronting its individual states: Besieged by determined but shadowy terrorist opponents with "no return address," states have no certain way of maintaining the security against armed attack that citizens expect the state to guarantee.

The United Nations certainly did not have any of the personnel needed to gather intelligence on activities and movements of suspected terrorists, nor to patrol border crossings or arrest alleged perpetrators—all of which were functions that governments should perform. Instead, in the aftermath of the September 11 attacks the Security Council acted to mobilize all its member states to put *their* personnel to work to suppress terrorist transit, training, recruitment, and financing. Resolution 1373 provided the mandate—drawing the language of its mandate, as noted above, from extant international conventions that many states had already ratified. The resolution also created a monitoring panel to oversee states' implementation of the mandates, the Counter-Terrorism Committee (CTC), and called on "all States to report to the Committee, no later than 90 days from the date of adoption of this resolution . . ., on the steps they have taken to implement this resolution."[13]

Not every state made its initial report within the first 90 days, but in a U.N. universe in which states only episodically respond to requests for reports from United Nations bodies, the response rate was extraordinary—in nine months, 150 nations had reported, and ultimately all 191 member states made at least one report to the CTC. Even Somalia's spectral "transitional national government" proudly reported its efforts (breaking up a pro-bin Laden demonstration in Mogadishu and an antiterrorist speech by its president on National Teachers Day), and pleaded for "urgent and adequate assistance from the international community to be able to comply with Resolution 1373."[14] States were encouraged to report not only by the urgency of the struggle against Qaeda-like global terrorism, but by the prospect of assistance from motivated donors to poor countries with weak antiterrorist capacities.

Since 9/11 the Council has devoted an ever-growing share of its time to terrorism issues. In the years before the East Africa embassy bombings in 1998, its only counterterrorism resolutions addressed the state-sponsored terrorism of Libya and Sudan. In the three years between the embassy bombings and the leveling of the World Trade Center, the Council adopted five antiterrorism resolutions, focused on al Qaeda and its Afghan protectors. In the four years following

September 11, the Security Council adopted 20 resolutions on terrorism.

Some of the flood tide of resolutions reflected politicized judgments or log-rolling. The Council embarrassed itself on March 11, 2004, by hastily adopting a resolution proposed by the electorally embattled Spanish government, just hours after deadly rail attacks in Madrid, declaring that the attacks were "perpetrated by the terrorist group ETA";[15] within three days Spanish investigators established incontrovertibly that the attackers were Moroccan-born jihadists. The Russian government, whose botched military counterattack on school hostage-takers in the North Ossetian town of Beslan resulted in the deaths of hundreds of schoolchildren, sought passage of a Council resolution that would show that it too could use its permanent seat on the Council to put its terrorist concerns high on the global antiterrorist agenda. Other members of the Council reshaped the text so that it would largely recycle previously agreed language from earlier resolutions without specifically mentioning the Beslan incident; its patina of substantive result was to create a Council working group to look into practical measures to be imposed on non-Qaeda terrorist groups, and inquire into the possibility of creating an international fund for victims of terrorism.[16]

The Council also felt pressure to produce a new statement on terrorism when it met at the head-of-government level during the 2005 World Summit. The presidents and prime ministers of the Council adopted a British resolution creating a new mandate on states: Not only are states obliged to bring terrorist *perpetrators* to justice, but they must also "prohibit by law *incitement* to commit a terrorist act" (emphasis added) and deny refuge on their territory to persons suspected of being guilty of such incitement. Yet, thanks to a climate in which harsh counterterrorism measures have drawn intense criticism for violation of international law, the Council felt compelled to add that "states must ensure that any measures" taken to implement the resolution "comply with all of their obligations under international law, in particular international human rights law, refugee law, and humanitarian law."[17]

The Human Rights Dimension

It is noteworthy that the Security Council—dominated as it is by the major powers most fiercely prosecuting the struggle against jihadist violence—should offer any caution at all on the need to keep counterterrorist measures within the parameters of international human rights law. But international concerns about the human rights dimension had been mounting as reports multiplied of harsh and sometimes indiscriminate repressive measures in the global "war on terror," including by the United States. The arc of an intensifying international debate could be traced in the General Assembly and would resonate in the U.N.'s human rights machinery.

In its first resolution on terrorism and human rights after the September 11 attacks, the General Assembly simply recycled previous language emphasizing how terrorism itself constituted a violation of the most basic of human rights—the right to life. It contented itself with its boilerplate reminder to governments that, in taking "all necessary and effective measures" to crack down on terrorism, they needed to respect "relevant provisions of international law, including international human rights standards."[18]

Just a year later, reports of human rights abuses in the U.S.-led "war" on terrorism—including secret detentions and proposed military commissions to judge detainees at Guantanamo—prompted the Assembly to focus on the risks to human rights of overzealous measures in the name of counterterrorism. The Assembly emphasized that "certain rights are recognized as non-derogable in any circumstances" (such as the bar to "torture or to cruel, inhuman or degrading treatment or punishment"); it exhorted governments, "while countering terrorism," to heed U.N. resolutions and treaty bodies on human rights; and asked the U.N. High Commissioner for Human Rights to examine the issue, "taking into account reliable information from all sources," and "provide assistance and advice to States, upon their request, on the protection of human rights and fundamental freedoms while countering terrorism."[19]

This early reaction to U.S. policies that even America's European allies found heavy-handed only revived Washington suspicions about the U.N.'s reversion to its congenital foot-dragging—proof, as it were, that the United Nations "seemed more worried about counterterrorist measures than about terrorism itself."[20] Indeed, as credible reports of serious abuses began generating indictments in Europe as well as media stories, the Assembly in 2005 went on record "deploring the occurrence of violations of human rights and fundamental freedoms in the context of the fight against terrorism."[21] By this point concern was growing even in some American circles that those prosecuting a "global war on terrorism" were showing reckless disregard for the fundamental standards of international law on human rights and war.

Concerns had started bubbling up in U.N. human rights bodies only months after the September 11 attacks. The expert committee monitoring compliance with the Convention Against Torture cautioned the states that were parties to the convention that most of its obligations cannot be derogated, including those prohibiting torture under all circumstances, those banning confessions extracted by torture being admitted in evidence (except as evidence against the torturer), and those barring cruel, inhuman, or degrading treatment.[22] By May 2006, the committee formally took testimony from a U.S. government delegation to rebut charges of American violation of the torture convention.[23]

As early as January 2002, reports about the situation of detainees held at Guantánamo drew the attention of the standing Special Rapporteurs of the U.N. Commission on Human Rights to report regularly on torture, on the independence of judges and lawyers, and on freedom of religion, along with the chairperson-rapporteur of the working group on arbitrary detention. Rebuffed in their request to visit the facility for private interviews with detainees, they issued a sharply critical report in early 2006 that stated flatly that "the continuing detention of all persons held at Guantánamo Bay amounts to arbitrary detention in violation of article 9 of ICCPR [international covenant on civil and political rights]"; called on Washington to "either expeditiously bring all Guantánamo Bay detainees to trial, in compliance with articles 9, paragraph 3, and 14 of ICCPR, or release them without further delay"; and insisted on prompt closure of the facility.[24]

During its 2004 session, the Commission on Human Rights adopted a resolution calling for appointment of an independent expert to report on how best to guard against rights abuses while vigorously prosecuting antiterrorist efforts. In his report, the expert (an American) noted the "considerable controversy" surrounding the stance of "one of the parties involved in the 2002 hostilities in Afghanistan" that detainees linked to terrorism were not entitled to the prisoner of war status under the Geneva conventions, and the sharp opposition of other states and the Red Cross to this argument.[25] The independent expert also noted that the Security Council's system for identifying and freezing assets of persons and groups involved in terrorism was too haphazard, putting at risk the right to property without due process: "no relevant Security Council resolution establishes precise legal standards governing the inclusion of persons and groups on lists or the freezing of assets, much less mandates safeguards or legal remedies to those mistakenly or wrongfully included on these lists."[26]

The expert's report was followed by a Commission decision in 2005 to appoint a special rapporteur, whose first report acknowledged difficulties in securing cooperation from several of the 11 countries from which he sought information or requested site visits.[27] The High Commissioner for Human Rights, Louise Arbour, followed with her own report on human rights and counterterrorism that focused on "two phenomena today which are having an acutely corrosive effect on the global ban on torture and cruel, inhuman or degrading treatment"—secret detentions of terrorism suspects in unknown locations, and "the trend of seeking 'diplomatic assurances' allegedly to overcome the risk of torture" when suspects are transferred to countries where risks of torture are perceived to be high.[28]

United Nations Agencies

While the U.N.'s political bodies have long tackled terrorism issues through norm-setting and treaty legislation (in the General Assembly) and antiterrorist mobilization of member states plus enforcement measures against egregious offenders (in the Security Council), the United Nations was long never thought to have an operational role in combating terrorism. Not only did the U.N. have no intelligence-gathering capabilities to bring to the counterterrorism table, but its reputation as a leaky sieve where no secret stays secret ensured that counterterrorism authorities in member states would not dream of a serious U.N. operational role.[29]

Only after the World Trade Center attacks were the system's leading contributors galvanized into seeking ways to make the U.N. operationally useful, by monitoring states' antiterrorist efforts and keeping sustained pressure on them to collaborate effectively against international networks. The Security Council became one locus of this effort though its subsidiary bodies; the Vienna-based U.N. Office on Drugs and Crime became the other, through a Terrorism Prevention Branch. The diffusion of responsibilities has meant there is no single "center" to U.N. antiterrorism efforts, despite considerable operational activity.

The Counter-Terrorism Committee established by Resolution 1373 has been the political nerve center of U.N. antiterrorist efforts, largely because it speaks for the Security Council and especially the Council's permanent membership. In a departure from the traditional practice of selecting only elected, two-year members of the Council to chair its subsidiary bodies, the CTC's first chairman was Britain's permanent representative to the United Nations, Jeremy Greenstock. Greenstock envisioned the CTC as:

> a switchboard, a catalyst and a driver of other institutions to do their work in a globally coordinated way. . . . It is our job to make sure that member States contribute to this activity, that international institutions coordinate with each other in a global system.[30]

The "catalytic" role developed out of the reporting process that the Council required of member states. As already noted, every member state complied with the Council mandate to report on the measures each had put in place to fulfill the antiterrorism mandates contained in Resolution 1373—its domestic legislation, law enforcement capabilities, and the deficiencies the state could not remedy on its own. After an analysis of each report, the CTC might follow up with probing questions about the adequacy of the steps taken or promised, sometimes in an extensive dialogue. For instance, the CTC engaged in multiple exchanges with Syria, a frontline state in the struggle with terrorist groups; on the third volley, among many other questions on which it continued to press Syrian officials, it warned that Syria's laws concerning terrorist financing "do not correspond to the requirements needed"—and Syrian authorities responded by submitting amendments to the country's money-laundering statute to the International Monetary Fund for the Fund's comments before final promulgation.[31] In other cases the CTC has found deficiencies in a state's ability to control movements or people or finances, where outside training and funding appear necessary; it has no capacity to supply either, but refers the need to national or international agencies that have.

Initially dependent on staff lent from Council member governments (especially Britain), the CTC assembled a tiny international staff to deal with the flood of reports from member states. Inevitably the sense of urgency that prevailed in the autumn of 2001 diminished over time (accelerated perhaps by deepening resistance to what many viewed as the broader direction of U.S. policy by the Bush administration under cover of its proclaimed war on terrorism—a "war" drawing ever fewer enlistments abroad, or even at home). By 2004, with reporting fatigue clearly setting in, the Council felt a need for "revitalization" of the process, creating a Counter-Terrorism Committee Executive Directorate as "a special political mission" reporting to the Council, under an executive director appointed by approval of the Security Council.[32] With the appointment of Spaniard Javier Rupérez as the first executive directorate, U.N. antiterrorism efforts at last had a face as well as a mandate. The CTC reporting process, however, was already largely exhausted; by 2006, the issue was how to fill in the gaps—of either material resources or political determination—in those countries that were still not doing all they should. As one analyst noted, "while the CTC may be making headway, it may be proceeding up a cul-de-sac."[33]

The Counter-Terrorism Committee, after all, is simply tasked with monitoring states' capacity to fulfill the Council's antiterrorism mandates, not with sanctioning those that have not complied. It has steadfastly refused to name governments that CTC members believe are willfully noncompliant. Nor does the CTC maintain any list of organizations or individuals proscribed as terrorist. That function, however, another Security Council subsidiary body has assumed—the sanctions committee created to monitor enforcement of the Taliban–Qaeda sanctions imposed under Resolution 1267 in 1999, which required states to impose sanctions against al Qaeda, Osama bin Laden specifically, and persons and groups associated with them, specifically including the Taliban. After 9/11, the United States and occasionally other governments presented the committee with names of terrorist groups and individuals that states would be obliged to ban, bar, or arrest, with over 400 names inscribed by the committee. But the lack of a consistent process for evaluating names proposed for the list (or for removing them if suspicions prove wrong) has undermined the sanctions committee's authority, and several Arab governments have stoutly rejected American efforts to list groups combating Israel as al Qaeda associates. The sanctions committee has not reported any instance of a government willfully sheltering al Qaeda associates, however. While this could represent the usual U.N. aversion to naming names, it is likelier that the 1267 committee's monitoring staff has concluded that the cause of countries' lax enforcement of sanctions genuinely lies in the non-performing states' lack of capacity rather than of political will: al Qaeda has microscopically few, if any, allies among governments.

Far away from the Security Council and its subsidiary bodies toils the Terrorism Prevention Branch of the Vienna-based U.N. Office on Drugs and Crime, mandated to provide technical assistance to the many member states that lack the resources or experience to bar their doors to terrorist groups. The work of the terrorism branch is a classically unthreatening U.N. provision of services to member states that want them and that the CTC says need them. The office has provided legal advisory services on a direct bilateral basis to 22 countries deficient in their legal codes; its regional workshops have trained officials from scores of other countries.[34] Fourteen countries have provided the voluntary contributions to finance its technical assistance activities since creation of the terrorism branch, which totaled just $1.6 million in 2005;[35] the General Assembly provides assessed financing of $950, 000 from the U.N.'s regular budget for terrorism branch staff, with additional staff provided by donor countries.[36] Its limited funding levels allow the branch to meet the assistance needs of only a fraction of the states with certifiably weak capacities; others get bilateral assistance directly from wealthier countries.

Prospects Ahead

The high-level panel that Secretary-General Kofi Annan appointed to assess the international community's capacities to address security threats of the new century (and in so doing to entice back into the U.N. collective security system its most powerful member state, which seemed on the brink of defecting) identified the terrorist threat as particularly urgent. Strikingly, in its analysis and recommendations the panel revived a dimension of the terrorism issue that major powers had effectively eliminated from the pronouncements of U.N. political bodies for more than a decade: "root causes." The panel called for the Secretary-General to promote a "comprehensive strategy that incorporates but is broader than coercive measures," pegged first on dissuading the disaffected from resort to terrorist violence by "working to reverse the causes or facilitators of terrorism."[37] The panel proposed that the Security Council deal with defiant states—those that obstinately refuse to cooperate on antiterrorist measures despite having the capacity to act—by adopting "a schedule of predetermined sanctions for State noncompliance." And it proposed to cut the Gordian knot that has tied up negotiations on a comprehensive convention against terrorism by offering a general definition of "terrorism" focused on an intention "to cause death or serious bodily harm to civilians or non-combatants."[38]

None of these recommendations of the panel won adoption at the political level during the General Assembly's year of "reform." All continue on the table, or at least in the shadows, for refinement and possible action in the future.

The Secretary-General did, to be sure, lay out a comprehensive strategy for U.N. action in an address before the international summit on democracy, terrorism and security in Madrid in March 2005.[39] Annan carefully eschewed terms that would provoke Washington's governing conservatives; the only "root cause" of terrorism, he averred, was terrorists' belief that surprise attacks on civilians are effective. He noted that the "right to resist occupation . . . cannot include the right to deliberately kill or maim civilians." But key governments were adamant against reintroducing any hint of the pre-1993 debate on "underlying causes," and the final Summit Outcome document adopted in September made no mention of causes, facilitators, political grievances, or occupation, even to rebut them; there was just the faintest hint of "conditions conducive to the spread of terrorism," and praise for "initiatives to promote dialogue, tolerance and understanding among civilizations."[40] Addressing political grievances that might be "conducive" to terrorism (not a serious option with messianic Islamists) thus won the faintest sanction as part of the U.N. antiterrorism toolkit. On the other hand, the notion of predetermined sanctions against countries judged laggard in their counterterrorism efforts drew fierce opposition from smaller and weaker countries, and was stillborn.

The high-level panel's proposal to break the deadlock on the definition of terrorism, creating a victim-based recognized standard in international law on which to ground binding obligations to suppress violent networks free of political selectivity and double standards, added a new dynamic to the treaty negotiations in the General Assembly's Sixth Committee, but did not break the deadlock in time for the 2005 summit. A majority of states have supported language that brands as a terrorist act one that intentionally causes death or serious injury "to any person" with the purpose of sowing fear in the population or a segment of it in order to advance political ends, or that causes serious damage to property, a government facility, or the environment, especially if it results in "major economic loss." But with violent conflict between Israelis and Palestinians on the upswing since 2001, Arab countries have remained adamant that violent actions taken against "foreign occupation" not automatically trigger a "terrorist" designation.

The high-level panel did not contest the right to resistance against tyranny or alien occupation. Rather, it insisted that "there is nothing in the fact of occupation that justifies the targeting and killing of civilians." The standard it accordingly proposed was that an act be "intended to cause death or serious bodily harm to civilians or noncombatants, when the purpose of such an act, by its nature or context, is to intimidate a population, or to compel a Government or an international organization to do or to abstain from doing any act."[41] Though some standard by which to judge what groups should be proscribed and their finances frozen is arguably needed, and this formulation seemed congruent with statements since 2001 from the Islamic Conference that attacks against innocent civilians are not acceptable forms of resistance and indeed contrary to Islam, mutual recriminations surrounding the summit negotiations ensured that the issue would remain on the table a while longer—perhaps until the Israeli–Palestinian conflict is settled.

The other major issue hanging over U.N. efforts against terrorism is the proliferation of units that have responsibility for distinct pieces of the whole, and their tangled accountability to political bodies. This is also true of national governments, of course, but governments execute a much wider range of activities than the U.N. ever will in order to protect their populations and their regimes from violent attack—running the gamut from police and intelligence-gathering to financial tracking, border controls, and airport and seaport security. Some have proposed consolidation of the separate subsidiary bodies of the Security Council; Costa Rica has called for a U.N. High Commissioner for Counterterrorism.

Part of the concern, however, is with the thin expertise of people working on terrorism issues in many international agencies. One critique notes that:

> the representatives on the CTC and other Security Council counter-terrorism-related bodies are usually political officers (regular diplomats or generalists), often with little or no background in the technical field of counter-terrorism. As a result, . . . the bodies, in particular the CTC, have tended to get unnecessarily consumed in negotiating process-oriented papers, and focusing on the political rather than the technical aspects of a particular issue.[42]

To strengthen the technical competence of international agencies to respond to international terrorist groups, some call for establishment of a new international agency to absorb the functions of the current Security Council committees and the Terrorism Prevention Branch in Vienna, either as a U.N. program, a new specialized agency, or an informal grouping of like-minded states, patterned after the Financial Action Task Force.[43]

Each formula for a successor agency has its infirmities as well as its advantages. The underlying issue, however, is whether the international community's mobilization against jihadist terrorism can be permanently sustained, or whether it will inevitably lose priority as public concerns ripen and change. There may be scant will to create a new agency if vigilant law enforcement is already close to success in breaking up today's terrorist networks, as some national leaders suggest.

Still, so long as cross-border terrorist networks are engaged in attacks on a wide range of countries, nations are almost certain to continue using the unique resources of global legitimacy and political efficiency that are the U.N.'s comparative advantage, especially in the Security Council. For the foreseeable future, the U.N.'s relevance is clear.

Endnotes

1. It was significant, of course, that the Partisans' acts of terrorism (for so they were branded by Axis authorities) in such places as France, Italy, Yugoslavia, and China were for the most part directed against officials and security forces, not against the civilian population—and were undertaken within the borders of the affected states, not abroad.
2. Despite fierce French objections to U.N. meddling, the General Assembly gradually involved itself in the Algerian conflict, progressing from a vague call for "a solution, in conformity with the purposes and principles of the Charter" (1957) to labeling the situation "a threat to international peace and security" and recognizing "the right of the Algerian people to self-determination and independence" (1960).
3. "Waldheim Bids U.N. Act on Terrorism," *New York Times* (13 Sep. 1972) p. 3.
4. General Assembly Resolution 3034 (XXVII), adopted 18 December 1972. The approved text provocatively "reaffirms the inalienable right to self-determination of all peoples . . . and upholds the legitimacy of their struggle, in particular the struggle of national liberation movements." After the vote, U.S. representative George Bush reported to Washington that Waldheim had lamented the Assembly's turning his terrorism initiative on its head, "identifying Algeria, Libya, Syria, and Iraq as particularly difficult." United States Department of State, *Foreign Relations of the United States, 1969–1976*, Volume V: United Nations, #108, "Telegram from the Mission to the United Nations to the Department of State," 20 December 1972.
5. General Assembly Resolution 40/61, adopted 9 December 1985.
6. General Assembly Resolution 48/122, adopted 20 December 1993.
7. General Assembly Resolution 49/60, adopted 9 December 1994.
8. The new positions represented half the professional staff posts made available to the new branch. Edward Luck, "The Uninvited Challenge: Terrorism Targets the United Nations," in Edward Newman and

Ramesh Thakur (eds.), *Multilateralism Under Challenge: Power, International Order and Structural Change* (Tokyo: United Nations University, 2005).
9. "Iranian, in U.N., Rebuffs Reagan on Cease-Fire," *New York Times* (23 September, 1987).
10. Joshua Black and Martin Skladany, "The Capabilities and Limits of the United Nations in Fighting Terrorism" (April 2000), reprinted in *Combating Terrorism: Does the U.N. Matter . . . and How* (New York: United Nations Association of the United States, 2002) p. 8.
11. Security Council Resolution 748, adopted 31 March 1992. The resolution also forbade arms sales to Libya, mandated a reduction in all Libyan diplomatic missions around the world, and required the shuttering of Libyan Airlines offices. The resolution provided enforcement to the Council's call two months earlier for Libya to respond to the three countries' demand for the suspects (Security Council Resolution 731, unanimously adopted 21 January 1992).
12. Security Council Resolution 1054, adopted 26 April 1996.
13. Security Council Resolution 1373, adopted 28 September 2001, Para. 6.
14. "*Report on the Action taken by the Government of Somalia to Implement United Nations Security Council Resolution 1373 (2001),*" S/2001/1287. The assistance sought by the transitional government was, however, much more focused on Somali reconstruction than on CTC priorities: Instead of assistance for money-laundering enforcement and tighter border controls, the Mogadishu authorities sought counterterrorism help for "rehabilitation and reconstruction of state institutions," "reconciliation and peace building," and "disarmament, demobilization and reintegration"—in short, the investment in overall peace building that despairing donors have withheld for a decade.
15. Security Council Resolution 1530, adopted 11 March 2004.
16. Security Council Resolution 1566, adopted 8 October 2004. The working group established under Resolution 1566 has rarely met and never produced recommendations.
17. Security Council Resolution 1624, adopted 14 September 2005. The resolution acknowledged that what governments might bar as "incitement" could conflict with "the right to freedom of expression," invoking the provision in the International Covenant on Civil and Political Rights allowing restrictions on freedom of speech and media only if legislated as necessary "for the protection of national security or of public order" (Article 19, Para. 3).
18. General Assembly Resolution 56/160, adopted 19 December 2001.
19. General Assembly Resolution 57/219, adopted 18 December 2002. The High Commissioner for Human Rights to whom the Assembly directed this request, Sérgio Vieira de Mello, was killed in the terrorist attack on U.N. offices in Baghdad eight months later.
20. Edward Luck, "Global Terrorism and the United Nations: A Challenge in Search of a Policy," p. 1, paper prepared for United Nations and

Global Security Initiative (United Nations Foundation), 2004, www.un-globalsecurity.org/papers_cat/terrorism_non_state_actors.asp#11.
21. General Assembly Resolution 60/158, adopted 16 December 2005.
22. CAT/C/XXVII/Misc.7, 22 November 2201; cited in the *Digest of Jurisprudence of the U.N. and Regional Organizations on the Protection of Human Rights While Countering Terrorism*, issued by the United Nations Commission on Human Rights.
23. "U.S. Defends Rights Record before U.N. panel in Geneva," *New York Times* (6 May 2006). In its report on the first day of the meeting between the committee on torture and the U.S. delegation, the British Broadcasting Corporation cited (5 May 2006, http://news.bbc.co.uk/2/hi/americas/4974852.stm) the observation of a Human Rights Watch representative that "this is the first time the United States is accountable for its record on torture with regard to some of the practices implemented after 9/11."
24. *Situation of Detainees at Guantánamo Bay*, Commission on Human Rights, E/CN.4/2006/120, 27 February 2006.
25. *Report of the Independent Expert on the Protection of Human Rights and Fundamental Freedoms while Countering Terrorism*, Commission on Human Rights, E/CN.4/2005/103 (7 February 2005), p. 10 (Para. 20). The independent expert was Robert K. Goldman, professor of law at American University; the country advancing the argument in controversy was the United States.
26. Ibid., p. 21 (Para. 63).
27. *Report of the Special Rapporteur on the Promotion and Protection of Human Rights and Fundamental Freedoms while Countering Terrorism*, Commission on Human Rights, E/CN.4/2006/98 (28 December 2005) p. 8. The rapporteur was Martin Scheinin of Finland.
28. *Protection of Human Rights and Fundamental Freedoms while Countering Terrorism: Report of the High Commissioner for Human Rights*, Commission on Human Rights, E/CN.4/2006/94 (16 February 2006) p. 2 (Para. 3).
29. It was not just counterterrorism officials in capitals who dismissed the U.N.'s capacity to be of any direct use in tracking down terrorist networks. When Secretary-General Kofi Annan established a policy working group of senior Secretariat officials to fashion forward-leaning recommendations for a vigorous U.N. role after the attacks in the United States, the group firmly stated that it "does not believe the United Nations is well placed to play an active operational role in efforts to suppress terrorist groups, to pre-empt specific terrorist strikes, or to develop dedicated intelligence-gathering capacities." *Report of the Policy Working Group on the United Nations and Terrorism*, A/57/273—S/2002/875, p. 5, Para. 9. Instead, the group concluded that the U.N. "should concentrate its direct role in counter-terrorism on the areas in which the Organization has a comparative advantage" (p. 2), such as norm-setting, human rights advocacy, development of model legislation, and inter-agency and intergovernmental cooperation.

30. United Nations Information Service, Round-up of Session, "*Vienna Symposium on Terrorism Adds More Momentum to Global Fight Against Terrorism,*" UNIS/CP/413 (http://www.unodc.org/unodc/en/press_release_2002-06-06_1.html).
31. *Fourth Report by the Syrian Arab Republic to the Counter-Terrorism Committee*, S/2005/265, Para. 1.1.
32. Security Council Resolution 1535, adopted 26 March 2004. Inevitably, the creation of an operational unit under the Security Council's control aroused suspicions in the General Assembly that the powerful were seeking to circumvent the larger body, which had one point of leverage to assert its authority: its control over the budget.
33. Luck, "The Uninvited Challenge," op. cit.
34. *Strengthening International Cooperation and Technical Assistance in Preventing and Combating Terrorism: Report of the Secretary-General*, A/60/164, pp. 7 and 12–13.
35. Op. cit., A/60/164, pp. 13–14. The three largest donors to the terrorism branch have been Italy, Austria, and Britain, which together have contributed half of the $6.1 million received over its short lifetime.
36. *Consolidated Budget for the Biennium 2006–2007 for the United Nations Office on Drugs and Crime*, E/CN.7/2005/12/Add.1, p. 42.
37. *A More Secure World: Our Shared Responsibility.* Report of the Secretary-General's High-Level Panel on Threats, Challenges and Change (United Nations, 2004), p. 48, para. 148. The panel specified "promoting social and political rights, the rule of law and democratic reform; working to end occupations and address major political grievances; . . . and stopping State collapse" as not only inherently important, but vital to removing "some of the causes or facilitators of terrorism."
38. Ibid., p. 52., para. 164
39. For the full text of Annan's remarks, see http://english.safe-democracy.org/keynotes/a-global-strategy-for-fighting-terrorism.html
40. *2005 World Summit Outcome*, General Assembly Resolution 60/1, para. 82.
41. *A More Secure World*, op.cit., para. 160 and 164.
42. Eric Rosand and Alistair Millar, *The Future of Multilateral Counter-Terrorism: The Case for an International Counter-Terrorism Body* (New York: The Century Foundation, 2006).
43. *The Future of Multilateral Counter-Terrorism*, op. cit.

7
Negotiating with Terrorists*

Peter R. Neumann

Dirty Deals

The argument against negotiating with terrorists is simple: Democracies must never give in to violence, and terrorists must never be rewarded for using it. Negotiations give legitimacy to terrorists and their methods and undermine actors who have pursued political change through peaceful means. Talks can destabilize the negotiating governments' political system, undercut international efforts to outlaw terrorism, and set a dangerous precedent.

Yet in practice democratic governments often negotiate with terrorists. The British government maintained a secret back channel to the Irish Republican Army even after the IRA had launched a mortar attack on 10 Downing Street that nearly eliminated the entire British cabinet in 1991. In 1988, the Spanish government sat down with the separatist group Basque Homeland and Freedom (known by its Basque acronym ETA) only six months after the group had killed 21 shoppers in a supermarket bombing. Even the government of Israel—which is not known to be soft on terrorism—has strayed from the supposed ban: in 1993, it secretly negotiated the Oslo accords even though the Palestine Liberation Organization (PLO) continued its terrorist campaign and refused to recognize Israel's right to exist.

---

*"Negotiating With Terrorists" *Foreign Affairs*, 86 (1), 2007. Reprinted with permission from *Foreign Affairs*.

When it comes to negotiating with terrorists, there is a clear disconnect between what governments profess and what they actually do. But the rigidity of the "no negotiations" stance has prevented any systematic exploration of how best to conduct such negotiations. How can a democratic government talk to terrorists without jeopardizing the integrity of its political system? What kinds of terrorists are susceptible to negotiations? When should negotiations be opened?

The key objective for any government contemplating negotiations with terrorists is not simply to end violence but to do so in a way that minimizes the risk of setting dangerous precedents and destabilizing its political system. Given this dual goal, a number of conditions must be met in order for talks to have even a chance of success. Assuming that negotiations are appropriate in all cases would be no more valid a theory than one that assumes they never are.

Who?

The first and most obvious question for any government considering negotiations is whether the terrorists it faces can make good negotiating partners. Bruce Hoffman, of Georgetown University; William Zartman, of Johns Hopkins University; and other experts believe that terrorists' stated aims and ideology should be the decisive factor in determining whether they might be willing to compromise. Hence, these experts draw a distinction between nihilistic terrorists, who have "absolute" or even "apocalyptic" goals (often religiously inspired) and for whom violence has become a perverted form of self-realization, and more "traditional" terrorists, who are believed to be "instrumental" or "political" in their aspirations and so have the potential to become constructive interlocutors.

This distinction between supposedly rational terrorists and irrational ones, however, is often in the eye of the beholder. If the IRA and ETA appear to be more rational than, say, al Qaeda, it is because their goals—nationalism and separatism—have a long history in Western political thought. The left-wing terrorists of the 1970s and 1980s—the West German Red Army Faction, for example, or the Italian Red Brigades—were seen as political because Marxism was a concept familiar to their targets. Al Qaeda's aim of re-creating an Islamic empire is no more absolutist (or realistic) than was imposing a nationality on a reluctant population or turning West Germany into a Marxist workers' republic. The difference is that al Qaeda's ideology has not become part of the twenty-first century's DNA and thus remains difficult to rationalize.

Rather than examining terrorists' stated ideology, policymakers should examine their thinking on the utility of violence. After all, it is terrorists' violent means rather than their particular political objectives that makes them uniquely problematic. Moreover, many terrorist groups did not start out as such; they resorted to violence when their political ambitions were frustrated or when they began to see violence as an instrument to further their cause. For such movements, the utility of violence sometimes diminishes, leading them to conclude that their aims might be better served by nonviolent agitation. No one in the IRA ever abandoned the organization's absolutist ambitions for a united Ireland, but at some point in the late 1980s, the group's leaders realized that their military campaign no longer furthered that aim, and so they began exploring alternatives.

It may be that religiously inspired groups—especially millenarian groups such as the Japanese organization Aum Shinrikyo—are less rational than the IRA. But the multifaceted identities of many others are often falsely reduced to their religious component. Although Hamas and Hezbollah both promote religiously inspired radical political ideologies, they derive much of their strength from their claim to represent particular ethnic groups. Not only do they have real-world constituencies they must satisfy; they have also demonstrated that they can modulate their use of violence against Israel according to more or less rational political assessments.

Another factor in deciding whether to negotiate with a terrorist group should be its level of internal cohesion. Although terrorists tend to portray themselves as belonging to tightly knit outfits, the conditions under which they operate—in particular, secrecy—make it nearly impossible for them to maintain a perfect chain of command. Even in relatively hierarchical organizations, such as ETA, authority is often decentralized and the leadership acts as little more than a coordinating body. In terrorist networks such as al Qaeda, the leadership hardly plays any operational role at all, merely providing ideological inspiration and moral sanction to its associated networks.

As a result, a government must consider not only whether the terrorist leadership will accept the terms of a settlement but also whether it can control its rank and file. Although the IRA's Army Council, the group's decision-making body, always enjoyed substantial formal powers, some IRA units—especially in rural parts of Northern Ireland—regarded with skepticism the peace initiatives of Gerry Adams, the longtime leader of the IRA's political wing, and ignored council directives demanding that operations be scaled down ahead of elections in the late 1980s and early 1990s. Had the IRA leadership merely insisted on its authority, the organization might have split up. Instead, it persuaded the skeptics to support Adams' plan with a mixture of subtle threats and deception, arguing that laying down arms was a ruse to, as the investigative journalist Ed Moloney has put it, "expose the Brits."

The IRA's Protestant counterparts failed to make good on their commitments because their leaders—although firmly committed to the peace process—proved unable to exert much influence over their constituents. Authority within the Ulster Defense Association, an umbrella organization for loyalist paramilitary groups, remained with local vigilante committees. By the time of the Northern Ireland peace process, the UDA had evolved somewhat, but most information continued to flow from the bottom up rather than from the top down, and the movement's political wing had little leverage. When the Belfast agreement, which created the Northern Ireland Assembly and committed all parties to "peaceful and democratic means," was concluded in 1998, a cease-fire held for a short while. But the political process stalled, and local commanders soon ignored their leaders and resumed the violence.

Additional difficulties arise when terrorists are sponsored by a state, in which case they may have little authority to make commitments without their backers' consent. In such situations, the negotiating government may decide that talking to the terrorists is futile and opt for negotiating with the sponsoring state instead. Before it makes this decision, however, it should thoroughly assess the relationship between the terrorist group and its state supporter. As Louise Richardson, a political scientist at Harvard University, points out, there are substantial differences between, say, the PLO, which has keenly preserved its internal autonomy despite accepting support from a number of states, and the Popular Front for the Liberation of Palestine–General Command, a breakaway pro-Palestinian organization that is little more than Syria's proxy. For all its imperfections, the PLO is a political player with whom negotiations might make sense, whereas the PFLP-GC has too little authority to be a credible interlocutor.

When?

Whether negotiations with a particular terrorist group are advisable is also a function of timing. For talks to succeed, a terrorist group must be at a strategic juncture: questioning the utility of violence but not necessarily on the verge of defeat. The Harvard law professor

Alan Dershowitz and other commentators believe that negotiations are always a bad idea: they should only be considered when terrorists are on the verge of giving up—at which point the terrorists might as well be finished off. In the real world, however, matters are rarely as clear-cut. Terrorists are accustomed to continued, substantial personal sacrifice, and when threatened with defeat, some of them might decide to further escalate the violence, wagering that they have little to lose from one last push. Analysts such as Jerrold Post, director of the Political Psychology Program at George Washington University, have even identified this situation as one of the scenarios in which terrorist organizations may be tempted to resort to weapons of mass destruction. So, as paradoxical as this may seem, it may sometimes be better to open talks with terrorists before they are on the verge of defeat.

Even then, governments must tread carefully. Governments eager for progress may be too quick to jump at any sign of a strategic juncture. This impulse may be well intentioned, but it can turn out to be counterproductive. Take the Colombian peace process in the late 1990s, a good example of how such eagerness can backfire. In 1998, the government in Bogotá agreed to establish a demilitarized zone in which the Revolutionary Armed Forces of Colombia (known as the FARC) could operate without interference from the security forces. The establishment of the zone was granted even before the FARC had agreed to sit down at the negotiating table, let alone end its military campaign. Buoyed by the government's offer, FARC hard-liners went on the offensive, seeing the zone as a golden opportunity to formalize the quasi-governmental authority they already enjoyed in much of the country. The negotiations turned out to be a farce, and in 2002 the government eventually decided to end the experiment, ordering the military to reoccupy the territory it had ceded. Before seizing what seems like an opportunity, therefore, a government must first carefully assess whether a critical mass within the terrorist organization questions the utility of violence. The government might not be at leisure to wait until a full consensus has emerged, but it must not move forward until the peace seekers within the terrorist group have the balance of influence in their favor.

It is because of these concerns that a government should begin formal negotiations only after the terrorist group has declared a permanent cessation of violence. Insisting on such a declaration spurs the politically minded among the terrorists to achieve internal consensus. As a litmus test of the terrorists' intentions, such a declaration also makes it easier for the government to trust that negotiations are meaningful. In terms of maintaining the government's stability, a permanent cease-fire represents a public commitment to which the terrorists can be held and for whose breach they can be sanctioned. Crucially, it helps maintain the democratic protocol, establishing in the minds of the terrorists (and of all others who consider the political use of violence) that the government will not allow major outcomes to be influenced by the use of violence. Lastly, it may help reinforce the perception that the negotiations represent a unique historical opportunity and thus may generate valuable political momentum toward resolving the conflict.

How?

Even when dealing with a terrorist group that is ready for negotiations, there is no guarantee that a talks process will succeed. What, then, should a government's posture be? For terrorism experts such as Paul Wilkinson, of the University of St. Andrews, the risk of appearing weak and undermining a government's political system during negotiations is so great that the government should make "no concessions." This argument is the logical extension of the doctrine of "no negotiations"—and like it, it fails to address the many practical difficulties of trying to end violence while safeguarding the credibility of a government's political system.

Moty Cristal, a negotiator at Camp David for the Israeli government, has argued that one viable tactic is for governments to shift the terms of the negotiations from the terrorists' political demands to their personal fate. This might not be possible unless the terrorists are all but defeated, but it is a useful distinction in many instances. Governments can split negotiations into two tracks and consider two types of concessions. Primary concessions would relate to the terrorists' stated demands, secondary concessions to their personal fate. Both sets would be negotiated in parallel, but whereas secondary concessions would be discussed in direct negotiations between the government and the terrorists, primary concessions would have to be part of a broader process that would subject the terrorists to a democratic mandate, secured through elections for a constitutional assembly or a similar body.

The distinction between these two tracks is essential. Terrorists seeking primary concessions aim to alter the political arrangements under which the state operates, and no self-respecting democracy can allow a small group of once-violent conspirators to impose constitutional change, even after it has ostensibly renounced violence. On the other hand, terrorists will have little incentive to engage in negotiations unless they feel constitutional change is at least a possibility. The only way to resolve this tension is to grant primary concessions only in the context of a broader settlement involving all the major parties—and in which the terrorists participate on the basis of a democratic mandate—so that the concessions become an extension of the polity's will.

An additional advantage of putting together a broad, multiparty process is that it exposes the terrorists to democratic practices. The terrorists will have to subject their political program to the public's judgment in elections, and—once negotiations have begun—interact and engage with their opponents' concerns, build coalitions, and strike compromises. The case of the IRA demonstrates that such an apprenticeship in democracy can be an invaluable means of easing the transition from violence to conventional politics. As recent research has shown, the IRA's continued dialogue with political parties helped soften the group's position on key matters; in the middle of the negotiations, Adams is even reported to have said that the conflict in Northern Ireland required "a more complex response than simply the imposition of one nationality over another." Dialogue also gave the movement an incentive to shift resources from the armed struggle to the building of its electoral capability.

Governments will inevitably encounter tremendous difficulties in constructing an inclusive negotiations process. Terrorists will be reluctant to become just one of many political actors in negotiations. The government might have to bring on board some opposition parties, which could be tempted to exploit the situation for their own political gain. The difficulty of getting such parties to participate is often a major obstacle to talks. In Spain, for example, the current Socialist government has pushed back the starting date for negotiations with ETA. Although ETA has observed the cease-fire it declared in March 2006, the opposition Conservatives have firmly opposed any talks until ETA is fully demobilized. Conscious that any outcome emerging from a noninclusive process might be seen as illegitimate, the government has been left in a near-impossible situation. It seems to have no choice now but to hope that a sense of historic opportunity will eventually compel the opposition to join the process.

In contrast to that of primary-track negotiations, the purpose of secondary-track talks is relatively straightforward: to ensure an orderly demobilization of the terrorist group. But such discussions often turn out to be a negotiator's worst nightmare. This is especially true of negotiations on personnel-related matters, which often lead to amnesty-like arrangements for prisoners and terrorists on the run. No matter how conditional or sophisticated the form of their release, allowing convicted murderers to go free will invariably be at odds with the government's pledges never to give in to terrorists' demands, and such a deal could be impossible to sell to the public. Even so, securing such arrangements is in the government's best interest. They strengthen the hand of the peace seekers within the terrorist group and remove a pretext for dissidents to justify returning to violence. They also provide a strong incentive for terrorists to give ground on primary-track issues. It is for this reason (as well as to placate a skeptical public) that governments have traditionally insisted on tying concessions in this area to progress in all others. In the end, the public may be convinced of the need for secondary concessions only if it has a strong desire for closure and fears that a historic opportunity for peace will be lost unless there is an agreement. And so it is the government's ability to manage public expectations as well as the competing interests of the terrorists and the government's opposition that will determine the likelihood that negotiations will succeed.

The Next Good Friday

In some cases, such as that of al Qaeda, the chances for a negotiated solution are slim. Osama bin Laden and Ayman al-Zawahiri, al Qaeda's ideological powerhouse, have offered cease-fires to governments in the United States and Europe, but it is unclear whether the organization's local commanders would honor them. There is no sign that al Qaeda has changed its thinking on the utility of violence. And it is hard to conceive of a viable process of primary negotiations in which al Qaeda could be included. Al Qaeda has global aspirations and no firm territorial base, and there is no clearly defined territory in which its aims could be satisfied through constitutional means. Under these conditions, opening negotiations would be a counterproductive move: it would provide al Qaeda with political legitimacy while undermining both moderates across the Muslim world and the negotiating governments themselves.

Even when all the necessary conditions are met, negotiations will not be easy. As the Arab-Israeli peace process and talks in Sri Lanka have shown, attempts to bring about negotiated settlements often provoke violent challenges both from the in-group (dissident factions of the terrorist group or reactionary elements of the government's security forces) and from outsiders (rival or splinter groups). Moreover, postsettlement situations tend to be fragile long after the negotiations have been concluded. Issues such as the reintegration of combatants into society, the conduct of reconciliation processes, and the stabilization of new political institutions keep policymakers busy for years after a peace agreement has been signed.

The best example of how negotiations can be conducted successfully is undoubtedly those with the IRA. By the late 1980s, much of the IRA's leadership had concluded that alternatives to the armed struggle had to be explored. And although large parts of the organization were not yet ready to swap the bullet for the ballot box, the leadership possessed enough influence and cunning to cajole IRA skeptics into going along with the new strategy. The political process, which evolved throughout the 1990s, was complicated and often torturous, but its breadth and the British government's insistence that the IRA relinquish violence as a precondition for political participation protected the democratic framework.

Whether this example can be emulated in the cases of ETA, Hamas, and Hezbollah remains to be seen. The circumstances in each situation are vastly different. But whatever the particular ideological or geographic background, no negotiations process can even get started without strong indications that the terrorists are serious about ending their armed struggle. ETA, whose desire to move away from violence appears strong and consistent, is most likely to follow in the IRA's footsteps. But Hamas and Hezbollah still appear to have some way to go before arriving at a strategic juncture. Hezbollah, although under pressure to disarm, has little reason to forgo force, especially given the popularity of its armed campaign against Israel last summer. Hamas may be somewhat closer to an inflection point. Having won the Palestinian parliamentary elections in early 2006, it has a real incentive to make politics work. At the same time, elements of the leadership do not seem ready to do so. If it wants to capitalize on the enormous political opportunities that its strong electoral performance has created, Hamas must now forge a strong internal consensus for starting negotiations with Israel.

A separate but related issue is whether democratic governments can do anything to bring about the conditions under which negotiations with terrorists might succeed. And they can. Democratic governments should hold out the promise of giving terrorists a stake in the political process, but only if the terrorists agree to play by democratic rules. They should try to buttress the politically minded among terrorists while refraining from doing anything that could strengthen the hard-liners. Most important, they must remain firmly opposed to the use of violence for political ends. Negotiations can sometimes be an exit strategy for terrorists who have second thoughts about their campaigns. But governments must always be clear that committing to democratic principles is the price terrorists will have to pay.

8

Anti-terrorism Legislation: Civil Liberty and Judicial Alteration[1]

Laura K. Donohue[2]

Introduction

The phrase "civil liberty" at the time of the American founding carried a meaning different than today. It related to the right of the people to constitute government. Popular sovereignty lay at the heart of the concept—the people as the source of state legitimacy. A quasi-nationalist-republican form of government followed. The legislative, executive, and judicial branches each answered to the people, albeit in different ways. The Framers considered all three branches responsible for the protection and interpretation of the constitution. But the almost immediate adoption of a bill of rights and a series of legal cases helped the judicial branch to emerge as the primary guardian of rights.

In this way, as both an expression of popular sovereignty, and the protector of the entitlements of the people, consideration of the impact of counterterrorism on civil liberties ties directly to the judiciary. All too often, however, in the United States and in other liberal, democratic states constructed on similar principles, analyses center on the substantive decisions of the courts in upholding or invalidating laws with an impact on individual rights—not on the rules and structures of the judiciary itself.

This chapter breaks ranks by focusing on counterterrorism and the evolution of judicial structures. The United States' experience in this regard—the adoption of special rules for pursuing terrorist cases—is far from unique. The Republic of Ireland maintains Special Criminal Courts, the Republic of Turkey operates State Security Courts (Devlet Güvenlik Mahkemesi), and Israel draws on Courts Martial. The United Kingdom, for its part, also uses special tribunals—and it is this Diplock system that provides the case study for this chapter.

In 1973 the Diplock courts rose from the ashes of a spectacularly unsuccessful effort to intern paramilitaries and reduce violence in Northern Ireland. The tribunals carried the virtue of emphasizing the rule of law—and criminalizing political conflict. They eliminated the possibility of juror intimidation (by eliminating juries altogether). And they introduced important safeguards that made it easier for defendants to appeal decisions. However, the Diplock courts also suffered from a number of important weaknesses: the elimination of juries in the context of history undermined their legitimacy and counteracted efforts by the state to involve the minority community in governance of the Province. Simultaneously, the system embraced relaxed evidentiary standards for confessions, inferences from silence, and statements by police officers. The inclusion of a broad range of offences, moreover, meant that even non-terrorist crimes fell under their jurisdiction, representing a transfer of extraordinary powers to ordinary criminal law.

These weaknesses led to repeated calls to close the courts; however, successive governments, both conservative and liberal, refused to do so. In the interim, a number of informal and formal adjustments were made to the system. This chapter looks at these alterations and continued criticism of the Diplock courts and their operation, particularly post-9/11.

The elements highlighted in this chapter, while drawn from the British experience, are not unique to the U.K. Other countries too have altered due process to answer the threat of terrorism. Relaxed evidentiary rules and important shifts in the burden of proof apply on the basis of the type of crime charged. Special procedures on both sides of the Atlantic and across the English Channel affect habeas corpus. Client-attorney privilege too elsewhere has been altered. Additionally, in many countries, on the basis of a preliminary designation or the nature of the crime charged, the right to jury trial can be suspended.

While there are arguments that support these alterations, they carry risks for liberal, democratic states embroiled in a battle against terrorism. This chapter concludes by highlighting the unique challenges posed to the British judicial system by more recent threats and offers a series of observations that resonate with the Irish Special Criminal Courts, the Turkish DGMs, the Israeli courts martial, and the proposed American military tribunals.

The United Kingdom

"[O]ur society is based on the liberty of the individual. It is what we fight to protect."

Lord Falconer of Thoroton, QC, *HL Debs*, 26 Mar 2003, cols 851–54

In his chronicles of the kings of England, Sir Richard Baker described King John as a man who "neither came to the crown by justice, nor held it with any honour, nor left it peace."[3] Yet, but for this dismal performance, the 1215 Magna Carta—the Great Charter and forerunner of constitutional democracy—might never have been signed. This document secured for freemen the protection of the common law. Once granted, King John's subsequent effort to circumvent these liberties led to his death.

The Magna Carta guaranteed that no freeman would be imprisoned, exiled, "or in any way destroyed . . . except by the lawful judgment of his peers or by the law of the land."[4] Justice would be swift.[5] And punishment would be proportionate to the degree of the offense.[6]

These principles are so fundamental to the British judicial system that it cannot be conceived of without them. It is not that liberty rights are never infringed. But, as Lord Falconer proclaimed, "Any limitations on individual freedom must be proportionate to the threat; they must be sanctioned by law and cannot take place on an ad hoc basis; and they must be implemented in a way which ensures that there are safeguards and that the activities of the executive are subject to monitoring, scrutiny and accountability."[7] He continued, "If limitations are implemented excessively, the framework must ensure that the monitoring, scrutiny and accountability arrangements are likely to identify and remedy such excesses. In other words, if protections are put in place they must be effective."[8]

This framework dominates the United Kingdom's approach to counterterrorism. In the post-9/11 environment, however, it has come under increasing strain. The 2001 Anti-terrorism Crime and Security Act, rushed through Westminster in the wake of the attacks, instated the indefinite detention of foreign nationals. The 2003 Criminal Justice Act expanded the length of time terrorist suspects could be held to 14 days, forcing the U.K. to enter a derogation to the European Court of Human Rights. The Law Lords, when the statutes came before them, found the provisions incompatible with the 1998 Human Rights Act—not because of their substance, but because they applied only to foreign nationals, making them discriminatory. The Labor Government responded with the 2005 Prevention of Terrorism Act, which allowed for control orders—a form of house arrest—to be imposed on citizen and non-citizen alike.

The London bombings in July 2005 were enough to remind the state of the growing threat from Islamist organizations. Labour tried to extend detention without charge to 90 days, but was defeated. Subsequent efforts to prevent individuals from rallying converts to the cause, however, succeeded: the 2006 Terrorism Act outlawed the glorification of terrorism, incitement to terrorism, and acts preparatory to terrorism, while increasing the time suspects could be held to 28 days.

These more recent provisions have not appeared out of thin air: they are part of a much longer dialogue within the United Kingdom about how to accommodate the unique challenges posed by terrorism. For most of the 20th century Westminster did not directly deal with violence in Northern Ireland; instead, a devolved provincial parliament, Stormont, operated. In 1972, however, alarmed at the growing unrest that came to a head in the civil rights movement, the British Parliament assumed Direct Rule. Accordingly, the section begins with a discussion of the judicial alterations introduced in 1973. These prove exceedingly relevant, as the special rules then introduced, and modified over the next three decades, continue to regulate both terrorist and, to some extent, non-terrorism-related cases.

Internment and Executive Detention

Westminster inherited the Troubles in the wake of a disastrous effort to detain those involved in violence. In 1971 Operation Demetrius resulted in the imprisonment of hundreds of innocent people. Violence in the province spiraled: in the four months preceding the sweep, eight people died from Troubles-related violence. In the four months following internment, 114 individuals were killed.[9] From 78 explosions in July, the number jumped in August to 131, followed in September by 196.[10] Efforts to control the violence by re-arming the local police force failed. By the end of the year, more than three times the number of deaths from the previous year had occurred.[11]

In concert with the rising number of detainees, complaints of ill treatment suddenly increased. Allegations that men had been forced to run barefoot over barbed wire and broken glass, had their scrotums slammed in drawers, and had been severely beaten began to circulate.[12] To get detainees to talk, security forces used wall-standing, hooding, noise, a bread and water diet, and sleep deprivation—techniques developed by the British military in Malaya, Cyprus, Brunei, and elsewhere.[13] Father Dennis Faul, a Catholic priest and civil rights activist, placed his phone number in an advertisement in the *Irish News* and declared himself available for advice.[14] He subsequently documented twenty-five coercive methods of questioning used in Holywood and Girdwood Barracks, which included physical beatings, injections, electric shocks, burns, and security forces urinating on prisoners, as well as psychological methods such as interrogators wearing surgical dress, playing Russian roulette with the detainees, and threatening the prisoner's family members.[15]

As complaints of mistreatment grew more frequent, the British Government commissioned an inquiry into methods of interrogation. Sir Edmund Compton, Mr. Edgar Fay, and Dr. Ronald Gibson reported in November 1971 that "physical ill-treatment took place."[16] But, they continued, "we are not making a finding of brutality on the part of those who handle these complaints."[17] They explained, "We consider that brutality is an inhuman or savage form of cruelty, and that cruelty implies a disposition to inflict suffering, coupled with indifference to, or pleasure in, the victim's pain."[18]

This understanding of brutality—having sadistic undertones—presented a rather extreme position, and one not widely shared by either human rights organizations or the communities in the North. Internment discredited, upon the proroguement of Stormont, the first Secretary of State for Northern Ireland, William Whitelaw, began to review the cases of all 900 individuals still interned. A renewed IRA campaign in July 1972, however, convinced Whitelaw that in the short term it would be unwise to abandon indefinite detention. For the long term, though, a different solution was needed. Westminster appointed Lord Diplock to focus on the horizon.

Diplock

Lord Diplock, described upon his death as "a formidable intellect and one of the greatest judicial craftsmen of his generation,"[19] did not shirk from prominence. The London *Times* described him as "a powerful, if not always a sympathetic, judge at every level of his career. His manner was tensely analytical, and—although never discourteous to Counsel who appeared before him—he never left them in any doubt about his intellectual superiority. . . . "[20] He took the central chair in the House of Lords, instituting the practice of issuing only one leading judgment where there were no dissents—and often writing them himself.[21] It was thus entirely consistent with his character that Lord Diplock should be comfortable recommending the suspension of jury trial in Northern Ireland and replacing it with a single judge tribunal.

Recommendations

The problems Lord Diplock had to address were many: internment had not only allowed for coercive interrogation practices, but it had brought the criminal justice system in Northern Ireland into disrepute. Yet the regular judicial system, as constituted at the time, appeared insufficient to meet the unique challenges posed by terrorism: for one, the courts systematically discriminated against Catholics. A study by Tom Hadden and Paddy Hillyard in 1973, for instance, found that in political cases, the court denied bail to 79 percent of the Catholics who came before it, but only 54 percent of the Protestants.[22] Part of the problem was the make-up of the judiciary. Judges were almost entirely drawn from the majority community. Even as late as 1976, Protestants held 68 of the 74 senior court appointments.[23] In 1972 Lord Justice O'Donnell became only the second Catholic member of the High Court bench. It took 14 years for the next Catholic, Michael Nicholson, to be appointed.[24] Juries, in turn, acquitted approximately 15 percent of Protestant defendants, to only 5 percent of Catholics.[25] Fr. Dennis Faul, legal advisor to the Northern Ireland Civil Rights Association, explained that the minority community was "afraid of the Courts: they believe the judicial system as it operates in the blatantly sectarian conditions of life here is loaded against them."[26]

Lord Diplock, however, appeared somewhat immune to the minority community's concerns. In his final report, published December 20, 1972, he suggested that the judiciary and the courts had, "in general held the respect and the trust of all except the extremists."[27] This view might have stemmed in part from the nature and limited extent of information provided to the commission. The inquiry lasted just seven weeks, in the course of which it received only three written submissions. Almost all of the evidence was oral and heard in

London—520 kilometers from Belfast.[28] Lord Diplock made only two trips to the Province, in the course of which he only met with the security forces and those administering the judicial system. And almost all the witnesses were drawn from the majority community.[29]

Nevertheless, Lord Diplock, for other reasons, did not consider the ordinary court system an adequate alternative to internment—which could not be relied upon in the long term as an effective way to address violence. Diplock expressed strong concern about the possibility of juror intimidation resulting from the strong social control paramilitaries wielded in the Province. And he pointed to perverse verdicts to underscore his concerns. Seven recommendations followed.

First, Diplock proposed that powers of arrest be extended to the army. For four hours the military ought to be able to hold individuals without charge, up to 28 days on remand. Second, Diplock claimed that magistrates were susceptible to intimidation and recommended that decisions for bail be transferred to high court judges. Third, he advocated that the burden of proof be shifted for firearms and explosives discovery: where found, the defense would have to prove that he or she was not aware of the presence of the weapon. Fourth, he suggested that standards be lowered for admissions to make them consistent with Article 3 jurisprudence of the European Convention of Human Rights. The English Judges' Rules currently in operation provided a higher bar: under them, any admission made in the course of a situation meant to induce confessions was considered involuntary and could not be admitted into court as evidence.[30] Fifth, Diplock advocated the suspension of the 1922–43 Civil Authorities (Special Powers) Acts, as well as capital punishment—both of which marked the Unionist control of Northern Ireland 1922–72. Sixth, he suggested that written affidavits be accepted from murdered witnesses, to try to protect against paramilitaries covering their tracks by killing those who might testify against them. (This recommendation appears to have come directly from the shooting of Mr. Agnew, a bus driver, who was killed the day before he was supposed to testify in a political trial.) And seventh, Lord Diplock recommended that a single high or country court judge, without a jury, hear cases involving political offences.[31]

Reaction to Lord Diplock's report fell largely along party lines: Catholics roundly denounced it. The nationalist Social, Democratic, and Labour Party expressed dismay. Bernadette Devlin, a minute and fiery republican, observed, "We have not heard from the government, and certainly not from Lord Diplock, one concrete point of evidence to show that it is necessary" to suspend jury trial.[32] She challenged, "We have heard of packed juries. But where is the statistical evidence? How many packed juries have there been? What is the percentage of juries that have been packed one way or the other? If there have been perverse judgments, convictions, or acquittals, what is the percentage?"[33] Ian Paisley, the Democratic Unionist Party autarch, welcomed the findings but expressed outrage that Protestant juries could be anything *but* fair minded.[34] The *Economist* and the London *Times* ran editorials supporting the recommendations; while a *Criminal Law Review* article by Professor William Twining accused the report of being written in haste, poorly researched, and resulting in widespread panic.[35] The Government, for its part, accepted Lord Diplock's conclusions—while remaining "firmly committed to the restoration of law in Northern Ireland."[36] William Whitelaw vowed to "continue to bring suspected persons before the courts whenever possible."[37] The 1973 Northern Ireland (Emergency Provisions) Act channeled the Diplock recommendations into law.

Strengths of the Diplock System

Statistical gains almost immediately followed the Diplock reforms: the minority population viewed the changes as preferential to executive detention. A survey taken a year into the operation of the Diplock courts found that 55 percent of Catholics thought that the new system was better than internment—but only 5 percent of Protestants felt the same.[38] Whether a result of the Diplock courts, or other steps taken under Direct Rule, after their institution, violence in the Province fell.[39] Simultaneously, convictions increased: in the first five years, murder convictions rose from 9 to 77; woundings from 142 to 499; and robbery from 791 to 1839.[40]

These were not the only perceived strengths of the new system: Criminalization, the elimination of possible juror intimidation, and retention of the adversarial system with additional safeguards offered important advantages to the state in its battle against terrorism. This section briefly considers each.[41]

Criminalization as a Counterterrorist Strategy

Perhaps most importantly, the use of the judicial process instead of executive action can be seen as a way of criminalizing the state's counterterrorist program. In the midst of a violent movement, this signaled a return to normalcy and undercut the political claims of those engaged in terrorist violence. It could be argued, in response, that the situation required not criminalization, but a political solution—and so efforts to criminalize it masked a more effective approach to ending the violence.[42] But the immediate criminalization of violence does not mean that political solutions to underlying grievances could not be (and indeed, later were) simultaneously pursued. Over the long term, the continued use of the system, however, signaled a lack of confidence in the people to be able to perform their juror functions. This may have undercut efforts to build confidence in the rule of law in Northern Ireland—an issue at the heart of the Troubles after decades of abuse. Nevertheless, there are other ways to signal this that suggest further movement towards normalcy: for instance, the state later increased the number of offences that could go to jury trial.

Elimination of Juror Intimidation

The system also offered other strengths: by eliminating juries the issue of juror intimidation (whether or not it was occurring at that point), simply disappeared. Although no evidence was offered by Lord Diplock or the government at the time, there had been documented instances of witness intimidation—and in a place as intimate as Northern Ireland, the suggestion that, in the presence of well-organized, purposive, and violent organizations, it could not extend to jurors, would be somewhat naïve.

There may have been other ways to address this phenomenon—such as *in camera* proceedings—but as a device for eliminating the possibility of juror intimidation, it did accomplish its task. This concern, moreover, has proven no less pressing as peace has emerged in the province—paramilitaries have moved into organized crime and continue to intimidate the local population.[43]

Safeguards in View of the Adversarial Model of Adjudication

The Diplock reforms did not alter the adversarial nature of the judicial system. Instead, although it removed jury trial, it included some safeguards that protected the adversarial nature of the proceedings. For instance, by making the judges triers of fact, they became more sensitive to the background circumstances of each case. To protect against self-bias, early on in the system, judges informally began vetting depositions before forwarding them to a different trial judge.

This prevented them from being in the rather awkward position of having to instruct themselves to ignore at least some portion of information that should not have made it to them in the first place. (This circumstance, however, as I return to in the next section, could not altogether be avoided—highlighting one weakness in the system). Judges became freer to state their views on the cases coming before them prior to trial—with the result that proceedings tended to be shorter than full-blown jury trials and less contest-oriented. The interactions between the judge and counsel were more frequent than ordinary trials, creating a "problem solving" approach—similar to that adopted during the sentencing phase of regular proceedings. This meant that more focus was placed on the issues in contention.[44]

Charges of case-hardening frequently assailed the Diplock courts: acquittals decreased, for instance, from 53 percent in 1984 to 29 percent in 1993. During the same period, acquittal rate for jury criminal trials was 49 percent in 1984 and 48 percent in 1993.[45] By 1993, reports circulated that the conviction rate had hit 85 percent.[46] But a scholarly inquiry into the system found that the percentage of convictions did not actually increase. Judges did tend to be more intrusive, and the defense did not have as many options for challenging the merits of the prosecution's case. However, the judges narrowly ruled on the specific charges before them. John Jackson, studying the system, found, "The most interesting consequence of this approach was that counsel indicated to us that their preference for one form of tribunal over the other depended on the particular kinds of evidence or issue involved in the case."[47] In sexual assault cases, judges might prove more sensitive than jurors to the shortcomings of identification evidence—making defending attorneys more amenable to have the case tried before a Diplock judge. Jackson added, "Significantly, however, defense counsel said that if they had a choice they would opt for a jury nine times of ten, because in matters of credibility it was easier to persuade a jury to entertain a doubt as to the defendant's guilt."[48]

Even as he suspended trial by jury, Lord Diplock tried to try to retain the core of this adversarial approach. He offered two ways to compensate: the judges became required to issue detailed, reasoned judgments in support of their convictions, and the defendant was granted an automatic right of appeal on grounds of either fact or law.[49] The importance of these safeguards is not to be under-estimated. The written judgments, for instance, required more discipline in the fact-finding phase of the trial. Judges proved to be sensitive to potential reversals by the Court of Appeal. Appellate courts tended to reverse

Diplock convictions more frequently than jury courts—most likely due to the requirement that the judges write out the findings of fact, making it easier to challenge the conclusion.[50] Judges consequently went to some lengths to ensure the strength of their facts.[51] There were limits, though, as to how far the trial judge was required to go. *R. v. Caraher* provides a salient example.

Armagh, near Crossmaglen, is bandit country—a staunchly republican area, with a long history of sniper attacks using large-calibre rifles. In April 1997, security forces found a stolen Mazda 626 rigged with a metal plate that could be used as a firing platform, then a shield, in a barn. Residue of gunpowder was found in the back of the car—while another car held traces of PETN (one of the components of the plastic explosive, Semtex). A trailer with a false bottom hid two rifles, an AKM and a Barrett .50 inch caliber rifle with a magazine, a telescopic sight, and three rounds of .50 ammunition. Security forces found another 50 live rounds of ammunition designed for the Barrett, (which had been fired), as well as two balaclavas. Two cell phones that worked in border area and could only receive incoming calls also were in the barn, as well as two CB radios switched to the same channel and ready for use (not channel 9, as CBs turn on to automatically, but channel 26). Three men were there when the security forces arrived, with another man sighted running away. The police caught him and found a pair of gloves near him that forensics later showed had been both in the barn and on the man, Michael Caraher. Although it was a warm day, Caraher was wearing two sets of clothes, and a spanner in his pocket (although a common size) fit the secret compartment in the trailer.

In deciding the case, the judge carefully laid out the set of facts from which he had inferred that the men had been associated with an illegal operation: the four men happened to have arrived simultaneously at the barn from different places. The firing platform on the Mazda would have been obvious—and it was not likely that the terrorists who had prepared the operation would have just left when four strangers showed up. The gates, moreover, had been barred from the inside.[52]

Specifically in relation to Caraher, the judge looked at the material facts: he tried to run away, he gave a false name initially, he was sporting the layered look, he carried a wrench fitting the trailer, and a call had been made to him from one of the mobile phones found in the barn six days before the incident. Caraher had given a detailed written statement, but he had only said he was on the way to see a friend—not why he was there. When confronted with the evidence,

Caraher had remained silent, leading the trial judge to conclude, "In my judgment the inference to be drawn is clear, that he could not if he gave evidence substantiate his story, which is not only unconvincing but altogether false, or explain those facts."[53]

Caraher appealed based on the detailed reasoning required in Diplock cases. He said that the judge had not shown the relative weight of the factors he had considered—nor had he indicated how many were necessary to cross over the threshold of guilt.

The appeals court drew a line: it asserted that judges are not required to do either of these when giving a judgment.[54] This did not mean that the facts relied upon or the manner of reliance were immune from scrutiny. Later in the same decision, for instance, the court disputed the judge's reliance on the telephone call made to Caraher from the mobile phone in the barn. This pushed Lord Justice Nicholson to go back to *R. v. Gibson*, which provided guidance on what to do if a material fact later turned out to be not strong enough for the judge to rely on it. Nicholson wrote,

> [I]f a judge states a number of reasons for convicting an accused and if he states that one reason is, or two reasons are, the main reason or reasons, and then states other reasons, and it then transpires on appeal that a main reason or the main reason is invalid, does it follow that the conviction is unsafe and unsatisfactory. In considering this question we are of opinion that where the judgment of a trial judge in a Diplock Court contains a defective and erroneous finding the position is broadly akin to a misdirection of fact by a trial judge to a jury. Where there is such a misdirection of fact the test in determining whether the conviction is safe and satisfactory is whether the jury would inevitably have convicted if the summing-up had not contained the misdirection . . .[55]

Here, the Appeals court relied on the strong fact pattern—and the inference from silence. Nicholson wrote: "[I]n our view there was a strong prima facie case against Caraher . . . Accordingly the judge was entitled to draw the inference from Caraher's failure to give evidence that he could not substantiate the story which he told the police and that it was not only unconvincing but altogether false and that he could not explain the facts which pointed towards his involvement in the arms find."[56]

Caraher shows how the written opinion describing the facts on which the judge relied to reach his judgment, and the automatic right of appeal on either fact or law, provided a protection for individuals accused in the Diplock system and protected the adversarial nature of the proceedings. Despite these safeguards, however, and the virtues of the Diplock courts in criminalizing terrorist conduct and eliminating concerns about juror intimidation, important weaknesses assailed the system.

Weaknesses of the Diplock Reforms

The Diplock reforms suffered from important weaknesses, not least of which centered on perceived fairness: Catholics were more likely than Protestants to know about the judicial changes—and they were more likely to perceive them as imbalanced. One study found that, a year into the operation of the courts, 63 percent of Protestants and 79 percent of Catholics were aware of abolition of jury trials. Of these, a disproportionate number of Catholics still found incredible the suggestion that people received a fair trial (88 percent of Catholics as opposed to 27 percent of Protestants).[57]

These perceptions were rooted in the rules and procedures of the Diplock Courts themselves. First, jury trials had a special place in the British judicial system, and their suspension, particularly in the face of little to no evidence of juror tampering, immediately gave rise to questions of fairness. It created an adversarial deficit, and it disengaged the minority community at a time the state sought to involve it further in governance of the region. Simultaneously, alternative and unexplored ways to address the concern existed. Second, changes in rules of evidence related to confessions, inferences from silence, and membership in proscribed organizations undermined due process. Emphasis shifted from pre-arrest gathering of evidence to post-arrest interrogation to obtain information.[58] And allegations of mistreatment during pre-trial interrogation skyrocketed: from 180 complaints in 1975, the following year the number increased to 384—while the total for 1977 and 1978 together approached 1100.[59] Third, the automatic inclusion of cases related to scheduled offences, and ever-expanding list of crimes considered such, meant that even non-terrorist cases could be tried in this manner. The procedural shifts, moreover, crept over into ordinary criminal law. And the erosion of the criminal justice system standards led to miscarriages in justice that became prominent symbols that undermined the legitimacy of the state. This section briefly considers these concerns.

Suspension of Jury trial

What has perhaps become lost to history is that single judge tribunals, far from being an exception in Ireland, were used with some regularity in the 18th and 19th centuries. What made them extraordinary was, particularly, their 19th century embrace by Westminster and application to a part of the United Kingdom under direct control of Parliament. This was closer to home than previous initiatives—and it went to the heart of the protections, enshrined in the Magna Carta, that were widely seen as a protection against despotism. Juries, moreover, were seen as keeping the law honest, "because they oblige lawyers and judges to deal with what is right and wrong by the standards of the general public, as well as what is the letter of the law."[60] By jettisoning juries, the courts ran the risk of being seen "as another tool in the battle by the state to maintain order and its own legitimacy."[61]

The importance of jury trial was recognized in Parliament: "Governments have always faced a critical dilemma. On the one hand, they have to be seen to address the public's anxiety and anger about crime. They have to show that they are on the case. Procedural reform is temptingly available to them for that purpose." The Lord continued, "On the other hand, they realize that they are the custodians of a precious framework of individual liberties, containing safeguards that, once curtailed, are seldom, if ever, restored. They certainly are part of our national heritage and I believe strongly that preserving them has far more than a mere historic or antiquarian importance. . . . trial by jury for serious offences remains a fundamental feature of the balance that we strike, as it has for centuries. We have always placed it in the scales on the side of freedom."[62]

Such sentiments were not limited to the second chamber. Mr. Robert Marshall-Andrews suggested in the House of Commons that "The great benefit of jury trial is not simply that it is fair and perceived to be fair, and that it involves the citizen in the process of justice, but that it is profoundly modern. It is one of our most ancient rights and liberties, but also the most modern . . . The citizen is empowered, and thereby enabled." He tied the necessity of a jury trial to the United Kingdom's adversarial system: "We are an adversarial people. Like the court, the Chamber is an adversarial arena. That is the way we do business. . . . The principle of our jury system is that the state brings its case, but must prove it in front of the citizen. To suggest that one can create an inquisitorial system by simply ripping out jury trial is the precise equivalent of claiming that one can remove the wheels from a car and thereby create a boat." It was hard to corrupt an entire jury, for "Corrupting, bullying, bribing or intimidating 12 people is almost impossible."[63] Moreover, efforts to try to "bribe, bully, cajole or intimidate judges" would be misplaced—as "they have nothing to do with the findings of fact at the end of the trial."[64] And by only seeing the evidence legally allowed by a separate process, the juries only saw the result, making their judgments untainted by erroneously produced evidence.[65]

By withdrawing the jury, what may be termed an "adversarial deficit" ensued.[66] It eliminated the procedural device created to give a defendant a meaningful opportunity to contest the charges and to ensure that guilt derived solely from evidence presented in the courtroom. With no separate, decision-making authority, the judge became (perhaps unknowingly) tainted.[67]

Additionally, if, as a counterterrorist aim, the goal of the British government was to engage the minority population in constitutional politics, eliminating juries can be seen as somewhat counterproductive.

With jury trials a fundamental aspect of the common law tradition, moreover, alternative ways to address the potential intimidation of jurors existed. For instance, a new offence of intimidating juries, or the retrial of defendants acquitted by juries could have addressed the problem. (These mechanisms, in fact, became built into the system through the 1996 Criminal Justice (Northern Ireland) Order 1996 and the Criminal Procedure and Investigations Act 1996.[68]) Jurors could have had their identity masked, or sat *in camera*—and the jury pool could have included people from a broader regional representation.[69]

This is not to say that juries do not themselves have weaknesses: Juries can be seen as "unrepresentative, inefficient, cumbersome," and insensitive to the complexity of the law. Their decisions may be arbitrary, based not on evidence but on emotion—with the result that guilty people end up being acquitted. Lord Justice McDermott claimed in 1995, "The growing number of cases, many of them of great gravity, which are aborted by reason of the nature of pre trial press and media coverage, adds to my anxiety that jury trial may no longer be the best and fairest mode of trial."[70] Indeed, much has been made of the potential movement away from the jury trial. But as David Sheldon recognized, "the ability of the jury to return unexpected or perverse verdicts may be regarded as one of the strengths of the system, since it demonstrates the independence of the jury from the state, and provides a check on the discretion of the prosecutor."[71]

The system is built on the idea that it is better to let the guilty man off than to send the innocent one to prison.[72] What is critical then about the counterterrorist judicial structures adopted in Northern Ireland is the extent to which they undermine this principle.

Relaxed Evidentiary Rules

Importantly, the Diplock Courts did not only suspend jury trial, but the rules of evidence altered to increase the probability that the defendant would be convicted. The admissibility of confessions, waiving of the right to silence, and admitting police officer statements as evidence of membership of illegal organizations, all came into play. While formulated to respond to very real concerns about the particular threat posed by paramilitary suspects—such as the difficulty of getting witnesses to come forward and the problems associated with interrogating individuals trained in counter-resistance techniques, the reforms also carried important negative repercussions such as altering the type of evidence sought by the security forces and increasing the likelihood of coercive interrogation, which contributed to undermining the perceived legitimacy of the system.

WEAKENING OF VOIR DIRE[73]

Widespread intimidation plagues the Northern Irish judicial system. As one Member of Parliament from the region put it in Westminster, "The real issue in Northern Ireland with the administration of justice is not the difference between a Diplock court and a jury court but whether the evidence exists to take cases forward and whether people engage in conspiracies to deny, destroy and prevent evidence."[74] The absence of witnesses meant that the state had to find other ways to convict terrorist suspects. It took a multitrack approach: first, relaxing the standards for the admissibility of confessions, second, allowing for extended pre-trial detention in order to obtain the necessary information, and third, allowing for conviction on the basis of uncorroborated evidence by informers turned Queen's evidence—namely, through Supergrasses. Each of these alterations carried a heavy price.

Under the common law, confessions were admissible only where they were voluntary. The state altered this rule for cases of suspected terrorism, making confessions admissible unless there was clear evidence that the interrogator deliberately forced the defendant to confess. The Diplock courts, moreover, allowed for "a moderate degree of physical maltreatment" to obtain a confession.[75] In other words, just because a statement was involuntary, it did not mean that it had to be excluded.[76]

The Northern Ireland (Emergency Provisions) Act subsequently allowed for the exclusion of confessions where "appropriate ... in order to avoid unfairness to the accused or otherwise in the interests of justice."[77] Under the statute, any violence on the part of interrogators was considered "unfair".[78] "A moderate degree of physical maltreatment" and "violence" thus book-ended the acceptable limits of interrogations.[79] In 1998 the incorporation of the European Convention of Human Rights into domestic law established an outright ban on torture as well as cruel, inhuman or degrading treatment.[80]

In parallel to the relaxed standards regarding the admissibility of confessions, the 1973 Northern Ireland (Emergency Provisions) Act et seq, and the 1974 Prevention of Terrorism (Temporary Provisions) Act et seq, provided for lengthy periods of detention prior to charge. Under the Prevention of Terrorism Act, the police could arrest a suspect for 48 hours, and then extend detention for up to five days on order of the Northern Ireland Secretary of State.[81] As soon as arrest was given effect under the PTA, the suspect became subject to EPA provisions limiting access to solicitors on notification of arrest.[82] Most individuals detained were later released without charge. In other words, these powers became a way to gather information.[83] Lengthy interrogation periods were widely believed to be critical to isolating suspects and encouraging them to provide information.[84]

These unsupervised periods provided the opportunity for abuse. Noel Bell, of the Armagh Four, wrote of his experiences, "I was slapped on the face, punched repeatedly on the chest and testicles until I fell to the floor. I was repeatedly told how I was supposed to have committed this murder on a guy I didn't even know. To cut a long story short, I was physically and psychologically tortured, brainwashed and degraded until I put my name to a prepared statement in order to get peace."[85] His father, Norman Bell, said, "Before this happened I did not really believe some of the nationalist accusations about the RUC." Their families said that the four men saw the RUC as friends—"unlike nationalist activists, who are often specially schooled in countering interrogation techniques."[86]

Indeed, between 1976 and 1986, physical abuse during interrogation was a common feature of the Northern Ireland security system.[87] Confessions obtained through such methods were routinely accepted by the courts[88]—even when challenged.[89] And even for cases that did not move into the realm of abuse, the isolation of suspects over the period of pre-trial detention impacted due process in the subsequent proceedings.

Calls for the closing of interrogation centers, however, went unmet.[90] And most claims against the RUC were settled out of court, with 86 percent of the complaints withdrawn.[91] (The independent commission for police complaints said this was because lodging complaints was a counterinsurgency tactic—not because they were further intimidated by RUC.[92])

Even as abuses continued, the courts increasingly relied solely on confessions made during interrogation for convictions. One study conducted in 1980 found that 86 percent of the evidence presented against suspects in the Diplock system consisted of statements made during interrogations—yet only 30 percent of this was supported by additional evidence.[93] Just over a decade later another study found that most Diplock prosecutions relied upon confessions by the defendant. In 85 percent of the cases, the statements were uncorroborated—with a conviction rate of around 95 percent.[94]

A number of prominent cases emerged, in which, as a result of uncorroborated confessions, miscarriages of justice were widely believed to have resulted. The Beechmount Five, for instance, were convicted entirely upon purported confessions. No witnesses had been produced, nor had any forensic evidence linked the accused to the crime—despite exhaustive searches and seizure of all the clothes the defendants owned. One person had been interrogated for 48 hours over a period of six days.[95] A clinical psychologist said the accused was "abnormally vulnerable" in conditions of intensive questioning.[96]

One Catholic commented about the tenor of the times, "We saw men we knew to be innocent being convicted in Crumlin Road courthouse and sent to Long Kesh (prison) for years. We had absolutely no confidence that we would be released, although we knew we were innocent."[97] The community, in the meantime—because of the suspension of juries—had no role in the decision-making process.[98] And, as the case of the Armagh Four demonstrated, it was not just the minority community that became further estranged from the judicial structure.

In a further effort to address the lack of witnesses, in the 1980s, the British government began using an informer system, in which blanket immunity was granted for giving evidence. In essence, courts began accepting the uncorroborated testimony of known paramilitaries—who could continue to act with impunity. Between November 1981 and November 1983, the Royal Ulster Constabulary arrested some 600 people fingered by seven Loyalist and 18 Republican "supergrasses."[99]

Amid accusations that the supergrass procedures had become show trials, the British government defended the system. Douglas Hurd argued in Commons, "There is no reason in principle to reject evidence simply because it comes from an accomplice who has given evidence to the police. That evidence has to be weighed in the scales of justice. If a court rejects accomplice evidence it does not show the decision to prosecute was wrong, any more than acquittal in a case involving a member of the security services show the case should not have been brought."[100] He referenced the Baker Report on the Emergency Provisions Act, which had broadly endorsed evidence from informers.[101]

In the end, the supergrass system collapsed. After three years, the percent of acquittals—either in the first instance or on appeal—had hit 72.5 percent.[102] Part of the problem was that individuals could use the system to settle old grudges. The evidence was often sketchy at best. And some witnesses ended up retracting their statements—assumedly under pressure from the paramilitaries. Not all witnesses turned Queen's evidence were particularly successful at avoiding reprisals; and the paramilitaries demonstrated a remarkably dogged response. In 1999, for instance, fourteen years after he had informed on his compatriots under interrogation, Eamon Collins was stabbed to death in Newry.[103]

The problems with witness intimidation did not end with the advent of the peace process. If anything, as paramilitaries moved into organized crime, intimidation became even more of an issue.[104] Adrian Bailey, West Bromwich, West stated in Parliament, "We are now witnessing the transformation of groups with a political ideology who carried on the sustained intimidation of local communities into groups that are specifically focused on common-or-garden criminality using techniques that they have honed to perfection over the years."[105] Bailey continued, "There is a huge body of evidence to demonstrate that many cases that could be won in court are lost because the original complainant or plaintiff decides not to give evidence. We all know that that happens because of threats to potential witnesses' personal safety. It is a requisite of any law-abiding society that people who want to act on behalf of the community and carry out their responsibilities be given some sort of protection."[106]

Nigel Dodds from North Belfast explained, "[Terrorist organizations in Northern Ireland] are involved in a range of illegal activities and impose their authority on vulnerable people who feel intimidated and are often unable to speak out against such a reign of terror. . . . [They] are becoming ever more sophisticated in their dealings. As one avenue of operation closes down, another opens up."[107] Roy Beggs from East Antrim noted that the Peace Process has had little effect: "One only has to read the newspapers to see that paramilitary activities remain rife within both traditions: murders, threats, beatings and enforced exiles are reported almost daily. Terrorism clearly remains a feature of life for many in Northern Ireland. Furthermore, there is increasing evidence that despite the ceasefires, paramilitary activity not only continues but has expanded in recent years to include such organized crime activities as fuel smuggling and counterfeiting."[108]

Jane Kennedy, the Minister of State at the Northern Ireland Office, related how paramilitaries still shoot children for "punishment"—when in reality they are simply consolidating their power.[109] Another MP discussed the case of Harry McCartan, a youth who had been convicted of joy riding. The UDA "used six-inch nails to impale his hands to a wooden fence and beat him mercilessly with nail-studded baseball bats about the head, arms, hands and legs. When received at the Royal Victoria Hospital late that day he was so badly bloodied that his father could only identify him by a tattoo."[110] In 2002 alone, 13 children under age 17 had been shot by Loyalists, and another 12 by republicans—and threats of shootings, beatings, mutilation, and exile continued.[111]

Calls for a more robust witness protection program, however, have been slow to yield results.[112] There are two issues here of note: first is the lack of procedural protections during the trial itself. Although public inquiries and inquests in Northern Ireland regularly granted anonymity to witnesses, the same did not exist in relation to the trial itself.[113] While video links were used for child witnesses, the same was not provided to adults. These and other weaknesses led the Northern Ireland Human Rights Commission to conclude that there "is not a very satisfactory set of procedures for dealing with informers and accomplices." It continued, "Money payments and other inducements in kind for informers are not subject to any form of public supervision and in cases where they are made there is a tendency to conceal the process from the courts and to avoid calling the informer to give evidence. Where an informer or accomplice is potentially willing to give evidence, on the other hand, there is no way in which the eventual outcome can be promised or predicted with any certainty."[114]

The second issue of note is the question of resources available to witnesses after the proceedings have concluded. ACC White has been very critical of the latter—and has suggested that the current program actually serves as a disincentive. He explains,

> The individual ... is moved into a council estate, given a minimum sum of money in terms of what he would be entitled to as an unemployed person. If he is a businessman he gets absolutely no money to re-establish himself and is required to sell his own business within the Province if he can and he must employ his own lawyer to do that. His house will be taken off him under the emergency provisions ... so he gets the bare minimum for what that house is worth ... if you have to go on the run leaving behind your whole social fabric and getting nothing to replace that, you do not really have much of a choice as a businessman. When you do the sums in your head you just roll over and pay.[115]

The Criminal Evidence (NI) Order 1999 made provision for witnesses in the courtroom proceedings, but it failed to address the witness protection issues writ large. This led one government report to conclude that the programs in the United States and Italy were superior.[116] More recently, in 2003 the Home Office made some proposals to address this issue—as did a task force on racketeering in 2002–3. The Northern Ireland Office also commissioned a study by Professor Ron Goldstock, to look at how prosecution witnesses believe they have been treated, particularly during the trial proceedings. The results of these studies have yet to yield effective implementation.[117]

ALTERATIONS IN THE RIGHT TO SILENCE

Beyond the elimination of juries and relaxed rules of evidence in relation to confessions, the Criminal Evidence (Northern Ireland) Order 1988 limited suspects' right to silence. Although a defendant could not be compelled to give evidence on his own behalf, where an individual refused to give evidence at trial, the court or jury may "draw such inferences from the failure as appear proper" and "on the basis of such inferences treat the failure as, or as capable of amounting to, corroboration of any evidence given against the accused in relation to which the failure is material."[118] Similar inference could be drawn during the trial where an individual failed or refused to account for objects, marks, and the like, where a police officer believed such items could be attributed to participation in the commission of a criminal offence and, once the constable informed the person of his beliefs and asked him to account for the presence of the object, the person still failed or refused to do so.[119] The order further included as a basis for inference at trial a defendant's failure or refusal to account for her presence at a particular place.[120]

The allowance of inference from silence in Northern Ireland in the 1988 order was not limited to Diplock courts; it applied across the board to all criminal cases. The measure required the judge to warn the accused of the presumption of guilt upon a refusal to testify. But in 1994 a new statutory instrument required only that the judge be satisfied that defendant was aware that an inference could be drawn.[121] This rule stands in stark contrast to *Miranda v. Arizona* and the United States' 5th Amendment protection against self incrimination interrogations where custody might result.[122] In the context of the increasing tendency of the courts to allow evidence when it points to the defendant's guilt, this development is particularly concerning.[123]

In 1996 *Murray v. U.K.* brought this power before the European Court of Human Rights. The ECHR found that right to silence is central to the protections of Article 6; but this does not mean that the court cannot draw inferences from a defendant's failure to provide an explanation. However, the judge cannot rely only on the inference for conviction.[124] Because the Diplock Courts do supply a reasoned judgment, the inference is more transparent than it might otherwise be. A short example will here suffice.

In the *Caraher* case, discussed above, the trial judge also found the defendant guilty of the shooting of a security force member. Two men from the Irish Republican Army had taken over Gerard and Paula Sheridan's home at 13 Carrickasticken Road, and held the family against their will. One had a rifle; two went to the back yard, heard a bang, then the men left. Security forces found a dog kennel that had been moved along the wall and footprints found on the top of it that matched Caraher's boots at the time of the arrest. The soles of the boots had been damaged in a pattern that matched Caraher's shoes. Another individual said Caraher had pulled the trigger. According to the appellate court, the "learned trial judge" wrote in response to the defendant's claim that the case relied upon an inference from Caraher's failure to give evidence,

> I do not accept this submission. There was nothing from which one might suppose that other people might have stood on the roof of the kennel for other purposes at other times. Nor was there anything which might explain how Caraher's

footprints could have got on to the roof at some other time. He did not put forward any suggestion to this effect in his written statement . . . and he did not give evidence at trial. I consider it justifiable in these circumstances to draw the inference, which in my view is obvious, that he did not give evidence because he could not produce any explanation consistent with innocence for the finding of his footprints on the roof of the dog kennel.[125]

The detailed reasoning provided by the judge thus helped to clarify the role of inference in the final decision.

In the event of a return to jury trial, however, the ability to read prejudice into refusal to answer would present difficulty. One commentator has suggested, to overcome this, that the judge provide a firmly worded direction to the jury—but there are problems with this as well: for instance, how far into fact-finding does the judge go when a jury is present? On the other hand, what kind of effect exactly would it have on juries (if any)?[126] Another solution might be to let the jury pause occasionally through the trial to deliberate. The risk here is prejudgment, but might prevent ignorance/lack of understanding as the trial progresses.[127] Nevertheless, in some situations a charge to the jury may not be sufficient to offset bias—in these cases, judges may be able to discharge entire juries, or individual jurors.[128]

It is not, however, always so clear what role inference plays—nor does its presence bolster belief in the justice of the system. The Casement Park trials, in which three men—Pat Kane, Michael Timmons and Sean Kelly—were convicted in a joint trial in March 1990, relied on bad film footage, the judicial assumption that the IRA was present in Casement Park, and an inference of guilt from one defendant's silence. One report looking at the incident said, "One is left with the simple feeling that these men did not stand a chance. We found judicial assumptions about the men which were so negative that they verged on outright prejudice."[129] Other groups criticized the Casement Park trials on similar grounds.[130]

Inference from silence is not limited to *Caraher* or the Casement Park Trials. On the contrary, it has routinely been used where defendants have refused to testify.[131] What makes it particularly notable is that it does not just apply to terrorist crime; in Northern Ireland, it applies across the board. And six years after its introduction in the province, a similar provision went before the House of Lords as part of the Criminal Justice and Public Order Bill—with the intent to apply the inference to the whole of the United Kingdom. Parliament blocked the measure at the time, claiming it infringed civil liberties. While the incident does suggest a double standard within the United Kingdom, efforts to apply the powers beyond the contours of terrorist crime speak to the tendency of many of the provisions to extend beyond political violence.

EVIDENCE OF MEMBERSHIP OF A PROSCRIBED ORGANIZATION

The admissibility of confessions and right to silence were not the only relaxed standards. In 1998 the Provisional IRA detonated two bombs in the town of Omagh, killing 28 people.[132] The state responded with the Criminal Justice (Terrorism and Conspiracy) Act 1998, which admitted the opinion of a police officer as evidence of membership in a proscribed organization.[133] Inference could be drawn from the statement that the accused was a member of the specified entity. The statute included three "safeguards": the individual giving evidence had to be at or above the rank of superintendent; the opinion had to be administered orally (which would in theory suggest cross-examination could occur), and the court could not solely rely on the police officer's statement for conviction.

In practice, however, the safeguards proved somewhat dubious. The rank of the individual testifying meant that the witness tended to be removed from direct contact with the defendant. Although the witness technically could be cross-examined, she could also claim public interest immunity to protect the source of the information. And while the oral testimony alone might prove insufficient for conviction, if combined with the inferences from silence, discussed above, such (relatively weak) evidence would be sufficient to find membership.[134]

Lord Diplock had considered similar measures and rejected them[135]—but this had little effect on Labour's later decision to incorporate the alteration. In doing so, Blair's government looked to the Republic of Ireland, which has placed a similar mechanism on the books. A series of judicial decisions in the Republic, however, had eviscerated the measures: while seen initially as a way to convict individuals who refused to recognize the courts, the judiciary later found that in the absence of evidence corroborating the police officer's statement, it would be insufficient as the sole reason for conviction.[136]

The incorporation of this provision into British law, moreover, gave rise to the significant possibility of incompatibility with the European Convention of Human Rights (discussed below). It also raised concerning issues about the insertion of the executive into the judicial realm. In other words, the strength given to the opinion of the security forces shifted the nature of the role of the police. Instead of bringing suspects to the law, they became the entity that determined guilt or innocence—without any public accounting to justify the conclusion. While the expansion in executive authority is a recurrent theme in counterterrorist law, its incursion into the judicial realm deserves greater attention.

Inclusion of Non-terrorist Related Offences

An additional concern in the operation of the Diplock Courts centers on the breadth of scheduled offences. Murder, manslaughter, riot, most nonfatal offences against the person, robbery, aggravated burglary, arson, firearms and explosives offences, membership of proscribed organizations, and other crimes, automatically come under the Diplock system.[137] As discussed above, in order to ensure that ordinary criminal cases are not heard in a Diplock court, the Attorney General bears the burden of certifying out each particular case. This has caused considerable controversy over time, with many commentators arguing that the cases must be certified in instead of out—but the basic structure remains. As a result, a number of non-terrorist cases end up in the terrorist courts.

In 1997, for instance, Mark Bellringer was convicted in a Diplock court for the manslaughter of a hairdresser. Bellringer had been present when another man, Christopher McMillen, had beaten Norman Harley to death with an iron bar.[138] Although non-terrorist related, the case went before a Diplock judge. In 2001 Thomas Dunbar robbed a post office near Claudy. After a 2-day hearing before Diplock Judge David McFarland, Dunbar was found guilty.[139] And in 2004 four men who, wearing wigs and false moustaches, had asked a cleaner at Gransha Hospital in Londonderry when the Securicor van would arrive, found themselves in front of Diplock Judge Gibson. They were judged guilty of attempted robbery, possession of a handgun and ammunition with the intent to endanger life, and four counts of falsely imprisoning four staff members at the hospital.[140] In 2005 a football fanatic, Stephen Irwin, found himself before the Diplock courts after slashing Mark Lee John Finlay's leg with a knife during the Irish Cup final at Windsor Park.[141] These, and other examples of seemingly ordinary criminal activity being found in the Diplock system proliferate.

While the percentage of cases certified out did increase in step with the Peace Process (see discussion, below), for much of the courts' history, cases unrelated or even only tangentially related to terrorism found their way onto the docket—somewhat nullifying the justification offered for the suspension of trial by jury. According to both the National Council for Civil Liberties and the Haldane Society, in the latter half of the 1980s and early 1990s, approximately 40 percent of the cases tried in the Diplock courts were not connected to paramilitary activity.[142]

The mid-1980s: Calls for an End to the Diplock Courts

With growing concern about the fairness of the Diplock tribunals, in the mid-1980s calls for the end to the regime increased. The number of defendants was growing annually—from 432 in 1983, by 1985 the number of individuals brought before the courts had reached 750.[143] Labour delegates at their annual conference agreed to a motion to eliminate the single-judge tribunals. Hugh Atkinson, from Croydon Northwest, dramatically (and rather inaccurately) claimed that they were no better than the Star Chamber: "We demand a return to trial by jury." He continued, "There are provisions in the judges' rules which will take account of any intimidation of jurors. Of course there will be problems, but those problems are nothing compared to the problems we will put ourselves in if we continue to support trial without jury. We should have no double standards on this. What is good enough for Britain is good enough for Ireland."[144] The Labour party narrowly approved the motion 3 million to 2,624,000.[145]

Labour raised the issue in Parliament as well. Peter Archer, during the debate on the Baker Report, for instance, criticized the Diplock courts and suggested it was time to return to jury trial.[146] The shadow Northern Ireland secretary, Archer, supported the Irish government's call for a three-judge tribunal to replace them.[147] Kevin McNamara, Labour spokesman on Northern Ireland, also demanded that the Government move to a three judge court.[148] McNamara claimed that emergency legislation was making the "search for peace" in Northern Ireland more difficult: it was increasing divisions and unjustifiably curtailing civil liberties in the Province. The only way to achieve an end to violence was to win the confidence of the people in the rule of law.[149]

The Standing Advisory Committee for Human Rights similarly supported a move to three judges for terrorist-related offences, with a reduction in the number of cases to be heard in special terrorist courts.[150] But it was the Irish Government that put the most pressure on the Tories to relinquish the Diplock reforms.

Peter Barry, the Irish Foreign Affairs Minister, and Alan Dukes, the Minister for Justice, raised the issue with Tom King, Britain's Northern Ireland Secretary, and Nicholas Scott, Minister of State, during talks at Stormont.[151] Dublin proposed an exchange: British reform of the tribunals in return for enhanced cooperation from Ireland on extradition.[152] The Republic cited the Anglo-Irish Agreement's commitment to improving the criminal justice system in the North to justify their insistence on the move away from a single-judge tribunal.[153] This adjustment also would have brought Northern Ireland into line with the South, where a three-judge tribunal sat in special criminal courts for terrorist cases. Decisions by these courts had to be unanimous.[154]

As Dublin began a frontal assault, the newspapers appeared rather optimistic. Headlines began "After Diplock" and articles discussed what new system would replace the old tribunals.[155] These celebrations proved premature, though, as the Conservative party held firm. Tom King, the Secretary of State for Northern Ireland, announced that the U.K. would not accede to demands for three judge courts—even if that meant that the Dáil would not ratify the extradition bill. In Ireland, opposition to ratification grew. Garret FitzGerald, former Irish prime minister, reiterated that the 1985 Anglo-Irish Agreement specifically committed Britain to judicial reforms. And he attributed the "Catholic lack of confidence in the administration of justice in the Province" in part to the Supergrass system.[156]

Margaret Thatcher angrily responded that the Diplock courts were not a bargaining chip.[157] Changes in the administration of justice in Northern Ireland were not up for debate. The Iron Lady went well beyond Tom King's assertion that U.K. was not "presently persuaded" by Dublin's call for three judges.[158] King came back within a week, one-upping Thatcher, threatening that Ireland's failure to implement extradition would have "serious implications" for British-Irish relations.[159]

Ireland finally capitulated, agreeing to the promise of future reforms from the United Kingdom. Although Fitzgerald tried to finesse it, Peter Barry, the former Irish Foreign Affairs Minister, put the point bluntly, saying that Ireland had failed to get any specific commitment that the U.K. would reform the Diplock courts.[160] Speaking from Wolfe Tone's grave, Charles Haughey hinted that the extradition treaty would not be ratified as long as the Diplock courts remained.[161] The *Guardian* crowed, "No single issue has caused so much heat and fury between London and Dublin in the two years of the Anglo-Irish Agreement than the Republic's demand for three judges rather than one to preside over the no-jury Diplock courts."[162]

Although Britain won the battle, the war continued. Irish politicians continued to press for a three judge tribunal to replace the courts. The British Government, for its part, brought in new measures meant to protect the rights of the accused: it introduced reasonable grounds of suspicion as a test for arrest, placed the onus for bail applications on the prosecution, clarified the judges' right to reject confession evidence, and increased the rights of suspects held in police custody. The *Guardian* reported, "It is understood that Mr. King, along with Mr. Douglas Hurd, the Home Secretary, and Sir Geoffrey Howe, the Foreign Secretary, favoured the introduction of three-judge courts on political grounds, but were vetoed by Lord Hailsham, the Lord Chancellor, who saw no reason why the judicial system in Northern Ireland should be changed because of political considerations."[163]

On January 16, 1986, Westminster approved amendments to the EPA, giving the Attorney General the discretion to schedule out cases related to kidnapping, false imprisonment, intimidation, damage to railways, and certain firearms offences, where they had no relation to terrorism.[164] At the behest of the Baker committee, the government also began publishing statistics on the operation of the courts.[165]

Informal Reforms and Persistent Critiques

Even as such formal mechanisms altered the Diplock procedures in place, informal adjustments proved important in mitigating some deficiencies.

It will be recalled, for instance, that one problem with the tribunal was that it combined in one person the roles of fact finder and arbiter of the law. Where prejudicial evidence might be presented, the judge was placed in the curious position of having to instruct herself to disregard certain material. Although Parliament did not pass a specific legislative provision to address this, the judiciary informally began the practice of having a different judge deal with the admissibility of evidence to prevent the trial judge from serving in this capacity. Depositions came to be "scrutinized by one judge in advance of the trial by another with a view to excluding any prejudicial material."[166] A similar mechanism came to be applied to issues of admissibility that would otherwise be attended by the judge alone, and to decisions on whether to reveal sensitive material to the defense—as well as to requests for disclosure.[167]

Another weakness was the tendency of Diplock courts to catch non-terrorist cases in their remit. While providing the possibility of the Attorney General scheduling out cases went some way towards addressing this concern, the fact remained that many ordinary criminal cases were still considered in their first instance within the counterterrorist framework. The number of cases de-scheduled, however, steadily grew: from 51 per cent of some 908 offences, in 1996 the number reached 85 per cent of some 1,522 offences.[168] This led one parliamentarian to suggest that the Attorney General had adopted a de facto policy of scheduling in—further signaling a return to normalcy.[169] Indeed, in the mid-1990s the number of defendants in the Diplock courts suddenly plummeted.[170] Even cases that appeared to be paramilitary in nature ended up outside the Diplock system.

In February 1996, for instance, right after the Provisional IRA's attack on Canary Wharf, armed police responded to an alarm at Holmes Cash and Carry in Belfast. There they found a lorry with Dublin plates on it and around £1 million worth of cigarettes in the back. The police arrested eight men at the scene, all of whom were described in Westminster as "IRA members or associates."[171] The Attorney General, Sir Nicholas Lyell, de-scheduled the case, saying that it was not "related to the emergency."[172] The case subsequently went through seven juries: one collapsed under allegations of tampering, another folded when one juror became ill, and a third when one of the jurors turned out to know the family of one of the defendants. Two juries could not reach a verdict; another was stepped down for legal reasons. By the time the case reached the fifth judge, Mr. Justice Kerr instructed the jury to return a verdict of not guilty.[173]

The number of applications made for certifying out continued to increase into the early 21st century, with the majority of requests granted. In 2002, for instance, there were 1,365 offences for which applications to certify out were made.[174] The Attorney General refused only 149, granting 1,216. In 2003 the number of applications increased to 1,567. The Attorney General refused 236, granting 1,331.[175] Of nearly 500 people arrested in Northern Ireland under counterterrorist law between January and September 2004, more than two thirds had their cases scheduled out and tried by a jury.[176] By November of 2005, only some 5 percent of serious cases were being tried by Diplock judges—compared to more than 40 percent in 1985.[177]

Yet more informal reforms occurred. The Diplock courts, for instance, required that bail applications be submitted to a High Court judge, Court of Appeal, or trial judge.[178] While the purpose of these rules was to protect magistrates and others from increased security risks, the practical effect was to delay defendants' ability to apply for bail. (High Court judges do not sit over the weekend). The judiciary again found a way around the issue: Sir Robert Carswell, Lord Chief Justice, created Saturday sittings for the High Court.

Despite both formal and informal efforts to fix the structure, however, criticism persisted. Lord Carlile, for instance, repeatedly drew attention to the length of time that elapsed prior to detainees being tried.[179] Mark Durkan, the SDLP MP for Foyle, suggested that the Diplock courts provided "an excuse to question the legitimacy of the justice system, and to withhold co-operation with the police and due recognition of the administration of justice."[180] In his first media interview after more than 20 years as a Diplock judge, Lord Carswell noted the toll the system took on the judiciary: "It's very testing," he said. "It's very tiring. And, at the end of the case, there's not the catharsis of the jury verdict. Everybody just goes home. And then the really hard work starts." At that point, "Unless it's a very obvious case, the judge has to go through all the evidence, go through all the arguments, do any necessary reading or research and then write a judgment—with nobody else to lean on." He added, "Jurors have each other, [judges in] the Court of Appeal have a couple of other members to discuss the case with, but the non-jury trial judge is on his own."[181]

A number of prominent cases of miscarriage of justice further underscored the critics' concern. The Birmingham Six, Guildford Four, Maguire Seven, and others, became a blight on Britain's record.[182] At times this figured in politics beyond British borders—in 1988 Governor Michael Dukakis, for instance, an American Democratic presidential candidate, faulted the Diplock courts for being unfair and "inconsistent with the basic principles of justice."[183] He vowed, if he won office, to encourage federal judges to deny extradition requests if there was a risk that they would come before one of the single judge tribunals.[184] Conservative MP's condemned his remarks as "outrageous" and "ignorant"[185]—not unlike the current Bush Administration's answer to critique from Labour MPs about U.S. treatment of suspects in Guantánamo Bay.

However outrageous Dukakis' remarks might have been at the time, they were not isolated[186]—and at times reverberated within Britain itself. In 1983, for instance, Jimmy Smyth and 37 other republicans broke out of the Maze. U.S. agents caught him in California. Awaiting extradition, Smyth argued that as a republican he risked persecution and possible death in Northern Ireland. The Labour MP for Brent East, Ken Livingstone, testified on Smyth's behalf, referencing the unofficial "shoot-to-kill" policy in the north, and the unfairness of the judicial system in place.[187]

The incorporation in 1998 of the European Convention of Human Rights further highlighted concerns about whether and to what extent the Diplock system deviated from international norms. In his 1999 report on the operation of counterterrorist law, John Rowe noted that the presumption of innocence guaranteed by Article 6(2) of the ECHR may be incompatible with portions of both the EPA and PTA.[188] In the Divisional Court, Lord Bimgham granted a declaration of incompatibility on the basis that portions of the latter, in particular, violated the ECHR. The House of Lords allowed the DPP to appeal the case—finding not that the Divisional court was wrong, but that it lacked the jurisdiction to review a decision to proceed with a prosecution, unless there was some evidence of bad faith or dishonesty, or some other extraordinary condition.[189] Similarly, the European Court determined that hearsay that cannot be refuted was unfair.[190] If informer evidence were to be used during trial, it would have to be open to cross-examination. Here, the alterations in rules of evidence—and, in particular, the admission of inferences from a police officer's statement in support of the charge of membership in a proscribed organization—seems to fall afoul of the European standard. At the time the 1998 order passed, Lord Lloyd underscored the likely violation of the ECHR.[191] Additional concerns presented themselves: the inference from silence during interviews in the absence of a solicitor, for instance, were found by the European Court to violate a detainee's right under Article 6 of the ECHR, regarding fair trial.[192]

The Terrorism Act 2000 et seq.

The 1998 Good Friday Agreement pledged, wherever possible, a return to normalisation and an end to emergency provisions.[193] While this raised the issue of the future of the Diplock system, though, as Lord Carlile pointed out in 2000, the ordinary criminal justice system itself was in flux.[194] In the White Paper *Justice for All*, presented to Parliament in July 2002, the Labour Government argued for the suspension of jury trial for non-terrorist crime, where potential juror intimidation or complex and lengthy fraud cases presented themselves.[195] This initiative evolved into the Criminal Justice Act 2003, which allows for the judge to suspend juries where evidence of a "real and present danger" exists that jury tampering may take place.[196] Diplock reforms, intended for terrorist challenge, had crossed over to ordinary criminal law.

It was not at all clear, moreover, that the Diplock courts themselves would no longer be needed. Despite progress made in the peace process and continued ceasefires from the Provisional Irish Republican Army and the Ulster Volunteer Force, terrorist activity continued in Northern Ireland—preserving Lord Diplock's concerns.[197]

According to the British Government, in 2003, for instance, more than 70 bombing incidents and more than 300 terrorist-type attacks took place in the Province.[198] Beyond sheer acts of violence, Lord Carlile reported in 2004,

> [P]aramilitary organizations still exercise very significant social and economic influence over communities. On both sides of the sectarian divide there is a clear danger of intimidation within living and working neighbourhoods. Armed robberies remain at a high level, and the raising of money for paramilitaries by various intimidatory methods remains part of the picture.[199]

Sinn Féin's entry into constitutional politics failed to prevent Martin McGuinness, a member of the party's Ard Comhairle (National Executive) and MP for Mid Ulster, from issuing a thinly-veiled threat: the return of exiles would not be acceptable.[200]

And intimidation still clearly extended to the judicial system: Labour reported, for instance, that between 2002 and 2003, the government recorded 58 instances of witness intimidation—twice the number of the previous year. Between 2003 and 2004, attacks on prison officers and their families and members of the police forces continued. A survey found that 68 per cent of the young offenders being held at Hydebank had been "subject to paramilitary threats, banned from a particular area, beaten or ... shot."[201] One third considered themselves still at risk. The Minister of State, Northern Ireland Office, Jane Kennedy, commented, "With such figures in mind, I am afraid there is every reason to expect that jurors in scheduled cases would face similar intimidation. Indeed, I am reminded of Lord Diplock's own observation that a frightened juror is a bad juror, which means that a person need not actually be at risk to undermine the system, but need only perceive themselves to be so. Therefore, I do not believe that the time is right to reintroduce trial by jury in scheduled cases."[202]

Efforts to normalize, then, had to be balanced against continued security concerns. With this in mind, Labour commissioned Lord Lloyd of Berwick to look into the contours that permanent counter-terrorist law might take, in the event that political violence ceased in Northern Ireland. Lloyd recommended the repeal of all temporary powers and their replacement with permanent measures that applied to all of the United Kingdom. With the current EPA set to expire in August 2000, in December 1999 Labour laid the 1999 Terrorism Act bill before parliament. In light of continued violence in Northern Ireland, Labour said it was not ready to dispense with temporary provisions altogether. Most relevant to our current discussion, section 75(1) continued the use of a single judge tribunal for the prosecution of scheduled offences.[203] Subject to annual renewal by orders made under affirmative procedure, the Diplock provisions and other temporary powers in part VII (which applied only to Northern Ireland) could only be renewed for five years before returning to Parliament for consideration.

In April 2003 the British and Irish Governments issued a Joint Declaration laying out the steps that would be taken towards normalization and demilitarization in Northern Ireland.[204] Annex 1 specified the "repeal of counter terrorist legislation particular to Northern Ireland."[205] This translated into Part VII of the Terrorism Act 2000. The trigger for normalization hinged on an end to terrorist campaigns and the institution of paramilitary decommissioning—and then, in July 2005, the Provisional IRA formally ordered an end to the armed struggle.[206]

The Secretary of State for Northern Ireland, Peter Hain, responded within days with a two-year plan for stepping down the British military presence in the province—and an announcement that jury trials would be reintroduced as part of the normalization of affairs in Northern Ireland.[207] Entirely predictably, the Irish Government, SDLP, and Sinn Fein—all of whom had been scathing in their condemnation of the tribunals—greeted the announcement with open arms.[208] In contrast, the Unionists were outraged.[209] The DUP slammed the announcement as "a surrender to the IRA."[210] The Rev. Ian Paisley called Hain's plan, "a scandalous betrayal of those who have given their lives to protect the community."[211] Reg Empey, Ulster Unionist leader, denounced it as "deplorable."[212] Even the Alliance Party was "alarmed."[213]

Labour backpedaled. A week after the initial announcement, the Government unveiled plans for special pre-trial, single-judge courts in Northern Ireland which would be able to consider secret evidence and whether the case before it should go to a jury.[214] Accusations of duplicity screamed across local papers.[215] But the Government appeared to consider the concerns raised by unionists and others to be well-founded: the problem of intimidation remained.[216] General John de Chastelain, the chair of the independent Commission on Decommissioning verified in September that PIRA had disarmed,[217] but a bitter and violent feud between the PUP and the UVF, and republican paramilitary activity continued.

Thus, while the province was moving towards normalization, significant security concerns remained. It was into this context, that the temporary counterterrorist provisions, which included the Diplock courts, came up for review. (They were due to expire in February 2006, unless re-enacted by primary legislation.) Labour scheduled the second reading of the Terrorism (Northern Ireland) Bill for October 2005. The Government tried to walk the line between encouraging political progress and ensuring security in the Province. The solution was to set a shorter expiry period for the operation of the Diplock courts and the admissibility of oral evidence from police officers regarding membership in proscribed organizations. From annual renewal with a five year limit, the Government reduced the duration to 18 months, with possible further extension for just one more year. Additionally, where before the Attorney General had the authority to schedule cases out for certain offences, the new legislation gave him the ability to remove *any* case from the Diplock system.[218]

The House of Commons' research paper that accompanied the bill noted, "The use of non-jury 'Diplock courts' in Northern Ireland has always been controversial and the general issue of scheduling particular offences for special treatment has been much criticized over the years."[219] Indeed, the traditional opponents of the system decried the continued use of juryless courts: the Committee on the Administration of Justice, the Northern Ireland Human Rights Commission, and others argued for a complete repeal of Part VII of the Terrorism Act. Brice Dickson, the Human Rights Commissioner, was "unconvinced that the danger of intimidation of those called for jury service justifies the continuing scheduling of offences."[220] He expressed concern about the lack of evidence presented by the state of specific instances of intimidation.

Nationalist politicians too found the Government's position unconvincing. The SDLP opposed the extension of powers that had undermined the minority community's faith in the rule of law.[221] Dr. Alasdair McDonnell, SDLP MP for Belfast, observed that their implementation had "alienated a whole community." Extensive use of stop-and-search authorities, coerced confessions, and extended detention had led to miscarriages of justice.[222] The Diplock courts, moreover, had "degraded" justice.[223]

Again and again the legitimacy of their judgments was called into question by the use of unreliable informer evidence and mass trials, which led to unjust outcomes. All of that, and the failure of the judiciary to tell it exactly as it was in cases such as the Widgery tribunal and the appeals of the Guildford Four and the Birmingham Six, served only to discredit the law in the eyes of the nationalist community. The result was . . . that such abuse of justice and maladministration plays right into the hands of those who care nothing for the law and care only about bringing chaos on to the street.[224]

The rule of law was at stake: "If we get the law wrong, we make an ass of the law and play into the hands of the very people we want to hold to account. Time and again, the people we were trying to hold to account scored one propaganda coup after another as even the most obviously guilty were able to garner sympathy when prosecuted in no-jury courts. Quite often, because of the malfunction of the law, they were able to walk away."[225] He concluded,

That is the bitter legacy of emergency law in Northern Ireland. The emergency law undermined the real, honest rule of law—the very law it was meant to protect—and, even more fundamentally, undermined the safety of the public, which we are meant to guarantee. That is the legacy. It is one that the Government should heed before they rush in on another front tomorrow, when they attempt to introduce three months' detention before trial and a whole raft of draconian measures that will serve only to alienate rather than to create security.[226]

Many commentators, however, took a considerably different tack.

Lord Rooker, the Minister of State for the Northern Ireland Office, claimed, "There is no question that [Diplock Courts] have served the people of Northern Ireland well."[227] Even for those who recognized the limitations of the Diplock system, continued violence proved a cause for concern. Laurence Robertson, a Conservative English MP, noted that in the six months prior to the bill's introduction, there had been 69 shootings, 70 paramilitary assaults, and six murders in the Province.[228] Gregory Campbell, DUP and MP for East Londonderry wanted to extend the courts until 2012 to send "a clear message to those who engage in terror that the legislative process will counter any of their activities."[229] He cited personal knowledge of cases where the prosecution had "collapsed because witnesses were intimidated by terrorist suspects and organizations."—and noted the continued potential "for members of juries to be open to such intimidation."[230] Diplock courts provided a sort of "insurance policy."[231] At best, "The Government were being over-optimistic and over-ambitious."[232] At worst, by sending the "wrong signals", Labour was actually responsible for continuing violence in Northern Ireland. Moreover, the reduced timeframe gave terrorists hope that in the future they would not just be able to intimidate witnesses, but jurors as well.[233] And it signaled that British subjects in Northern Ireland were second-class citizens within the U.K.: not because of an abridgement of trial by jury, but because the state would not first eliminate intimidation before restoring jury trial.[234] In addition, any effort to back off the Diplock system meant that the Government was not, as it claimed, tough on terror.[235] The DUP's Sammy Wilson crowed, "The Bill illustrates the schizophrenic approach of the Government to terrorism."[236]

It was not, however, just political violence that was a problem. Lord Carlile saw similar concerns in relation to organized crime and the increasingly murky relationship between paramilitary organizations and sophisticated criminal enterprises:

> There were also numerous serious criminal offences of a non-terrorist nature in which there appears to have been or may well have been a strong terrorist link. Whilst this is hard to prove, it seems reasonably clear that syndicated crime with a paramilitary connection (albeit sometimes remote) *is a clear and potentially permanent part of the criminal intelligence picture of Northern Ireland* . . . [237]

What made Lord Carlile's words remarkable was the underlying suggestion that extraordinary powers may indefinitely be required in Northern Ireland to deal with even ordinary, albeit "syndicated" crime. The arguments, then, first put forward by Lord Diplock specifically in relation to terrorist violence, were being applied to the ordinary criminal law system to deal with loosely- or non-political activity.[238]

In the end, although recognized as "controversial", Parliament decided that Diplock courts, "may still be necessary to deal with cases of witness and jury intimidation."[239] The Government resisted calls for a three-judge tribunal, citing potential costs to the taxpayer, delays in the criminal justice system, and lack of increased confidence in the judicial system.[240]

Concluding Remarks

Even as calls for the repeal of the Diplock courts persisted,[241] their use both in relation to Northern Ireland and other possible threats expanded. The incorporation of a single-judge tribunal option for cases of complex and lengthy fraud trials, or where juror intimidation appeared likely, brought the antiterrorist provisions into mainstream criminal law. Simultaneously, the July 7, 2004 bombings demonstrated that other terrorist threats exist within the United Kingdom.

On the one hand, Islamist organizations represented a fundamentally different type of challenge: the bombers did not operate within a population anywhere near the percentage or numbers that the republican or loyalist organizations do in Northern Ireland; nor did they have such a long history of violence within the U.K. Nevertheless, it is conceivable that such groups—or, indeed, even organized crime, which evinced less political ambition—might try to intimidate potential jurors in cases brought to trial.

Even before the July 7, 2005 bombing, the first Islamist case reached the Diplock courts, raising fresh questions about their appropriateness and sufficiency for a different type of threat. In December 2005 an al Qaeda suspect, Abbas Boutrab, was tried in Northern Ireland.[242] Twenty-seven years of age, Boutrab had come to the U.K. seeking asylum. He was found guilty of possessing and collecting information connected to terrorism. The security services seized 25 computer disks in his flat that contained information on how to make bombs, smuggle explosives on board an aircraft, and construct a silencer for an M16 or AK assault rifle.[243] Boutrab had obtained the data from the Internet on a computer in Belfast Central Library.[244] The FBI, with whom the Police Service Northern Ireland shared the information, demonstrated how it could have brought down an airplane.[245] In addition to computer disks, the security services found circuit boards, a stethoscope, grinding tools, various clamps, grips and spreaders, and a stolen Nokia pay-as-you-go telephone at Boutrab's residence.[246] Justice Ronald Weatherup expressed concern that Boutrab was plotting something with "even more chilling consequences than the decades of paramilitary violence in Northern Ireland."[247] Although Weatherup sentenced Boutrab to six years' imprisonment, Boutrab had already spent two years on remand, making his release in a year's time possible.[248]

Sentencing issues aside, the U.K. is not the only state facing potential al Qaeda affiliated terrorist attacks. In the United States, prior to 9/11 the ordinary court system provided the forum for prosecuting jihadists. But post-9/11 the Bush Administration announced their replacement with military tribunals for the prosecution of individuals captured in Afghanistan, Iraq, and elsewhere. For U.S. persons, or those apprehended within domestic bounds, domestic courts remained the primary avenue for charging individuals—albeit with slightly different rules.

As the foregoing discussion demonstrates, some changes, such as relaxed evidentiary standards, suspension of juries, and inferences from silence, are shared by other states. While some of the alterations benefited the U.K., for instance, by reinforcing rule of law, criminalizing the conflict, eliminating the potential of juror intimidation, and allowing for appeals of fact or law, many characteristics of the system undermined its effectiveness. The suspension of juries went against cultural expectations and further distanced the minority community from the state. Relaxed standards of evidence and extended detention periods shifted the emphasis to confessions. Failure to ensure witness protection resulted in more coercive interrogation techniques. Simultaneously, the state allowed adverse inferences to be drawn from silence. It also weakened the standards of proof for membership of proscribed organizations, shifting security forces into a judicial role.

Together, these led to miscarriages of justice and a crisis of legitimacy in the system as a whole. The inclusion of non-terrorist related crimes meant that those accused of even ordinary crime found themselves without important protections—going to the heart of the fundamental principle of innocent until proven guilty. Some of these procedures, moreover, brought the U.K. into conflict with its international obligations—agreements to which the country acquiesced, in part, assumedly, to bind others to similar standards.

Whilst there is not sufficient space here to go into similar analyses of the United States' counterterrorist judicial system, or to Turkey's DGMs, Israel's courts martial, or the Republic's Special Criminal Courts, these lessons may prove equally relevant to their experiences. What makes them particularly important in the contemporary environment is the absolute centrality of the judiciary and the rules under which it operates to the protection of civil rights in the liberal, democratic state.

Endnotes

1. Laura K. Donohue, *Terrorism and Trial by Jury: The Vices and Virtues of British and American Criminal Law*, 59 STAN. L. REV. 1321 (2007). Reprinted with permission from *Stanford Law Review*.
2. Special thanks to Paul Lomio and Christine Su for help acquiring the materials used in this paper.
3. John, Lackland (AD 1199–1216), available at: http://www.britannia.com/history/monarchs/mon28.html
4. 1215 Magna Carta, cl. 39, available at: http://www.cs.indiana.edu/statecraft/magna-carta.html
5. Ibid., cl. 40 (stating, "To no one will we sell, to no one will we refuse or delay, right or justice").
6. Ibid., cl. 20.
7. Lord Falconer of Thoroton, QC, HL Debs, 26 Mar 2003, cols 851–54.
8. Ibid.
9. *Sunday Times*, 1972: 269, cited in Charles Carlton, "Judging without Consensus: The Diplock Courts in Northern Ireland," *Law & Policy Quarterly*, 3, 2 (1981) 225–42.
10. Laura K. Donohue, *118 Counter-terrorist Law and Emergency Powers in the United Kingdom 1922–2000* (2000).
11. Michael McKeown, *Two Seven Six Three: an Analysis of Fatalities Attributable to Civil Disturbances in Northern Ireland in the Twenty Years between July 13, 1969 and July 12, 1989* (1989).
12. Author interviews with former detainees, in Londonderry, Northern Ireland, 1993.
13. Ireland v. U.K. (Application No. 5310/71) (1976), the Compton Report, the Gardiner Report, and other documents discuss these techniques.
14. Monsignor Denis Faul, Obituary, *Timesonline* (June 22, 2006), available at: http://www.timesonline.co.uk/article/0,60–2236881,00.html
15. John McGuffin, *The Guineapigs* (1974, 1981), chapter 9. Note: this book, written by an East Belfast Protestant-turned-anarchist/republican, who was interned in the early 1970s, was initially published by Penguin. The publisher sold out of the first run of 20,000 copies. A week into the first edition, Reginald Maudling, Home Secretary, banned the book, which was later reprinted in the United States by Minuteman Press. See http://cain.ulst.ac.uk/events/intern/docs/jmcg74.htm; and http://www.irishresistancebooks.com/guineapigs/guineapigs.htm
16. *Report of the Inquiry into Allegations Against the Security Forces of Physical Brutality in Northern Ireland Arising Out of Events on the 9 August 1971*, Session 1971/72 Cmnd. 4823, para. 23.
17. Ibid.
18. Ibid.
19. Michael Zander, "Diplock, the Non-jury Judge," *Guardian* (London), (Oct. 15, 1985).
20. "Obituary of Lord Diplock," *The Times* (London), (Oct. 16, 1985).
21. Ibid.

22. Tom Hadden & Paddy Hillyard, *Justice in Northern Ireland; A Study in Social Confidence* (1973).
23. Charles Carlton, *Judging without Consensus: The Diplock Courts in Northern Ireland*, 3 Law & Policy Quarterly, 225–42. (1981).
24. Joe Joyce & Paul Johnson, Irish Minister Deplores Diplock Changes, *Guardian* (London), Jan. 6, 1986.
25. Hadden & Hillyard, *supra* note 17. See also Charles Carlton, *Judging without Consensus: The Diplock Courts in Northern Ireland*, 3 Law & Policy Quarterly, 225–42. (1981).
26. *Irish Times*, Dec. 2, 1969.
27. *Report of the Commission to Consider Legal Procedures to Deal with Terrorist Activities in Northern Ireland*. Dec. 1972, Cmnd. 5185. [hereinafter Diplock Report]
28. Cities Located Close to London, timeanddate.com, available at: http://www.timeanddate.com/worldclock/distances.html?n=136.
29. Donohue, *supra* note 8, at 126.
30. See Reg. v. Flynn and Leonard (Belfast City Commission May 24, 1972) and the Queen v. Gargan (Belfast city Commission, May 10, 1972), digested at 23 Northern Ireland Legal Quarterly 343 (1972) and quoted in Joseph W. Bishop, Jr., *Law in the control of Terrorism and Insurrection: the British Laboratory Experience, Law & Contemporary Problems*, 42 (1978), 140–201, at 172.
31. Diplock Report, *supra* note 22. See also John D. Jackson & Sean Doran, *Conventional Trials in Unconventional Times: The Diplock Court Experience*, 4 Crim. L. F. 503.
32. HC Debs, April 17, 1973, Vol. 855, col. 305.
33. Ibid.
34. Charles Carlton (1981), "Judging without Consensus: The Diplock Courts in Northern Ireland," Law and Policy Quarterly, 3, pp. 225–42.
35. Ibid.
36. HC Debs, 855, 277; Apr. 17, 1973.
37. Ibid.
38. Boyle, 1975: 144–50.
39. Charles Carlton (1981), *Judging without Consensus: The Diplock Courts in Northern Ireland*, Law & Policy Quarterly, 3, pp. 225–42.
40. Ibid., at 234.
41. In 1972 the United Kingdom created the position of Director of Public Prosecution (DPP), which has the authority to bring or drop charges against an accused. The DPP takes into account the probability of conviction as well as whether the trial is in the public's best interest. Where the trial is to proceed, the defendant is served with committal papers while in custody. Where it is not a terrorist charge, the initial hearing is before a magistrate, who will determine whether probable cause supports the charge. Lesser crimes are heard and summarily disposed by the magistrate—who can sentence defendants for up to 12 months in jail and fine them up to £2,000—or order the defendant to make restitution. For non-Diplock trials, the defendant has up to 12 peremptory jury challenges; the prosecution does not have any. Although

the goal is to return a unanimous jury verdict, if no agreement has been reached after two hours, the jury is authorized to return verdicts of 10–12 or 11–1. That is for non terrorism related cases. For terrorist charges, the rules are different. In accordance with Diplock's recommendation, only a High Court or Crown Court—not a magistrate—is authorized to grant bail. The file goes not to the DPP, but to the Attorney General, who makes sure that at least one scheduled offense is being charged. The Attorney General has twenty four hours to decide whether to retain the case in the Diplock court. Carol Daugherty Rasnic, *Northern Ireland's Criminal Trials without Jury: the Diplock Experiment 5 Ann. Surv. In'l & Comp. L.* 239, at 244–45.

42. See, e.g., David Sharrock, *Justice "going through motions"*, Guardian (London), June 9, 1992, at 4.
43. See, e.g., Terrorism Financing (Northern Ireland); discussion of Financing of Terrorism in Northern Ireland—Fourth Report from the Northern Ireland Affairs Committee, Session 2001-2, HC 978-I and the Government's response thereto, Sixth Special Report, Session 2001-2, HC 1347; Westminster Hall, Jul. 10, 2003, cols 3111WH-348 WH. See also Laura K. Donohue, 'Anti-terrorist Finance in the United Kingdom and United States,' *Michigan Journal of International Law*, Vol. 27, No. 2, Winter 2002, 303–435.
44. John D. Jackson, *The Restoration of Jury Trial in Northern Ireland; Can we Learn from the Professional Alternative?* 2001 *St. Louis-Warsaw Trans'l* 15, at 19.
45. Jackson & Doran at 35, Table 2.2.
46. In Belfast, Confession if Good for the Crown, *New Jersey Law J.*, Apr. 12, 1993, at 17. Of only nine judges, six were drawn from strong Unionist backgrounds. David Sharrock, *Justice "going through motions"*, Guardian (London), June 9, 1992, at 4.
47. Ibid.
48. Ibid.
49. John D. Jackson, *The Restoration of Jury Trial in Northern Ireland; Can we Learn from the Professional Alternative?* 2001 *St. Louis-Warsaw Trans'l* 15.
50. Jackson & Doran at 276–79. See also Carol Daugherty Rasnic, *Northern Ireland's Criminal Trials without Jury: the Diplock Experiment 5 Ann. Surv. In'l & Comp. L.* 239.
51. John D. Jackson, *The Restoration of Jury Trial in Northern Ireland; Can we Learn from the Professional Alternative?* 2001 *St. Louis-Warsaw Trans'l* 15.
52. R. v. Caraher, The Court of Appeal in Northern Ireland, NICC3072 (Transcript), Sept. 29, 2000 (Nicholson LJ).
53. Ibid.
54. Citing *R. v. Thain*, Lord Justice Nicholson wrote, "Where the trial is conducted and the factual conclusions are reached by the same person, one need not expect every step in the reasoning to be spelled out expressly, nor is the reasoning to be carried out in sealed compartments with no inter-communication or overlapping even if the need to arrange

a judgment in a logical order may give that impression. It can safely be inferred that, when deliberating on a question of fact with many aspects, even more certainly than when tackling a series of connected legal points, a judge who is himself the tribunal of fact will (a) recognize the issues and (b) view in the entirety a case where one issue is interwoven with another." (Ibid., citing R v. Thain (1985) 11 NIJB 31 at p. 60.)
55. Ibid. (citing R. v. Gibson and Lewis (1986) NIJB 1 at p. 29).
56. Ibid. The court similarly relied on the trial court's recounting of the fact pattern and subsequent inference from silence to tie Caraher to the shooting of Constable Ronald Galwey at Forkhill, Co. Armagh. I return to this case, below.
57. Charles Carlton (1981), *Judging without Consensus: The Diplock Courts in Northern Ireland*, Law & Pol'y Quarterly, 3, pp. 225–42.
58. See Grier, and Foley, Thomas P, Public Security and Individual Freedom: The Dilemma of Northern Ireland, *Yale Journal of World Public Order*, Vol. 8:284, 1982.
59. Foley, Thomas P, Public Security and Individual Freedom: The Dilemma of Northern Ireland, *Yale Journal of World Public Order*, Vol. 8:284, 1982.
60. Lords Handard, 21 Nov. 2002, Address in Reply to Her Majesty's Most Gracious Speech, cols 520–44, at 520 (quoting from White Paper, Justice for All, prepared by Bar Council and Criminal Bar Association).
61. John D. Jackson, *The Restoration of Jury Trial in Northern Ireland; Can we Learn from the Professional Alternative?* 2001 St. Louis-Warsaw Trans'l 15, pp. 17–18.
62. Lords Hansard, 21 Nov. 2002, Address in Reply to Her Majesty's Most Gracious Speech, cols 520–44, at 520.
63. HC Debs, Dec. 4, 2002, cols 962–68, col. 964.
64. Ibid., at cols. 964–65.
65. Sarah Spencer & Fran Russell, *Agenda: Breaking the Diplock—A three-judge system*, Guardian (London), Aug. 17, 1987.
66. Professor Mirjan Damaska, Yale: two ideal types of adjudication: adversarial and inquisitorial: Mirjan R. Damaska, Evidentiary Barriers to Conviction and Two Models of Criminal Procedure: A Comparative Study, 121 U. Pa. L. Rev. 507, 513 (1973) There may be ways to increase the adversarial nature of Diplock courts—such as stricter enforcement of rules of evidence, limits on the trial judge's exposure to incriminating, inadmissible evidence, and encouragement of more passive judicial fact-finding. But these do not entirely bridge the gap created by suspending jury trial. Sean Doran, John D. Jackson, Michael L. Seigel, *Rethinking Adversariness in Nonjury Criminal Trials*, 23 Am. J. Crim. L. 1.
67. Damaska, *supra* note 64.
68. Art. 47(1) of the Criminal Justice (Northern Ireland) Order 1996 and 54–57 of the Criminal Procedure and Investigations Act 1996. John D. Jackson, *The Restoration of Jury Trial in Northern Ireland; Can we Learn from the Professional Alternative?* 2001 St. Louis-Warsaw Trans'l 15.

69. See Steven Greer & Antony White, Aboishing Diplock Courts 74–75 (1986), C. Gearty and John A. Kimball, Terrorism and the Rule of Law 56–57 (1995) and Lord Lloyd of Berwick, Inquiry into Legislation Against Terrorism, para. 16.18 (1996); and Jackson, supra note at 23.
70. Michael Finlan, *Northern appeals judge says trials by jury may be less fair than trial by impartial judge*, Irish Times, Oct. 30, 1995, at 6.
71. David Sheldon, *Making Harsh Judgments on the Jury System*, Scotsman, Nov. 16, 1995, at 17.
72. Ibid.
73. Unlike in the United States, in the United Kingdom and Ireland, *voir dire* refers not to impaneling a jury, but to determining the admissibility of confessions.
74. HC Debs, Oct. 31, 2005 (pt 14), cols. 653–56, Mark Durkan, MP Foyle, SDLP, col. 654.
75. R. v. McCormick and Others (1977) 105, 111 (McGonigal, J.)
76. Ibid.
77. Northern Ireland (Emergency Provisions) Act §11(3).
78. Northern Ireland (Emergency Provisions) Act, §11(2)(b).
79. Carol Daugherty Rasnic, *Northern Ireland's Criminal Trials without Jury: the Diplock Experiment* 5 Ann. Surv. In'l & Comp. L. 239.
80. Kevin Boyle, Tom Hadden, & Paddy Hillyard, *Ten Years On in Northern Ireland* (1980).
81. Prevention of Terrorism (Temporary Provisions) Act, § 14.
82. These provisions contradicted international norms. E.g., the U.N. Report of the 8the United Nations Congress on the prevention of Crime and the Treatment of Offenders, U.N. Doc. A/Conf. 144/28, at 127 (1990), stated, "All arrested, detained or imprisoned persons shall be provided with adequate opportunities, time and facilities to be visited by and to communicate and consult with a lawyer, without delay, interception or censorship and in full confidentiality."
83. Although the NI(EP)A also allowed a constable to arrest suspects on reasonable grounds, security forces, for the most part, did not use this authority, preferring the more lenient powers in the PTA. See Fionnuala Ni Aoilain, Legal Developments: the Fortification of an Emergency Regime, 59 Alb. L. Rev. 1353.
84. See, e.g., Miranda v. Arizona, 384 U.S. 436 (1966) (quoting from the interrogation manual).
85. Kieran Cooke, *Echoes of Guildford for the Armagh Four*, Financial Times (London), Nov. 16, 1989, at 10.
86. Ibid.
87. Gerard Hogan & Clive Walker, Political Violence and the Law in Ireland (1989), p. 101.
88. John Jackson & Sean Doran, Juries and Judges: A Vew from Across the Atlantic, Crim. Just, Winter 1997, at 15, 17 (1997). See also Howard J. Russell, *New Death Breathes Life into Old Fears: The Murder of Rosemary Nelson and the Importance of Reforming the Police in Northern Ireland*, 28 Ga. J. Int'l & Comp. L. 199.

89. See, e.g., R. v. Harper, 1990, N. Ir. 28, 30 (defendant made two written statements during interrogation, on the basis of which he was convicted; he appealed the case, saying that the confessions had been obtained through oppressive techniques. The court above quashed the appeal, saying that it was up to the trial judge to determine whether confessions ought to be admitted as evidence.) See also R. v. Dillon and Another, 1984 N. Ir. 292, 292 (finding that as long as the confession was voluntary, it could be admitted); and Denis Campbell, 18 jailed Irishmen 'may be innocent', *Irish Times*, July 17, 1992, at 4 (reporting on Thomas Green, life sentence in 1986 for murder at loyalist drinking club, who signed incriminating statement right before they took him to hospital with an anxiety attack).
90. See, e.g., David Sharrock, *Call to Halt Ulster Murder Trials*, *Guardian* (London), June 9, 1992 (reporting that the Haldane Society, a prominent group of socialist lawyers, was calling for the closure of RUC interrogation centres—as well as reform of the Diplock courts. Their report said, "The Diplock Courts are failing to secure reliable convictions based on properly tested evidence.") In July 1995 the U.N. Human Rights Committee urged that Castlereagh interrogation be closed; it remained open.
91. David Sharrock, *Justice "going through motions"*, *Guardian* (London), June 9, 1992, at 4.
92. Ibid.
93. Kevin Boyle, Tom Hadden, & Paddy Hillyard, *Ten Years On in Northern Ireland* (1980).
94. In Belfast, Confession if Good for the Crown, *New Jersey Law J.*, Apr. 12, 1993, at 17. See also United Kingdom/Northern Ireland Human Rights, U.S. Department of State, Jan. 31, 1994 (citing a human rights organization that had found a 50 percent higher conviction rate in Diplock courts in 1991).
95. In Belfast, *supra* note 92.
96. Ed Neafsey, *Northern Ireland Trial Notebook*, *New Jersey Law J.*, Nov. 8, 1993, at 16.
97. Ibid.
98. Ibid.
99. Jackson & Doran, *Judge without Jury* (1995) at 44. The term comes from R. v. Turner, 61 Cr. App R67 (1975) (in which one woman testified against various alleged co-conspirators in a series of robberies 1968–71).
100. *Parliament: Informer Evidence defended/Northern Ireland Secretary Hurd defends 'supergrass' evidence in Ulster trials*, *Guardian* (London), Dec. 21, 1984. The comments in the House of Commons occurred Dec. 20, 1984.
101. Ibid.
102. Three Men on the Bench, *Guardian* (London), Aug. 28, 1987.
103. Jim Dee, *One-time IRA Member who Penned Tell-all is Found Murdered*, *Boston Herald*, Jan. 28, 1999.

104. See, e.g., Select Committee on Northern Ireland Affairs, Fourth Report, June 26, 2002, at para. 130, noting that 46 percent of the victims in extortion cases request no police action to be taken for fear of reprisal; another 39 percent later withdrew their complaint and said they had not been contacted by extortionists—although the assessment suggested that in such cases 'it is strongly suspected that the victim has, in fact, acceded to the extortionists' demands.'
105. Terrorism Financing (Northern Ireland); discussion of Financing of Terrorism in Northern Ireland—Fourth Report from the Northern Ireland Affairs Committee, Session 2001–2, HC 978-I and the Government's response thereto, Sixth Special Report, Session 2001–2, HC 1347; Westminster Hall, Jul. 10, 2003, cols 311 WH–348 WH, at col. 311 WH.
106. Ibid., at col. 315 WH.
107. Ibid., at col. 327 WH.
108. Ibid., at col. 316 WH.
109. Ibid., at col. 317 WH.
110. Ibid., at col. 322 WH.
111. Ibid., at col. 322 WH (Barnes).
112. See, e.g., ibid., at col. 329 WH (Nigel Dodds, Belfast).
113. Response of the Northern Ireland Human Rights Commission to the Home Office Disscussion Paper on Counter-terrorism Measures: Reconciling Security and Liberty in an Open Society, NIHRC, Aug. 2004, p. 8.
114. Ibid.
115. Select Committee on Northern Ireland Affairs, Fourth Report, June 26, 2002, para. 131, quoting ACC White.
116. Select Committee on Northern Ireland Affairs, Fourth Report, June 26, 2002. The report suggested, "We find the picture of support for potential witnesses presented to us by the PSNI very disappointing. The level of personal sacrifice required of the individual, as it was described to us, is unreasonable; it makes the individual and potentially his or her family victims twice over. It is not surprising that so few are currently willing to make a stand. We believe that the Government, in conjunction with the Executive where appropriate, must look again at the type and level of resources it makes available to support potential witnesses before, during and after cases which go to trial." Select Committee on Northern Ireland Affairs, Fourth Report, June 26, 2002.
117. Jane Kennedy, Terrorism Financing (Northern Ireland); discussion of Financing of Terrorism in Northern Ireland—Fourth Report from the Northern Ireland Affairs Committee, Session 2001–2, HC 978-I and the Government's response thereto, Sixth Special Report, Session 2001–2, HC 1347; Westminster Hall, Jul. 10, 2003, cols 341 WH–342 WH).
118. Criminal Evidence (Northern Ireland) Order 1988, SI 1987, §4 (provisions regarding evidence at trial), §3(2) (inference that may be drawn).

119. Criminal Evidence (Northern Ireland) Order 1988, SI 1987, §5.
120. Criminal Evidence (Northern Ireland) Order 1988, SI 1987. See also *No longer a state of emergency? The Lawyer*, Sept. 13, 1994, Vol. 8, No. 35, at 7. The right to silence in English law carries a rich history. In 1769 Sir William Blackstone wrote about "the English judgment of penance for standing mute": "the prisoner shall be remanded to the prison from whence he came; and put into a low, dark chamber; and there be laid on his back, on the bare floor, naked, unless where decency forbids; that there be placed upon his body as great a weight of iron as he can bear, and more; that he shall have no sustenance, save only, on the first day, three morsels of the worst bread; and, on the second day, three draughts of standing water, that shall be nearest to the prison door; and in this situation this shall be alternately his daily diet, till he dies, as the judgment now runs, though formerly it was, till he answered." Sir William Blackstone, *Commentaries on the Laws of England* (1769), vol. IV, chap. 25, p. 322.
121. Amendment to Article 4 of the Order accompanying Criminal Justice and Police Order Act 1994, §10, para. 1.
122. Carol Daugherty Rasnic, *Northern Ireland's Criminal Trials without Jury: the Diplock Experiment* 5 Ann. Surv. In'l & Comp. L. 239.
123. John D. Jackson, *The Restoration of Jury Trial in Northern Ireland; Can we Learn from the Professional Alternative?* 2001 St. Louis-Warsaw Trans'l 15, at 23.
124. Murray v. U.K., 22 Eur. H.R. Rep 29 (1996).
125. R. v. Caraher, The Court of Appeal in Northern Ireland, NICC3072 (Transcript), Sept. 29, 2000 (Nicholson LJ).
126. John D. Jackson, *The Restoration of Jury Trial in Northern Ireland; Can we Learn from the Professional Alternative?* 2001 St. Louis-Warsaw Trans'l 15, at 24.
127. Ibid., at 26–27.
128. Ibid.
129. David Sharrock, *Call to Halt Ulster Murder Trials, Guardian* (London), June 9, 1992.
130. See, e.g., ibid. (citing CAJ).
131. David Mason, *Ulster Still Taints Britain's Human Rights Record—Amnesty, Press Association*, July 9, 1992.
132. Omagh bombing kills 28, BBC News, Aug. 16, 1998, available at: http://news.bbc.co.uk/1/hi/events/northern_ireland/latest_news/152156.stm
133. Criminal Justice (Terrorism and Conspiracy) Act 1998, c. 40.
134. Northern Ireland Human Rights Commission, comments on the Incompatibility of the Emergency Laws in Northern Ireland with International Human Rights Law, December 1999.
135. Report of the Commission to Consider Legal Procedures to Deal with Terrorism Activities in Northern Ireland, Cmd. 5185 (1974), 12.
136. See e.g., O'Leary v. AG (1991 ILRM 454), The People v. Cull (Court of Criminal Appeal 1980) and The People (DPP) v. McGurk [1994] 2

IR 579. Cited in Northern Ireland Human Rights Commission, Comments on the Incompatibility of the Emergency Laws in Northern Ireland with International Human Rights Law, December 1999.
137. Jackson et al., *supra* note 108.
138. John Mullin, Six start flood of freed terrorists; 200 prisoners to be released in two months, *Guardian* (London), Sept. 12, 1998, p. 2.
139. Post office robber to be sentenced, *Belfast Telegraph*, Oct. 20, 2001. See also Guilty Man Picked out of identity parade, *Irish News*, Oct. 20, 2001, p. 13.
140. Nine Years for Man trapped by DNS, *Belfast News Letter* (Northern Ireland), Nov. 17, 2004, p. 10.
141. CUP Final Attack Judge told "Camera Cannot Lie", *Belfast News Letter* (Northern Ireland), Oct. 20, 2005, p. 12.
142. David Sharrock, *Justice "going through motions"*, *Guardian* (London), June 9, 1992, at 4; and Alan Travis, *Diplock Court Reform Agreed/ MPs approve amendments to Ulster Emergency Provisions Act*, *Guardian* (London), Jan. 17, 1986.
143. Although the British government introduced Diplock courts in 1973, it was not until 1983 that the state began to keep statistics. From a high of 354 Diplock cases in 1987, the number has since, on average, been on the decline.

Table 8.1

Year	Defendants	Cases
1983	432	—
1984	435	—
1985	750	—
1986	622	329
1987	743	354
1988	557	314
1989	461	277
1990	492	265
1991	433	206
1992	418	221
1993	427	256
1994	376	222
1995	453	237
1996	174	110
1997	149	94
1998	177	92
1999	108	73
2000	89	49
2001	62	45
2002	113	72
2003	110	71
2004	77	65

Bridget Prentice, Minister of State, Department for Constitutional Affairs, HC Debs, Dec. 5, 2005, col. 1054W. These numbers are reported differently in different sources. For instance, *Irish Times* said that in 1995, there were 418 people tried. It explained this increase as "a consequence of the considerable backlog of arrested and charged persons". Of the 418 people tried, 360 pleaded guilty, 58 pleaded not guilty, 23 of whom found not guilty. *Non-jury courts Tried 418 in North*, *Irish Times*, Apr. 3, 1996, at 9. Because of the discrepancy in numbers, I have cited those given formally in Parliament by the Minister of State.

144. Labour Party Conference: Withdrawal of Troops heavily voted down/ British troops in Northern Ireland, *Guardian* (London), Oct. 6, 1984.
145. Ibid.
146. *Parliament: Informer Evidence defended/Northern Ireland Secretary Hurd defends 'supergrass' evidence in Ulster trials*, *Guardian* (London), Dec. 21, 1984.
147. Hugh Carnegy, *Labour Call to Replace One-Judge Diplock Courts*, *Financial Times* (London), Dec. 4, 1986, at 16.
148. Robert Morgan, John Winder, Anthony Hodges & Peter Mulligan, *Labour Party Conference: Irish knot*, *Times* (London), Sept. 29, 1987.
149. Richard Ford, Parliament: *Emergency laws attacked—Minority "alienated"*, *Times* (London), Feb. 2, 1988.
150. Paul Johnson, *Shake-up for Ulster 'terror' courts urged/Administration of justice in Northern Ireland*, *Guardian* (London), Dec. 19, 1984; and Peter Murtagh, Diplock Courts "Need Three Judges", *Guardian* (London), Nov. 27, 1986.
151. *Talks Fail to Resolve Ulster Courts Issue*, *Financial Times* (London), Dec. 9, 1986, at 10.
152. Joe Joyce, British plan to End Diplock Stalemate, *Guardian* (London), Nov. 9, 1987. See also Philip Webster, *Thatcher Steps up Pressure on Extradition*, *Times* (London), Nov. 11, 1987.
153. *After Dipock*, *Times* (London), Oct. 23, 1987.
154. Ibid.
155. Ibid.
156. Martin Fletcher & John Cooney, *King resists Dublin call for three-judge courts*, *Times* (London), Oct. 31, 1987.
157. Sarah Spencer & Fran Russell, *Agenda: Breaking the Diplock—A three-judge system*, *Guardian* (London), Aug. 17, 1987. See also Greer and White, *Abolishing the Diplock Courts* (1986). Hugh Carnegy, *Irish Plea on Diplock Courts Refused*, *Financial Times* (London), Nov. 6, 1986, at 9. See also *Rebuff for Irish on Diplock*, *Times* (London), Nov. 6, 1986.
158. David Hearst, *Rift with Dublin widens over Diplock courts*, *Guardian* (London), Oct. 23, 1987.
159. King Issues Warning to Dublin on Extradition Bill, *Financial Times* (London), Oct. 22, 1987. See also David Hearst, Britain Confident Dublin Will Back Treaty, *Guardian* (London), Oct. 22, 1987.

160. Tom Lynch, *Conflict in Dublin on Diplock Deal, Financial Times* (London), Oct. 19, 1987, at 8.
161. John Cooney, *Haughey Links Treaty to Court Reform: Anglo-Irish Relations, Times* (London), Oct. 12, 1987.
162. David Hearst, *Diplock Courts Reform Sours Ulster Talks: The bone of contention at this week's Anglo-Irish meeting, Guardian* (London), Oct. 19, 1987. See also Sarah Spencer & Fran Russell, *Agenda: Breaking the Diplock—A three-judge system, Guardian* (London), Aug. 17, 1987. See also Greer and White, *Abolishing the Diplock Courts* (1986).
163. David Hearst, *Dublin encouraged by King's reforms; Irish government welcomes Ulster legal reforms, Guardian* (London), Nov. 10, 1986. See also James Naughtie, Hailsham Blocks Reform Plan for Diplock Courts, *Guardian* (London), Oct. 29, 1986; See also Nicholas Wood, *Hailsham Blocks Irish Move, Times* (London), Oct. 29, 1986 (claiming that Lord Hailsham was against it in opposition to other cabinet members and adding that Hailsham thinks interferes with British sovereignty, concerned about what would happen if split decision between the judges).
164. Alan Travis, *Diplock Court Reform Agreed/MPs approve amendments to Ulster Emergency Provisions Act, Guardian* (London), Jan. 17, 1986
165. David Hearst, Few Exercise Right of Diplock Appeal, *Guardian* (London), Aug. 4, 1987.
166. Response of the Northern Ireland Human Rights Commission to the Home Office Discussion Paper on Counter-terrorism Measures: Reconciling Security and Liberty in an Open Society, NIHRC, Aug. 2004, at 6.
167. Ibid.
168. Mr. Tony Worthington (Clydebank and Milngavie), HC Debs, Mar. 19, 1997: Column 1016–17.
169. Ibid.
170. Between 1992 and 1995 there were approximately 400 Diplock defendants per year. In 1996, however, the number dropped to 170, and in the first nine months of 1997, only 102 Diplock defendants stood trial. John Mullin, *The Trying Game, Guardian* (London), Jan. 20, 1998, p. 17. The numbers continued to decrease until they reached a low in 2001. Although the numbers have increased since then, they remain far below the levels present in the 1980s and early 1990s. See footnote 143.
171. Mullin, *supra* note 168.
172. Ibid.
173. Ibid.
174. Each application may relate to one person/one offence, one person with various offences, or various persons with same offence. The Terrorism (Northern Ireland) Bill, Bill 52 of 2005–6, Research paper 05/70, House of Commons Library, Miriam Peck, Home Affairs

Section, Oonagh Gay, Parliament and Constitution Centre, Gavin Berman, Social and General Statistics., Oct. 27, 2005, p. 14.
175. The Terrorism (Northern Ireland) Bill, Bill 52 of 2005–6, Research paper 05/70, House of Commons Library, Miriam Peck, Home Affairs Section, Oonagh Gay, Parliament and Constitution Centre, Gavin Berman, Social and General Statistics., Oct. 27, 2005, p. 14. Interestingly, the numbers appear to fall off in 2004: January through September of that year, of 638 applications made, the Attorney General refused 103 and granted the remaining 535. Ibid.
176. Angelique Chrisafis, *Guardian* (London), Jan. 31, 2005, 0.
177. Joshua Rozenberg, The Trials of being both judge and jury sitting in Northern Ireland's Diplock courts, Lord Carswell not only presided over cases but also delivered the verdicts, *The Daily Telegraph* (London), Nov. 24, 2005, p. 21.
178. Sec. 67(2).
179. Mr. David Lidington (Aylesbury, Con), col. 8; First Standing Committee on Delegated Legislation, HC Debs, Feb. 5, 2004, cols 3–12.
180. HC Debs, Oct. 31, 2005 (pt 14), cols. 653–56, col. 655.
181. Joshua Rozenberg, The Trials of being both judge and jury sitting in Northern Ireland's Diplock courts, Lord Carswell not only presided over cases but also delivered the verdicts, *The Daily Telegraph* (London), Nov. 24, 2005, p. 21. Carswell was the Lord Chief Justice in Northern Ireland, until becoming a Law Lord in 2003.
182. See, e.g., Gareth Parry, *UK News in Brief: Pub bombs case may be reopened*, *Guardian* (London), Oct. 20, 1987; and Joe Joyce, *Haughey Noncommittal on Details of Extradition Treaty with N. Ireland*, *Guardian* (London), Oct. 12, 1987.
183. Jamie Dettmer, *Storm over Dukakis Attack on Ulster Justice; US Presidential election*, *Times* (London), Nov. 2, 1988.
184. Ibid.
185. Ibid.
186. See, e.g., Boris Belitskiy, "Vantage Point", Moscow, BBC Summary of World Broadcasts, Nov. 1, 1988. See also: British government's move against 'right of silence' Part 1 The USSR, BBC Summary of World Broadcasts, Oct. 25, 1988 (stating "Indeed, Britain has already made a mockery of justice in Ulster by introducing the Diplock courts.")
187. Livingstone backs Maze Fugitive; Labour MP ignores concern of senior party members that court appearance will be seen as endorsing IRA terrorists, *Independent* (London), Oct. 8, 1993, at 2. Whether or not a shoot to kill policy existed at the time was a highly contentious issue. In 1984 allegations made in Parliament to this effect were denied by Nicholas Scott, the Junior Northern Ireland Minister. *Parliament: Informer Evidence defended/Northern Ireland Secretary Hurd defends 'supergrass' evidence in Ulster trials*, *Guardian* (London), Dec. 21, 1984 (stating "There is not, and never has been, a policy of summary

execution, or shoot to kill in Northern Ireland.") Although the Government instituted an inquiry into the matter, the results were suppressed. *Amnesty latest critic of the Stalker affair*, Times (London), Oct. 5, 1988.
188. Rowe specifically cited §13 of the EPA, and the equivalent provisions of the PTA 1989 §§16(a) and 16(b).
189. Northern Ireland Human Rights Commission, comments on the Incompatibility of the Emergency Laws in Northern Ireland with International Human Rights Law, December 1999. Two Lords (Hope and Hobouse) skeptical as to whether they were incompatible, but said could be incompatible in particular context. Lord Cooke said that he saw "great force in the Divisional Court's view that on the natural and ordinary interpretation [of section 16A] there is repugnancy [with Article 6(2)]." Stated, "On its face section 16A of the Act of 1989 enables a person to be found guity of a very serious offence merely on reasonable grounds of suspicion. It may be highly inconvenient that this should not be permissible . . . but at best it is doubtful whether Article 6(2) can be watered down to an extent that would leave section 16A unscathed."
190. Unterpertinger v. Austria (1986) 13 EHRR 175, at p. 184; Kostovski v. Netherlands (1989) 12 EHRR 434; and Windisch v. Austria (1990) 13 EHRR 281.
191. Lord Lloyd, HL Debs Sept. 3, 1998, col. 38 (stating, "Would [a conviction based in large part on the statement of a police officer] have the slightest chance of standing up in Strasbourg? . . . It would not have the slightest chance. It certainly would not stand up in our courts once the Human Rights Act comes into force.")
192. John Murrah v. U.K. (1996) 22 EHRR 29. See also Funke v. France (1993) 16 EHRR 297. The British Government responded to the decision with the introduction of Sections 30A(4) and 30A(6), which require the court to take account of whether the defendant had access to a solicitor before police questioning. Only where he did have access and remained silent, and the suspect could reasonably be expected to respond, can a court draw the inference of guilt. See Northern Ireland Human Rights Commission, Comments on the Incompatibility of the Emergency Laws in Northern Ireland with International Human Rights Law, December 1999.
193. See Good Friday Agreement, Security 2(iii)–(iv), available at: http://www.nio.gov.uk/agreement.pdf
194. Report on the Operation in 2001 of the Terrorism Act 2000, Lord Carlile of Berriew, para. 7.9, available at: http://pi.gn.apc.org/issues/terrorism/library/uk2001reportterrorismact.pdf
195. *Justice for All*, July 2002, CM 5563, paras 4.27–4.33; available at: http://image.guardian.co.uk/sys-files/Politics/documents/2002/07/17/Criminal_Justice.pdf
196. Criminal Justice Act 2003, c. 44, Part VII.

197. Security-related incidents in NI 1997/8–2005/6:

Table 8.2

Year	Shooting incidents	Bombings Incidents	Bombings Devices	Incendiaries Incidents	Incendiaries Devices
1997/98	245	73	91	6	6
1998/99	187	123	229	20	20
1999/00	131	66	86	5	5
2000/01	331	177	206	9	22
2001/02	358	318	407	5	6
2002/03	348	178	226	8	8
2003/04	207	71	80	3	3
2004/05	167	48	51	29	36
2005/06*	72	32	41	1	1

*As of 31st Aug.; source: PSNI stats.

Note that shooting incidents include terrorist shots, security force shots, paramilitary-style attacks with shooting, shots heard/later confirmed, other violent incidents where shots fired (e.g., armed robbery).

Source: The Terorrism (Northern Ireland) Bill, Bill 52 of 2005-6, Research paper 05/70, House of Commons Library, Miriam Peck, Home Affairs Section, Oonagh Gay, Parliament and Constitution Centre, Gavin Berman, Social and General Statistics, Oct. 27, 2005.

198. Jane Kennedy, Minister of State, Northern Ireland Office, col. 4; First Standing Committee on Delegated Legislation, HC Debs, Feb. 5, 2004, cols 3–12.
199. Carlile Report 2004, paras 2.9 and 2.10.
200. HL Debs, Northern Ireland (Monitoring Commission etc.) Bill, Sept. 12, 2003, (230912–03), cols 580–600; Baroness Park of Monmouth, col. 586.
201. Jane Kennedy, Minister of State, Northern Ireland Office, col. 5; First Standing Committee on Delegated Legislation, HC Debs, Feb. 5, 2004, cols 3–12.
202. First Standing Committee on Delegated Legislation, HC Debs, Feb. 5, 2004, cols 3–12; cols 5–6, Kennedy.
203. See also Terrorism Act 2000, §§66–80, for other rules applying to scheduled offences.
204. Joint Declaration of the British and Irish Governments, April 2003, p. 6, paras 18–19, available at: http://www.ireland.com/newspaper/special/2003/blueprint/blueprint.pdf
205. Joint Declaration of the British and Irish Governments, April 2003, p. 13, para. 9, available at: http://www.ireland.com/newspaper/special/2003/blueprint/blueprint.pdf
206. "The leadership of Oglaigh na hEireann has formally ordered an end to the armed campaign. This will take effect from 4 pm this afternoon. All IRA units have been ordered to dump arms. All Volunteers have

been instructed to assist the development of purely political and democratic programmes through exclusively peaceful means. Volunteers must not engage in any other activities whatsoever.... The Army Council took these decisions following an unprecedented internal discussion and consultation process with IRA units and Volunteers." BBC News, IRA Statement in Full, July 28, 2005.
207. Jury Trials to Return for Terror Cases, *Belfast News Letter* (Northern Ireland), Aug. 3, 2005, p. 11. See also Chris Thornton, Diplock Court system to be Ended, *Belfast Telegraph*, Aug. 2, 2005.
208. Sharon O'Neill, First steps to normalization—Diplock courts could be scrapped, *Irish News*, Aug. 2, 2005, p. 8.
209. David Sharrock, Unionists reject 'dangerous and dishonest move', *Times* (London), Aug. 2, 2005, p. 4.
210. Radical plan to cut security in North Unveiled, *Irish Times*, Aug. 2, 2005, p. 1.
211. David Sharrock, *supra* note 207.
212. Radical plan to cut security in North Unveiled, *Irish Times*, Aug. 2, 2005, p. 1.
213. David Sharrock, Unionists reject 'dangerous and dishonest move', *Times* (London), Aug. 2, 2005, p. 4.
214. Chris Thornton, Ulster to get secret courts, *Belfast Telegraph*, Aug. 10, 2005.
215. See, e.g., Double Standards, *Belfast News Letter* (Northern Ireland), Aug. 10, 2005, p. 1.
216. Shaun Woodward, Northern Ireland Security Minister, HC Debs on the Terrorism (Northern Ireland) Bill, Standing Committee, Nov. 9, 2005, col. 26.
217. http://www.independentmonitoringcommission.org/documents/uploads
218. But note that the bill *added* to the list of scheduled offences.
219. The Terrorism (Northern Ireland) Bill, Bill 52 of 2005–6, Research paper 05/70, House of Commons Library, Miriam Peck, Home Affairs Section, Oonagh Gay, Parliament and Constitution Centre, Gavin Berman, Social and General Statistics., Oct. 27, 2005, p. 12.
220. NIHRC submission, quoted in The Terrorism (Northern Ireland) Bill, Bill 52 of 2005–6, Research paper 05/70, House of Commons Library, Miriam Peck, Home Affairs Section, Oonagh Gay, Parliament and Constitution Centre, Gavin Berman, Social and General Statistics, Oct. 27, 2005, p. 12.
221. Dr. Alasdair McDonnell, SDLP, Belfast, South, Terrorism (Northern Ireland) Bill, discussion of continuance in force of Part VII of the TA 2000, Nov. 30, 2005, cols. 300–339.
222. HC Debs on the Terrorism (Northern Ireland) Bill, Standing Committee, Nov. 9, 2005, col. 27.
223. HC Debs on the Terrorism (Northern Ireland) Bill, Standing Committee, Nov. 9, 2005, col. 28.
224. Ibid.

225. Ibid.
226. Ibid.
227. Lord Rooker, Minister of State, Northern Ireland Office, Dec. 20, 2005, HL Debs, Col. 1681.
228. Laurence Robertson, HC Debs, Oct. 31, 2005 (pt 22), col. 686. The murder of Robert McCartney in a bar in January 2005 and suspicious lack of witnesses to come forward (around 70 people present in the pub claimed not to have seen anything) underscored both local and national concern at the continued intimidation exercised by paramilitary groups in Northern Ireland. See Shawn Pogatchnik, Police, sisters of Belfast man killed by IRA one year ago renew appeal for witnesses, justice, Associated Press, Jan. 31, 2006.
229. Terrorism (Northern Ireland) Bill, discussion of continuance in force of Part VII of the TA 2000, Nov. 30, 2005, col. 302. See also Mr. Donaldson, Member for Lagan Valley, Terrorism (Northern Ireland) Bill, discussion of continuance in force of Part VII of the TA 2000, Nov. 30, 2005, col 302 (stating, "It is not that we need politics to normalize; it is that we need society to normalize.")
230. Terrorism (Northern Ireland) Bill, discussion of continuance in force of Part VII of the TA 2000, Nov. 30, 2005, col. 302.
231. Terrorism (Northern Ireland) Bill, discussion of continuance in force of Part VII of the TA 2000, Nov. 30, 2005, col. 303.
232. Henry Bellingham, Conservative, MP for Norfolk, Terrorism (Northern Ireland) Bill, discussion of continuance in force of Part VII of the TA 2000, Nov. 30, 2005, col. 338.
233. Sammy Wilson, DUP, MP for East Antrim, Terrorism (Northern Ireland) Bill, discussion of continuance in force of Part VII of the TA 2000, Nov. 30, 2005, col. 339.
234. Ibid., at 307. See also, Nigel Dodds (Belfast, North, DUP): Terrorism (Northern Ireland) Bill, discussion of continuance in force of Part VII of the TA 2000, Nov. 30, 2005, col. 307 (stating, "We will not be treated as second-class citizens or accept a standard of democracy that others are not prepared to accept. We will move forward only on the basis of the cessation of all terrorism, the dismantling of all terrorist structures and the disbandment of all terrorist organizations.")
235. See remarks by Henry Bellingham (col. 338), Donaldson, and Sammy Wilson (col. 339), Terrorism (Northern Ireland) Bill, discussion of continuance in force of Part VII of the TA 2000, 30 Nov. 2005.
236. Terrorism (Northern Ireland) Bill, discussion of continuance in force of Part VII of the TA 2000, Nov. 30, 2005., col. 339.
237. Lord Carlile, Report on the Operation in 2004 of Part VII of the TA 2000, para. 2.9. (Emphasis added) See also ibid., para. 2.10.
238. But see comments by Fred Cobain, UUP, crediting the increased number of cases scheduled out of the Diplock system to the movement by paramilitaries into the criminal realm: "The reason why the cases are falling is that paramilitary activity is falling and the police are dealing with a lot of this through judge and jury courts. This involves

money laundering and drugs and people now have more confidence in the police and the courts. Dipock courts need to go away as quickly as possible." Michael McHugh, Axe Diplock by end of year: SDLP; Courts call as terror cases halve, *Belfast Telegraph*, Feb. 1, 2006.

239. Baroness Harris of Richmond, HL Debs, Dec. 20, 2005, col. 1677. See also Joe Churcher and Katherine Haddon, Anti-terror law extended, *Irish News*, Dec. 1, 2005, p. 9 (reporting that legislation passed).

240. HC Debs on the Terrorism (Northern Ireland) Bill, Standing Committee, Nov. 9, 2005, cols. 21–29. Note in relation to claims of cost: a written answer to Ulster Unionist Lord Laird noted in December 2005 that over the previous five years, the costs in personal security for those under "substantial or severe terrorist threat" ran to £45 million over the past 5 years, with some. Current year £7.5 million estimated for 2005. The number was expected to drop to £3.8 million for 2006. Brian Walker, New post-Diplock court system on way: Rooker, *Belfast Telegraph*, Dec. 21, 2005. Assumedly, unless the time to trial or in trial increased significantly, movement to a three judge tribunal would impact these costs.

241. See, e.g., First Standing Committee on Delegated Legislation, HC Debs, Feb. 5, 2004, col. 6; First Standing Committee on Delegated Legislation, Standing Committee, HC Debs, Feb. 8, 2005, col. 16 (both raising in Parliament the possibility of replacing the Diplock courts with a three-judge tribunal).

242. Man Guilty of Terror Plot in First Trial with Al-Qa'Ida Link, *Irish Independent*, Nov. 25, 2005.

243. Owen Bowcott, Algerian guilty of downloading bomb data, *Guardian* (London), Nov. 25, 2005, p. 6.

244. Man Guilty of Terror Plot in First Trial with Al-Qa'Ida Link, *Irish Independent*, Nov. 25, 2005.

245. Bowcott, *supra* note 241.

246. David Sharrock, Belfast's non-jury court tries Islamist suspect, *Times* (London), Sept. 9, 2005, p. 27.

247. Al Qaida terrorist may be out in a year, Belfast Telegraph, Dec. 21, 2005. See also John Murray Brown, Terror suspect faces non-jury trial, *Financial Times* (London, England), Sept. 9, 2005, p. 4.

248. Al Qaida terrorist may be out in a year, *Belfast Telegraph*, Dec. 21, 2005.

9

Human Rights and the Challenge of Terror

David Cole

The human rights movement, born from the ashes of World War II, has made astounding progress in just over sixty years. Human rights treaties addressing a broad range of subjects have been widely adopted and ratified. Regional courts now enforce human rights against once-sovereign nations, most notably the European Court of Human Rights and the European Court of Justice. Domestic courts in many nations treat human rights treaties as a part of their own domestic law, and binding on their own government officials. Dozens of new non-governmental organizations devoted to advocating on behalf of human rights are formed every year, and established organizations, such as Amnesty International and Human Rights Watch, are stronger than ever.

But the human rights movement is now facing its greatest test yet. The "war on terror" declared by the United States in the wake of the terrorist attacks of September 11, 2001, has seen the most world's most powerful nation, and formerly one of the world's principal exponents of human rights, adopt a nearly adversarial relationship to human rights standards. In the name of fighting terror, the United States has sought to redefine and water down the prohibitions on torture and cruel, inhuman, and degrading treatment; engaged in forced disappearances and indefinite detention without trial; exploited double standards, imposing treatment on foreign nationals that would not be acceptable if applied to its own citizens; and run roughshod over rights of association. Moreover, it has pressured other nations to take similar measures against terrorism—through formal international initiatives, such as the United Nations Security Council resolution on terrorist financing, to co-opting other governments to collaborate in renditions and coercive interrogations. Human Rights Watch announced in its 2007 World Report a conclusion that had long become evident to the rest of the world—that by its actions, the United States had forfeited its role as a voice for human rights around the world.[1]

Other countries have been more than willing to use the United States' actions as an excuse to adopt repressive measures of their own, targeting political opponents as terrorists and taking abusive measures against them.[2] Meanwhile, the United States has offered at best only muted criticism of such abuses, compromised by its own practices, and by its need to collaborate with rights-abusing nations.

The United Kingdom responded to 9/11 by adopting its own antiterrorism law, one provision of which authorized indefinite detention without charges or trial of foreign nationals suspected as terrorists. When that provision was declared incompatible with the European Convention on Human Rights, on the ground that it impermissibly discriminated against foreign nationals, Parliament responded by authorizing the imposition of "control orders," an often onerous form of house arrest, on the same "suspected terrorists," on the basis of secret evidence, and this time extended the law to British nationals as well. Most recently, the British government has sought to overturn a ruling of the European Court of Human Rights barring the deportation of suspected terrorists to countries where they face a substantial risk of torture or cruel, inhuman, or degrading treatment.[3]

Conor Gearty, head of the Centre for the Study of Human Rights at the London School of Economics, has asked, "Can human rights survive?"[4] The question is not merely rhetorical. As Princeton Professor Kim Scheppele has argued, the "war on terror" has produced the first major systemic international counter-force to the expansion and establishment of human rights.[5] The United Nations Security Council has called on all states to take measures against terrorism and against the financing of terrorism. While human rights are likely to survive, their character could well be fundamentally altered by the "war on terror," and their survival will depend upon the concerted efforts of human rights organizations and institutions, advocates, and, of course, states themselves.

In this essay, I will argue that while there is real reason for serious concern about the continued viability of human rights, there is also a basis for hope. Human rights have probably never been under a more serious and sustained attack. Thus far, however, they have proved their resilience in important ways. The conflict is ongoing, and the outcome is far from clear. But one of the often overlooked lessons of the first five years of the so-called "war on terror" has been that even the most powerful nation in the world is not free to sacrifice fundamental human rights in the name of fighting terrorism without incurring significant costs to its own efficacy. The United States' human rights abuses have undermined the legitimacy of its effort to ward off terrorist attacks, while simultaneously reinforcing terrorists' recruitment efforts. The Bush administration has viewed human rights as a check on the its ability to fight terrorism—after all, they do limit what a state can do in its own defense, and require it to fight, as Israeli Supreme Court Justice Aharon Barak has said, "with one hand tied behind its back."[6] The five years following the attacks of September 11 have seen extremely troubling compromises on human rights principles and commitments. At the same time, however, the United States has been forced to retreat from many of its most extreme policies. Moreover, the first five years of the "war on terror" have demonstrated that, properly understood, the moral authority of human rights can be a tool to fight terrorism, and that such moral authority is ignored at our peril.

Since the attacks of September 11, the Bush administration has treated human rights and humanitarian law obligations as obstacles to be evaded. In January 2002, Alberto Gonzales, then the President's chief lawyer, characterized the Geneva Conventions as "quaint" and "obsolete," and argued against their application to al Qaeda and Taliban detainees. Geneva Convention protections, it was said, would hinder interrogation efforts. The same concern led Gonzales to instruct lawyers at the Office of Legal Counsel, purportedly the constitutional conscience of the executive branch, to draft a memorandum narrowly construing the torture ban reflected in international and U.S. domestic law, in order to reassure CIA interrogators that they could act with impunity in coercively interrogating suspects. Among other things, the Office of Legal Counsel opined that threatening suspects with death is not torture, as long as the threat is not of imminent death, and that inflicting great physical pain is not torture, so long as the pain does not rise to the level associated with organ failure or death.[7] Among the specific tactics reportedly authorized by the Justice Department and employed by the CIA is "waterboarding," a process in which individuals are made to fear that they are drowning in order to induce them to talk.[8]

The August 2002 Office of Legal Counsel torture memorandum

was adopted in secret. It was leaked to the press and posted on the Web by the *Washington Post* in June 2004.[9] The memorandum sparked widespread criticism from scholars, lawyers, members of Congress, and human rights activists. By the end of 2004, as White House Counsel Alberto Gonzales was preparing for Senate hearings on his nomination to be Attorney General, the Justice Department formally repudiated the memo and issued a new one in its stead, adopting a much broader view of what constitutes torture.[10] The Justice Department was able to maintain its torture policy, in other words, only until that policy became public.

The Office of Legal Counsel memorandum addressed itself exclusively to the ban on torture, and did not even discuss "cruel, inhuman, and degrading treatment," also banned by the same international human rights treaty, the Convention Against Torture and Other Cruel, Inhuman, and Degrading Treatment or Punishment (CAT).[11] It was a real stretch to say that extreme physical pain, threats of death, and waterboarding do not constitute torture—but surely no one could argue that such acts are not "cruel, inhuman, and degrading," a lower standard of mistreatment. The European Court of Human Rights, for example, held in 1979 that five coercive interrogation tactics used by the United Kingdom to interrogate IRA suspects—stress positions, hooding, subjection to noise, sleep deprivation, and deprivation of food and drink—were not torture, but were nonetheless prohibited as "cruel, inhuman, and degrading treatment."[12] In order to evade this prohibition, the United States Justice Department secretly interpreted the CAT to protect only U.S. citizens from cruel, inhuman, and degrading treatment outside the United States, leaving foreign nationals outside our borders unprotected. Accordingly, as long as the suspect was foreign and the interrogation was conducted outside U.S. borders, the Justice Department reasoned, there was no barrier to employing cruel, inhuman, and degrading tactics. This interpretation remained a secret until January 2005, when Alberto Gonzales was being considered for confirmation as Attorney General of the United States.

The Justice Department's position was predicated on a strained interpretation of a "reservation" adopted when the Senate ratified the treaty in 1994. At that time, some had expressed concern that the substantive scope of the term "cruel, inhuman and degrading treatment" was unclear. The Senate adopted language stating that it understood the term to be coterminous with the kinds of conduct banned by the Fifth and Eighth Amendments to the U.S. Constitution, amendments that had had the benefit of years of judicial construction, and so were arguably less vague than the treaty prohibition itself. No one suggested at the time that this would mean that the United States would be free to inflict cruel and inhuman treatment on foreign nationals abroad.

After September 11, however, the administration reasoned that because the U.S. Constitution has generally been understood not to apply to foreign nationals beyond U.S. borders, then the treaty obligation undertaken in signing and ratifying the CAT also did not extend to foreigners held outside our borders. This reasoning turns human rights on its head. The very predicate of a "human" right is that it stems from the respect owed to every human being by virtue of their very humanity. Human dignity is universal, and is certainly not limited to those with American passports, or to those detained inside United States borders. The Bush administration interpretation struck at the very core of the idea of human rights—that certain rights must extend equally to all.

To its credit, when Congress learned of the administration's interpretation of the CAT, it overturned it by overwhelming margins, in an effort led by Republican Senator John McCain. The McCain Amendment affirmed that the ban on cruel, inhuman and degrading treatment applies to *all* persons, regardless of where they are held.[13] The Bush administration strongly opposed this measure, however, and while it could not defeat it altogether, it did ensure that the McCain Amendment contained no sanctions for its violation, and simultaneously obtained passage of another provision that denied enemy combatants the right to go to court to challenge their treatment, even if it is plainly cruel, inhuman, or degrading, or indeed outright torture.[14] Still, as a formal matter, Congress insisted that the *human* right not to be subjected to cruel, inhuman, or degrading treatment extends to all humans, not just Americans. And even if enemy combatants cannot seek review in the courts, the executive branch is nonetheless legally obligated to adhere to the McCain Amendment.

The struggle over the meaning of the CAT illustrates the lengths to which the Bush administration was willing to go to free up its agents from what it saw as too-restrictive human rights norms. But the fact that the Justice Department's interpretations were adopted only in secret, and were repudiated once they became public, illustrates the resilience of human rights norms. Both the exceedingly narrow interpretation of what constitutes torture ban and the limitation of the ban on cruel, inhuman and degrading treatment to foreign nationals were adopted in secret, no doubt because the administration feared the consequences if they sought to make such changes through an open deliberative process. At the end of the day, both positions were flushed out, and once they saw the light of day, were formally repudiated.

The particular tactic employed with respect to the ban on cruel, inhuman and degrading treatment illustrates a broader threat to human rights in the context of the "war on terror." The Bush administration strategy here, as in so many other areas since September 11, was to adopt a double standard—imposing on foreign nationals treatment that it did not inflict on U.S. citizens. Other examples include the military tribunals, which subject foreigners accused of terrorist crimes to a much less protective legal process than U.S. citizens accused of the same crimes, and the detention of enemy combatants at Guantánamo. The administration argues that because the Guantánamo detainees are foreign nationals held outside United States borders, they are entitled to no constitutional protection whatsoever. It has made the same argument that foreign nationals beyond our borders deserve no constitutional protection in defending lawsuits challenging its "rendition" of foreign nationals to third countries to be coercively interrogated. Such double standards are politically convenient, because politicians can say to the electorate: "You need not sacrifice your own rights in the name of greater security, because we are sacrificing the rights of someone else." When the "someone else" is a foreign national, the trade-off is relatively costless for the electorate and the representative, as foreign nationals have no vote, and therefore no effective voice in the political process.

The United States is far from alone in exploiting the citizen/noncitizen divide. The most extreme provision in the United Kingdom's post-9/11 antiterrorism legislation was also selectively targeted at foreigners, providing that foreign nationals suspected of terrorist involvement but not deportable could be held indefinitely without trial or charge. In 2004, however, the Law Lords, the United Kingdom's highest court, declared that law incompatible with the European Convention on Human Rights, precisely on the ground that it exploited an impermissible double standard.[15] The Law Lords reasoned that foreign terror suspects pose no greater danger than terror suspects who are British citizens, and therefore there was no rational justification for singling out foreign nationals for such treatment. Here, too, then, the government initially responded to the threat of terrorism by running roughshod over a fundamental principle of human rights, but was ultimately forced to back down in the face of the human rights principle.

In February 2007, the Canadian Supreme Court similarly invalidated antiterrorism legislation directed at foreign nationals.[16] The legislation in question permitted the Minister of Citizenship and Immigration and the Minister of Public Safety and Emergency Preparedness to issue a certificate declaring that a foreign national is inadmissible to Canada on grounds of security. The certificate could be based on secret evidence not disclosed to the foreign national. And issuance of the certificate resulted in an automatic 120-day detention of the foreign national once the certificate was approved by a judge. The Canadian Supreme Court declared that the law was inconsistent with the Canadian Charter, both because it permitted detention based on secret evidence, denying the foreign national a fair hearing, and because the 120-day detention period is arbitrary.

The American experience at Guantánamo Bay further illustrates that human rights are simultaneously under serious attack and more resilient than one might think. In January 2002, when the Department of Defense first started bringing enemy combatants to Guantánamo Bay, Cuba, its position was that the detainees were the "worst of the worst," and were deserving of no rights whatsoever. In fact, Guantánamo Bay was selected as the site for the prison camp precisely so that the government could argue that U.S. laws had no applicability there. The United States refused to provide any hearings or other process to the detainees, and beyond categorical assertions that they were "evil," refused to provide any public information about who was held there and why they were there. The United States government effectively claimed the right to hold the detainees forever, without even the most rudimentary legal protections, and without any access to courts at all.

Five years later, Guantánamo Bay has become an international embarrassment for the United States. International pressure mounted, as one after another the United States allies condemned Guantánamo and called for its closure.[17] The United States Supreme Court ruled that the detainees had a right to seek judicial review of the legality of their detentions, and hundreds of lawsuits were filed.[18] The Supreme Court's decision prompted the administration to grant "combatant status review" hearings to all detainees. Other courts required that the military afford the detainees access to their lawyers, and demanded that information about the detainees be released to the public. Over time, the military has released nearly 300 of the Guantánamo detainees, and even President Bush himself has said that he would like to close down the facility.[19] In short, the Bush administration sought to create a "human rights free zone" at Guantánamo, but learned to its dismay that it could not succeed in insulating its practices there from human rights scrutiny. That scrutiny in turn has compelled the administration to backtrack substantially from its original position and practices vis-à-vis the detainees.

The United Kingdom has seen similar actions and reactions. In the wake of the July 7, 2005 London subway and bus bombings, Prime Minister Tony Blair called for a number of antiterrorism measures with serious human rights implications. He proposed making it a crime to "glorify" terrorism through one's speech, and empowering police to hold suspects without charge for up to 90 days. Despite his party's lopsided majority control of Parliament, Blair's proposals faced stiff resistance. Ultimately he was forced to water down the glorification provision to the point that it essentially criminalizes incitement to violence, and had to accept a 28-day detention power, far short of the 90 days he wanted. Here, too, human rights concerns were voiced and taken seriously, and ultimately required the government to retreat from its initial proposals.

The story is of course more complicated. There are other examples of counterterrorism initiatives raising substantial human rights concerns that have elicited much less opposition, and seen far less retreat on government officials' part. In the name of cutting off funding for terrorists, for example, the United States and the United Nations have pressed for measures that effectively blacklist individuals and groups, often without fair processes or even any evidence of wrongdoing. Under U.S. law, for example, groups and individuals can be designated as "specially designated global terrorists" based on nothing more than a secret finding that they are "otherwise associated" with someone else on the designated list.[20] Once listed, all assets in the United States are frozen, and it becomes a crime for U.S. citizens or those under U.S. jurisdiction to engage in any transaction with the listed individual or group—regardless of the intent and effect of the transaction. Moreover, the law permits groups and individuals to be designated in an entirely secret process, without any notice or hearing. Once a designation is published, those listed can challenge their designation in court, but the party seeking review is not permitted to present evidence in its defense, and the government is free to justify its actions with secret evidence presented behind closed doors to the court, and not made available to the designated entity or its lawyers. Not surprisingly, no one has yet successfully challenged a designation.

Because terrorist financing is a global phenomenon, soon after the September 11 attacks the United States pressed the United Nations Security Council to adopt a resolution requiring member states to take measures in their own countries to penalize terrorist financing. If such measures were carefully targeted at those who intentionally fund terrorist activity, and insisted on fair procedures, they would not raise human rights concerns. But where, as in the United States, the law permits designations to be made entirely in secret, and then defended with secret evidence, and where the laws then criminalize any support to such designated groups, even where the support is neither intended to further, nor has the effect of furthering, terrorism, these terrorist financing laws become a modern mechanism for imposing guilt by association. Yet while some courts in the United States have invalidated some of the broadest aspects of terror financing laws,[21] and while some in Europe have complained about the fairness of their procedures, there has not been any substantial retreat by states on this front.

The most troubling example of human rights objections failing to take hold has been with respect to the United States' practice of "disappearing" suspects in the war on terror and holding them incommunicado in undisclosed secret detention centers around the world. "Disappearances," a practice made famous by the military junta in Argentina's "dirty war," involves the secret detention of individuals without any acknowledgment that they are being detained. In the Argentinean example, many of the "disappeared" were eventually permanently disappeared—secretly executed and dropped into the ocean or buried in secret graves. The United States' practice has not reached that extreme, but it has involved all of the critical elements of a "disappearance" nonetheless—the secret incommunicado detention of suspects for indefinite periods of time. When the *Washington Post* disclosed the existence of the CIA's "black sites," the story prompted widespread objections from Europe. When it was suggested that some of the secret prisons may have been in Europe, the European Union asked the United States to confirm or deny this and the European Commission launched an investigation.[22]

The Bush administration, however, has been entirely unapologetic about the practice. In September 2006, it acknowledged the existence of the program, and transferred fourteen men who had been detained in "black sites" to Guantánamo. President Bush made a national speech defending the program—including its use of what he euphemistically referred to as "alternative" interrogation techniques—on the ground that it had elicited valuable information that helped to identify other terrorists and to disrupt terrorist plots.[23] The program was brought to light only because a United States Supreme Court decision in June 2006, *Hamdan v. Rumsfeld*, had ruled that al Qaeda detainees were entitled to the protections of Common Article

3 of the Geneva Conventions, and the implication of that ruling potentially subjected CIA interrogators to criminal prosecution for war crimes. But instead of forswearing the practice of disappearances, President Bush pushed for and obtained authorization from Congress to go forward. In the Military Commissions Act (MCA) of 2006, Congress revised the scope of the War Crimes Act to limit it only to "grave breaches" of Common Article 3 of the Geneva Convention, thus leaving unspecified a realm of Common Article 3 violations that are not criminal. (Prior to the MCA, any violation of Common Article 3 was a felony). Upon signing the MCA into law, President Bush noted that one of its salutary effects would be the reopening of the CIA's secret detention centers. In this instance, a fundamental human rights violation was defended on the ground that it "worked," and Congress was asked to give its blessing to the practice, and obliged.

The extensive secrecy surrounding much counterterrorism policy makes it difficult to know the full extent of human rights violations that may be being committed in the name of national security, or to gauge the reaction of states to human rights complaints about their practices. For example, the Bush administration has received substantial criticism from human rights groups regarding its practice of "renditions," in which it abducts individuals from one country and takes them to a third country for interrogation. In many documented instances, the recipient country has been known to employ torture in interrogating suspects, and it appears that the very purpose of the rendition is to permit such tactics to be employed. In one of the most renowned cases, for example, the United States intercepted Maher Arar, a Canadian citizen, while he was changing planes at John F. Kennedy Airport in New York, en route to his home in Canada, and then deported him to Syria, where he was held without charges for more than a year and tortured.[24] What possible reason could the United States have for taking a Canadian citizen en route to his home country and forcibly redirecting him to Syria, other than the fact that Canada does not have a record of torturing its suspects, while Syria does? Yet because this entire program is carried out in secret, and outside the law, little is known about how the Bush administration has reacted to the outcry that the few publicized accounts have elicited. Moreover, when the administration has been challenged in U.S. courts for this practice on constitutional and human rights grounds, it has defended it by arguing that the program itself is such a secret that no judicial review of its legality is even possible.[25]

The record, in other words, is mixed. The fear of terrorism has led countries often identified as major proponents of human rights—

such as the United States and the United Kingdom—to compromise on the commitments that human rights treaties demand. At the same time, such compromises have had little demonstrable positive results in terms of thwarting terrorist attacks, while prompting widespread criticism throughout the world. That criticism has fed an anti-American sentiment that has never been higher. And that anti-Americanism in turn fuels the recruitment efforts of al Qaeda and its associates. When the photographs of torture and abuse at Abu Ghraib first appeared, some politicians in Washington expressed concern for the victims of the abuse depicted there. But everyone immediately identified the images as a disaster for the United States' image around the world, and, thereby, for the war on terror. That reaction may have been most acute with respect to the Abu Ghraib photographs—but the phenomenon is more generalizable. Each time the United States, the United Kingdom, or some other country compromises on the fundamental commitments of human rights, it produces a backlash that, in the long term, can only make the West more vulnerable to the very terrorism it fears most.

When Israeli Supreme Court Justice Aharon Barak wrote that a democracy must fight terrorism "with one hand tied behind its back," he went on to say that this was a strength, not a weakness, in the democratic state's arsenal.

> Even so, a democracy has the upper hand. The rule of law and the liberty of an individual constitute important components in its understanding of security. At the end of the day, they strengthen its spirit and this strength allows it to overcome its difficulties.[26]

Some might dismiss Justice Barak's views as overly optimistic. His career was forged in a long-term terrorist conflict, but talk about "spirit" can seem terribly abstract when one faces the threat of a large-scale terrorist attack. Yet terrorists are in the end aiming at their enemy's "spirit," and it may well be that adherence to the human rights principles that characterize a liberal democracy is a critical element in withstanding the effects of inevitable terrorist attacks.

Perhaps more to the point, however, the aftermath of 9/11 suggests that the democratic state confronting a terrorist foe must adhere to human rights not only to strengthen its own spirit, but to maintain its standing in the world community. Wholly apart from their effect on the spirit of the national community, human rights norms play a major role in how the rest of the world views the state's response to terror. The very fact that the most powerful nation in the world, confronting a relatively small terrorist group with few state backers, has had to retreat as much as the United States has on its counterterrorism policies, suggests that the human rights revolution of the past sixty years has indeed taken hold in important and resilient ways.

Endnotes

1. Human Rights Watch, *World Report 2007*, available at http://hrw.org/wr2k7; Nora Boustany, "U.S. Has Lost Credibility on Rights, Group Asserts," *Washington Post* (Jan. 12, 2007) A10.
2. Human Rights Watch reported in its *World Report 2003*:

    Washington's subordination of human rights to the campaign against terrorism has also bred a copycat phenomenon. By waving the anti-terrorism banner, governments such as Uzbekistan seemed to feel that they had license to persecute religious dissenters, while governments such as Russia, Israel, and China seemed to feel freer to intensify repression in Chechnya, the West Bank, and Xinjiang. Tunisia stepped up trying civilians on terrorism charges before military courts that flagrantly disregard due-process rights. Claiming that asylum-seekers can be a "pipeline for terrorists" entering the country, Australia imposed some of the tightest restrictions on asylum in the industrialized world. Facing forces on the right and left that have been designated terrorists, Colombia's new president, Álvaro Uribe, tried to permit warrantless searches and wiretaps and to restrict the movement of journalists (until the country's highest court ruled these measures unconstitutional).

    In sub-Saharan Africa, some of the mimicry took on absurd proportions. Ugandan President Yoweri Museveni shut down the leading independent newspaper for a week in October because it was allegedly promoting terrorism (it had reported a military defeat by the government in its battle against the Lord's Resistance Army rebel group). In June, Liberian President Charles Taylor declared three of his critics—the editor of a local newspaper and two others—to be "illegal combatants" who would be tried for terrorism in a military court. Eritrea justified its lengthy detention of the founder of the country's leading newspaper by citing Washington's widespread detentions. Zimbabwean President Robert Mugabe justified the November 2001 arrest of six journalists as terrorists because they wrote stories about political violence in the country. Elsewhere, even former Yugoslav President Slobodan Milosevic defended himself against war-crimes charges by contending that abusive troops under his command had merely been combating terrorism.

    Human Rights Watch, *World Report 2003*, Introduction; available at: http://hrw.org/wr2k3/introduction.html

3. The decision the U.K. seeks to overturn is *Chaha v. United Kingdom*, l22414/93 [1996] ECHR 54 (15 November 1996). See Human Rights Watch, *Dangerous Ambivalence: U.K. Policy on Torture since 9/11* (November 2006), available at: http://www.hrw.org/backgrounder/eca/uk1106/
4. Conor Gearty, *Can Human Rights Survive?* (Cambridge: Cambridge University Press, 2006).
5. Kim Lane Scheppele, "The International State of Emergency," paper given at the annual meetings of the American Sociological Association (August 12, 2006), Montreal, Canada.
6. Public Committee Against Torture v. State of Israel, HCJ No. 5100/94, (July 15, 1999), at p. 27, available at: http:\\elyon1.court.gov.il/files_eng/94/000/051/a09/9405100.ao9.pdf
7. Memorandum from Jay S. Bybee, Assistant Attorney General, Department of Justice Office of Legal Counsel, to Alberto R. Gonzales, Counsel to the President, Re: *Standards of Conduct for Interrogation under 18 U.S.C. §§ 2340–2340A* (Aug. 1, 2002), at 31.
8. Brian Ross, "History of an Interrogation Technique: Water Boarding", ABC News (Nov. 29, 2005), available at: http://abcnews.go.com/WNT/Investigation/story?id=1356870
9. Dana Priest, "Justice Dept. Memo Says Torture 'May Be Justified'," *Washington Post* (June 13, 2004) A1.
10. Memorandum for James B. Comey, Deputy Attorney General, Re: Legal Standards Applicable Under 18 U.S.C. §§ 2340–2340A (Dec. 30, 2004).
11. Memorandum for Alberto Gonzales, Counsel to the President, Re: Standards of Conduct for Interrogation under 18 U.S.C. §§ 2340–2340A, Aug. 2, 2002; reprinted in Mark Danner, *Torture and Truth: America, Abu Ghraib and the War on Terror* (New York: New York Review Books, 2004), 115.
12. Republic of Ireland v. United Kingdom, European Court of Human Rights, Series A, No. 25, 1979–90, 2 ECHR 25.
13. Detainee Treatment Act of 2005, Pub. L. No. 109–148 119 Stat. 2680 (2005).
14. Ibid.
15. A v. Secretary of State for the Home Department, [2004] UKHL 56.
16. Charkaoui v. Canada (Citizenship and Immigration), 2007 SCC 9 (February 22, 2007).
17. See, e.g., Lord Johan Steyn, "Guantanamo Bay: The Legal Black Hole", Twenty-Seventh F.A. Mann Lecture (November 25, 2003), available at: http://www.statewatch.org/news/2003/nov/guantanamo.pdf; Katerina Ossenova, "U.K. Attorney General Repeats Call for Guantanamo Bay Closure on U.S. Visit", *Jurist* (September 17, 2006), available at: http://jurist.law.pitt.edu/paperchase/2006/09/uk-attorney-general-repeats-call-for.php
18. Rasul v. Bush, 542 U.S. 466 (2004).
19. White House press conference (June 14, 2006), available at: http://www.whitehouse.gov/news/releases/2006/06/20060614.html

20. Executive Order 13,224 (September 23, 2001).
21. Humanitarian Law Project v. Gonzales, 380 F. Supp. 2d 1134 (C.D. Cal. 2005); Humanitarian Law Project v. United States Dept. of the Treasury, 2006 U.S. Dist. LEXIS 87753 (C.D. Cal. November 21, 2006).
22. "E.U. to query U.S. 'secret prisons'," BBC News (November 22, 2005), available at: http://news.bbc.co.uk/1/hi/world/europe/4461470.stm. European Commission Report on CIA Secret Prisons Released, available at: http://www.talkleft.com/story/2006/04/26/355/62134
23. White House, Office of the Press Secretary, "President Bush Discusses Creation of Military Commissions to Try Suspected Terrorists" (September 6, 2006), available at: http://www.whitehouse.gov/news/releases/2006/09/ 20060906-3.html
24. Canadian Commission of Inquiry into the Actions of Canadian Officials Relating to Maher Arar, "Arar Commission Releases its Findings on the Handling of the Maher Arar Case", press release (September 18, 2006), available at: http://www.ararcommission.ca/eng/ReleaseFinal_Sept18.pdf
25. El Masri v. Tenet, 437 F. Supp.2d 530 (E.D. Va. 2006).
26. Public Committee Against Torture v. State of Israel, HCJ No. 5100/94, July 15, 1999, at p. 27, available at: http:\\elyon1.court.gov.il/files_eng/94/000/051/a09/9405100.ao9.pdf

Index

7/7 attacks (2005), 3, 9, 34, 36–7, 104, 137, 164
9/11 attacks (2001), 1, 3, 8–9, 17, 33, 37, 41, 50, 66, 72–4, 76–9, 80, 82, 102–3, 138, 157–9, 161–2, 164, 167

A

abassiya (group feeling), 30
Abu Ghraib prison, 4, 20, 167
Adams, Gerry (Sinn Féin), 93–4, 97
Afghan Northern Alliance, 75
Afghanistan, 1–2, 15, 34, 37, 48, 65, 74–6, 79, 138
African Union, 22–3
Air India attack (1985), 71
AKP (Turkish Islamic Party), 44, 47, 66, 67
al Qaeda, 1, 27, 29, 32–4, 66, 72–6, 82, 92–3, 98, 137–8, 159, 165, 167
al-Azm, Sadiq Jalal, 53
al-Farabi, Abu Nasr, 54
Algeria, 18, 21, 55, 70, 71
al-hall huwa al-Islami (Islam is the solution), 46, 49
al-Jazeera television, 49
al-Mahdi army, 43, 47
almujtamaa ammadani (civil society), 30
al-Nahda (Tunisia), 55
al-Qaradawi, Yusuf, 49, 56
al-Sadr, Muqtada, 43, 47
al-Sirat al-Mustaqim (Straight Path), 63–4
al-Zawahiri, Ayman (al Qaeda), 98
Amnesty International, 157
Anglo-Irish Agreement, 127–8
Angola, 70
Annan, Kofi, Secretary-General, 14, 38, 83–4
anti-globalization movement, 36
anti-Shah struggle, 65
Anti-terrorism Crime and Security Act 2005 (UK), 103
appeals to UK courts, 102, 110, 112–13, 119, 122–3, 130–1, 135, 138
Arab-Israeli war (1948), 69
Arab-Israeli peace process, 98
Argentina, 10, 165
Aristide, Jean Bertrand (Haiti), 20
Aristotle, 45
Armagh Four (Diplock case), 117–18
assets, freezing of, 79, 85

Association of South East Asian
    Nations (ASEAN), 23
Aum Shinrikyo (Japan), 93
Australia, 35–6
authoritarian-liberal continuum, 16
autocracy in Arab states, 23, 45, 52,
    65, 68

B
Baathism, 48
Badr Brigades (Iraq), 43
Baghdad attack on UN (2003), 7, 69
Bahrain, 66
Baker Report (UK), 119, 126, 128
Barak, Aharon (Israeli judge), 159,
    167
Basque Homeland and Freedom. *See*
    ETA
Beechmount Five (Diplock case), 118
Belarus, 22
Belfast Agreement (1998), 94
Berlin nightclub attack (1986), 74
Bernadotte, Folke, Count, 7, 69
Beslan school attack, 77
Bildt, Carl (Swedish minister), 46
bin Laden, Osama, 1, 2–3, 27, 34, 64,
    66, 74–6, 82, 98
Birmingham Six (Diplock), 130, 135
Black September group, 70
Blair, Tony (UK PM), 124, 164
Bolivia, 21
Bosnia, 65
Boutrab, Abbas (Diplock case), 137
Brazil, 18
Brooks, Omar (Abu Izzadeen), 3
budgetary pressures on UN, 72
Burma, 23
Bush administration, 5, 13, 17, 19, 23,
    41, 44, 81, 130, 138, 159,
    161, 163, 165–6
Bush, President George W., 17, 20,
    22–4, 33–4, 163, 165–6
Bush, Laura, First Lady, 20

C
Canadian government, 163, 166
Canadian Supreme Court, 162–3
Caraher, Michael (Diplock case),
    111–12, 122–3
Carlile, Lord, reports by, 130–2, 136

Casement Park trials (Diplock), 123
Catholics (NI), 106–7, 113, 118, 127
Centre for the Study of Human Rights
    (UK), 158
Chavez, President Hugo, 18, 20
Chechnya, 65
Chile, 22
China, 18, 74
CIA (US), 159, 165–6
Citizens Against Terror (CAT), 37–8
Civil Authorities (Special Powers) Acts
    1922–43 (UK), 107
civil liberties, 8, 34, 36, 101, 124, 126
civil rights, 14, 20, 104–5, 138
civil society, 6, 15, 18, 23, 27–38,
    46–7, 55, 67
civility, 27, 29–30
clientelism, 48
Clinton, President Bill, 72
Club de Madrid, 3, 37–8, 45, 52, 55,
    84
coercive interrogation, 105–6, 116,
    135, 138, 158–60, 162
Cold War, 16, 18, 34, 74–5
Colombia, 18, 95
colonial rule, 7, 48, 70–1
Committee on the Administration of
    Justice (UK), 134
Community of Democracies, 14, 22
confessions, 79, 102, 107, 113,
    116–18, 121, 124, 128,
    135, 138,
Confucian values and democracy, 6
Constitutional Court (Palestine), 47
control orders (UK), 10, 104, 158
Convention Against Torture (CAT),
    79, 160–1
corruption, 23, 48
Costa Rica, 85
Cote d'Ivoire, 16
Council on Foreign Relations, 21
counter-terrorism, 36, 67, 80
    and the judiciary, 101–38
    counter-productivity of measures, 5,
        13, 17, 21, 115, 159, 167
    role of civil society, 27–38
    United Nations conventions, 73
    measures, 35–6, 76–8, 103, 108,
        133, 168
Courts Martial (Israel), 102–3

Criminal Evidence (Northern Ireland) Order 1988, 121
Criminal Evidence (Northern Ireland) Order 1999, 121
Criminal Justice Act 2003 (UK), 103–4, 131–2
Criminal Justice (Northern Ireland) Order 1996 (UK), 115
Criminal Justice (Terrorism and Conspiracy) Act 1998 (UK), 124
Criminal Procedure and Investigations Act 1996 (UK), 115
"Crisis of Democracy" meeting, 50–1
Cuba, 18. *See also* Guantánamo Bay
"cultural borrowing", 44, 55
cultural relativism, 49
"culture matters", 51, 56

D

Dar al-Islam (Abode of Islam), 64–5
Da'wa Party (Iraq), 43
dawla Islamiyya (Islamic state), 50
de Tocqueville, Alexis, 28, 31–2
debt relief assistance, 16
Declaration on Measures to Eliminate International Terrorism (UN, 1994), 71–2
decommissioning (NI), 133–4
democracy
  and civil society, 6, 28–9, 55, 67
  and Islamism, 6, 42, 51–2, 54, 56–7, 66
  as universal value, 5, 14, 52, 54
  benefits to citizens, 16
  definitions of, 14
  electoral process versus political culture, 42, 55
  externally imposed, 5, 15, 49
  fighting for, 18
  growth from within, 5, 15, 19, 21, 49
  human rights, 3, 13
  in Madrid Agenda, 3–4
  in practice, 14
  Muslims living under, 67
  quality of, 14
  resilience of, 16
  successful transition, 6
  to inhibit terrorism, 5
  trends in, 16–17
democracy promotion, 13, 35, 42, 50
  and Iraq war, 5, 19
  by Bush administration, 10, 13, 20, 41
  by European Union, 5, 44
  by international community, 13, 15–16
  by United Kingdom, 10
  guidelines for, 17–24
  role of civil assistance, 23, 35
  United States' interest in, 17
"democratic peace", 17, 51
democratic rule, 7, 19, 48–9, 99
Democratic Unionist Party (DUP), 108, 133, 135–6
derogation, 78–9, 104
despotism, 4, 56, 114
detention without trial, 10, 20, 34–5, 78–80, 103–5, 108, 116–18, 135, 138, 157–8, 162–6
Devlet Güğenlik Mahkemesi (DGM, Turkish courts), 102, 103, 138
Devlin, Bernadette, 107–108
dictatorship, 41, 43, 49–50, 54
Diplock, Lord, background of, 105–106
Diplock Inquiry (1972), 106–108
Diplock Courts (UK), 102–38
  abolition, calls for, 126–8
  "adversarial deficit", 113, 115
  and adversarial system, 108–10, 114
  and Islamist threats, 137
  and juror intimidation, 102, 107–9, 113, 115, 126, 131, 136–8
  and non-terrorist offences, 102, 104, 113, 125–6, 129, 132, 136, 137
  and proscribed organizations, 124–5
  appeal mechanism, 102, 110, 112–13
  Attorney General's role, 125, 128–9, 134
  bail applications, 106–7, 128, 130
  cases, 117–8, 111–12, 122–3, 130, 135, 137

certification mechanism, 125–6, 129
community, exclusion of, 118
comparison with jury trials, 110
criminalization as strategy, 108–109
criticism of, 130–1
evidentiary standards, 102, 113, 116–26
evolution of, 102
fairness, perceptions of, 108, 113, 116
informal reforms of, 128–31
Irish Government, influence of, 127
judges' experience of, 130
judge's multiple roles, 110, 128
legacy of, 135
legitimacy of, 102, 116, 130, 135, 138
maltreatment, sanction of, 116–17
origins, 102
"problem solving" approach, 110
safeguards, 109–13
strengths, 108–13
subsequent reduction of scope, 109
support for retention, 135–6
uncorroborated evidence, 116
vetting of dispositions, 109–10
weaknesses, 102, 113–26
written judgements, 110
Direct Rule (Northern Ireland), 104, 108
"disappearances" under Bush, 10, 157, 165–6
dissidents, 20, 31, 98
double standards, 84, 124, 126, 157, 162
Downing Street attack (1991), 91

E
Eastern Europe, 22, 31–2
education in civil society, 15–16, 36–7
Egypt, 2, 6, 13, 20, 42–3, 46–8, 55, 66, 74
elections, 5, 13–15, 19, 21, 28, 41–3, 46–7, 93, 96–7, 99
"enemy combatants", 4, 20–1, 161–3
Enlightenment, 53

Erbakan, Necmettin (Turkish PM), 67
ETA (Basque), 77, 91–3, 97, 99
European Convention on Human Rights (ECHR), 107, 117, 122, 124, 131, 158, 162
European Court of Human Rights, 104, 122, 131, 157–8, 160
European Court of Justice, 157
European Union (EU), 5, 8–9, 15–16, 22, 43–4, 66, 165

F
Fadhila Party (Turkey), 67
Falconer, Lord, 103
FARC (Colombian revolutionaries), 95
Faul, Father Dennis, 104, 106
fatwa (bin Laden), 2–3
Financial Action Taskforce, 85
financial aid to states, 16, 83
financial support of terror, 2, 73, 76, 81, 158, 164–5
FIS (Algeria), 55
freedom, 114
and Islam, 44–5
fundamental/universal, 29, 78, 161
limits on, 103
of association/assembly, 10, 14, 28, 54, 157
of expression, 14, 54, 157
of faith/religion, 47, 79
of press freedom, 14, 17, 28
political, 53–4
United States' view of, 17, 21
"freedom agenda" (Bush), 13
Freedom House, 16
fundamentalism, 6, 36, 42, 46–8, 50

G
G-77 democracies, 18
Geneva Conventions, 4, 79, 159, 165–6
Georgia, 16
Global Civil Society yearbooks, 29
"glorification" of terrorism, 164
Good Friday Agreement 1998 (Northern Ireland), 8, 131
Greek influence on Arabs, 44–5, 53–5
Guantánamo Bay base, 4, 20, 78–9, 130, 162–3, 165

Index 175

Guildford Four (Diplock case), 130, 135
guilt by association, 165

H
habeas corpus, 9, 102
Habermas, Jürgen, 30–1
Haiti, 20
hakimiyyat Allah (God's rule), 43, 45, 47, 49
Haldane Society (UK), 126
Hamas (Palestine), 5, 29, 33, 43–4, 46–7, 55, 57, 66, 93, 99
Hamdan v. Rumsfeld (US case), 165–6
Hariri, Rafik (Lebanon PM), 75
Hazaras (Shiite minority), 2
hegemony of West/US, 18, 23, 65
Hellenism, 44–5, 53–5
Hezbollah (Lebanon), 5, 55, 93, 99
Hitler, Adolf, 47
Hizb al-Tahrir (Jordan), 43
Holmes Cash and Carry (NI case) 129
house arrest, 10, 104, 158
hulul mustawradah (imported solutions), 45, 56
Human Rights Act 1998 (UK), 104
human rights, 4, 10, 18–19, 32, 35, 36–7, 71–2
  abuses of, 20, 78–9, 159, 161
  and challenge of terror, 157–68
  and UN Security Council, 77–80
  in Arab world, 47–8, 50–1, 54
  incorporation in domestic law, 117, 157
  promotion of, 13, 17, 20
  resilience of norms, 159, 161–2, 168
  under Bush, 20, 78–9, 157, 159–63, 166
Human Rights Watch, 157–8
humanitarian law, 37, 77, 159
Hungary, 22
Hurd, Douglas (UK minister), 119, 128
Hussein, Saddam, 43, 51, 69

I
Ibn Khaldūn Center, 55
Ibrahim, Saad Eddin, 6, 45, 55, 63–8
"illiberal democracy", 6
"imported solutions", 45, 49
in camera proceedings, 109, 115

incentives
  to promote democracy, 15, 23, 36
  to discourage terrorists, 97–9
incitement to terrorism, 77, 104
Independent Task Force, 21–2
India, 18, 22, 29, 48, 71, 74
Indochina, 70
Indonesia, 6, 34, 45, 55, 65–7
inference in judicial proceedings, 102, 111–12, 121–4, 131, 138
informer system (Northern Ireland), 116, 118–20, 127, 131
"innocent until proven guilty", 116, 138
Inter-American Democratic Charter, 20
International Center for Democracy Transition, 22
International Covenant on Civil and Political Rights (ICCPR), 79
International Institute for Democracy and Electoral Assistance, 14
International Monetary Fund, 23–4, 81
International Republic Institute, 22
Internment. *See* detention
intimidation of witnesses/jurors, 102, 107–9, 113, 115–16, 118–19, 126, 128, 131–2, 134, 136–8
Iran, 44, 46, 47, 51, 73
Iraq, 5, 15, 19, 20, 48, 49, 52, 65, 69
  constitution, 48, 52
  democratization, 21, 41–2, 47
  elections, 41–2, 44
  expulsion from Kuwait, 74
  human rights groups, 37
  internal politics, 43, 55
  internal strife, 33–4
  occupation of, 13, 19
  opposition to war, 36
  war, 19, 41, 50, 51
Irish Republican Army (IRA), 8, 91–4, 97, 99, 105, 123, 129, 133, 160
Islam
  all-encompassing nature, 63
  and democracy, 6, 41–57
  and Hellenism, 45

and Islamism, 41–57
as "perfect" religion, 63
classical, 30
"Golden Age", 64
mobilizing power of, 65
"of despotism", 56
struggles in name of, 65
Islamic Action Front (Jordan), 55
Islamic Conference, 85
Islamic Group, 2
Islamic
  groups opposed to violence, 66
  metaphor, power of, 65
  perceptions of democracies, 6, 27
  rationalism, need for, 54
  supremacy, 56
Islamism, 6, 41–57
  and democracy, 42, 52
  and Islam, 42, 45, 50, 52
  and religious fundamentalism, 47–8
  institutional versus jihadist, 43, 50, 52, 56
  redefinition of shari'a, 44
  totalitarianism of, 43, 47, 50
Islamist
  governments, 42
  Diplock case, 137
  parties, 21–2, 43–4
  rejection of civil society, 46
  terrorism against Algeria, 71
  view of rule of law, 51
Israel, 8, 43, 91, 96
  Courts Martial, 9, 102–103, 138
  hostility towards, 7
  military action, 34, 65
  opinion, 71
  violence against, 93, 99
Israeli-Palestinian conflict, 36, 43, 84–5
Italian cruise ships, attacks on, 70
Italy, 29, 121
Izzadeen, Abu (Omar Brooks), 3

J
Jamaica, 18
Japan, 93
jihad, 43, 47, 65, 67
  and Islam, 3, 44, 50, 56
  global, 51, 56

jihadist
  organizations, 5
  versus "institutional" Islamists, 43
  violence/terrorism, 71, 77, 86
jihadists, 5–6, 46, 52, 56, 138
Joint Declaration 2003 (United Kingdom and Republic of Ireland), 133
Jordan, 21, 43, 45, 66
juror intimidation, 9, 102, 107, 109, 113, 131, 137–8
jury trial, 102, 106, 108–10, 113–16, 126, 131, 133, 136

K
Kant, Immanuel, 32
Karimov, Islom (Uzbekistan), 20
Kashmir, 65
Khadduri, Majid, 54
Khaldūn, Ibn, 30, 35, 55
Khamenei, Ayatollah (Iran), 73
King, Tom (NI Secretary), 127–8
Korea, 6, 22
Kuwait, 66, 74
Kyrgyzstan, 16

L
Latin America, 10, 21, 30–1, 32
law enforcement, 3–5, 35, 81, 86. *See also* rule of law
Law Lords (UK), 104, 162
Lebanon, 13, 49, 55, 65, 75
liberty, 4, 17, 53, 103
Libya, 74, 76
Lithuania, 22
Locke, John, 4–5
Lockerbie bombing, 74
London attacks (2005), 3, 9, 34, 36–7, 104, 137, 164

M
McCain Amendment (US), 161
Madrid Agenda, 3–5, 10
Madrid attacks, (2004), 3, 34, 41, 51, 77
Magna Carta (1215), 103, 114
Maguire Seven (Diplock case), 130
Mali, 22
martyrdom, 64, 67
Mauritania, 23

Mazar-e-Sharif (Afghanistan), 2
media in civil society, 15–16, 36
migration, European fear of, 44
Military Commissions Act 2006 (US), 166
Military Tribunals (US), 9, 103, 138, 162
Mill, John Stuart, 4–5
Millennium Challenge Account, 23–4
Miranda v. Arizona (US case), 122
Moore, Barrington, 54–5
Morocco, 65–7
Mubarak, Preseident Hosni, 20, 74
Mugabe, President Robert, 18
mukhabarat (secret police), 55
Munich Olympics (1972), 7, 70, 74
Murray v. U.K. (ECHR case), 122
Musharaff, General Pervez, 20
Muslim Brothers, 42–3, 47, 49, 55, 64, 66–7
Muslim militancy, 63–8

N
Nasserism, 48
National Council for Civil Liberties (UK), 126
National Democratic Institute (US), 22
National Endowment for Democracy, 23
Nazi Party (NSDAP), 47
negotiations with terrorists, 8–9, 43, 91–100
neutrality of judiciary (NI), 106
Nicaragua, 21
Nicholson, Lord Justice, 106, 112
nizam Islami (Islamic system of government), 43
Nonaligned Movement (NAM), 18
"non-believers" as targets for terror, 33
Nongovernmental Organizations (NGOs), 5-6, 27–9, 31, 35, 37, 157
non-Muslim "other", 64–5
North Atlantic Treaty Organization (NATO), 70
North Ossetia, 77
Northern Ireland (NI), 8–9, 93–4, 97, 102–38. *See also* Diplock Courts
Northern Ireland Assembly (1998), 94
Northern Ireland Civil Rights Association, 106
Northern Ireland (Emergency Provisions) Act 1973 (EPA), 108, 117, 119, 121, 128, 131, 133
Northern Ireland Human Rights Commission, 120, 134
NSDAP (Nazi Party), 47

O
Office of Legal Counsel (US), 159–60
On Liberty (Mill), 4
"one man, one vote, one time", 21–2
Operation Demetrius (NI), 104
operational role of UN, 72, 80
Orange Revolution, 22
Organization of American States, 22
organized crime (Northern Ireland), 109, 119–20, 136
Oslo Accords (1993), 8, 71, 91

P
Paisley, Reverend Ian, 108, 133
Pakistan, 16, 20, 75
Palacio, Anna (Spanish minister), 46
Palestine, 7–8, 13, 34, 37, 41–3, 46–7, 49, 55, 65, 84–5, 99
Palestine Liberation Organization (PLO), 8, 71, 91, 94
Palestinian National Authority (PNA), 43, 47
Pan Am flight 103 (1988), 74
"paper factory" criticism of UN, 73
paramilitary organizations (Northern Ireland), 120, 126, 129, 132–7
parliaments in democracies, 14, 48
particularism, 49
Partisan resistance in World War II, 70
peace processes
 Arab-Israeli, 98
 Colombian, 95
 Northern Ireland, 94, 119–20, 126, 132
Philippines, 65
pluralism, 21, 47, 49, 54, 56
Poland, 22

political class and civil society, 36
political culture, 42, 45, 47, 51, 54, 56
political Islam. *See* Islamism
political rights in democracies, 14, 21, 79
politics, conflation with religion, 44
Polity IV index, 16
Popular Front for the Liberation of Palestine (PFLP), 94
Portugal, 22
poverty, alleviation of, 32, 37
"pragmatic idealism" (US policy), 17
press freedom in democracies, 14, 17, 28
Prevention of Terrorism (Temporary Provisions) Act 1974 (UK), 117
Prevention of Terrorism Act 2005 (UK), 104, 131
Protestants (NI), 94, 106, 108, 113
Provisional IRA, 124, 129, 132–4
public interest immunity, 124

Q
Qur' an (Holy Book), 44, 63

R
radio to counter extremism, 37
Reagan, President Ronald, 74
"realist" school of foreign policy, 17
reason
    and Enlightenment, 53
    common law of, 4
    in civil society, 27, 32, 35
Red Army Faction (West Germany), 92
Red Brigades (Italy), 92
Red Cross, 79
refugee law, 77
"regime change", 41
R. v. Caraher (Diplock case), 111–13, 122–3
R. v. Gibson (UK case), 112
religion, conflation with politics, 44
religious schools, 36
rendition under Bush, 158, 162, 166
Republic of Ireland, 124, 126–8, 133
    Joint Declaration 2003, 133
    Special Criminal Courts, 9, 102–103

Rice, Condoleeza (US Secretary), 17
right to silence (Northern Ireland), 121–4
rights of individuals, 29, 78, 161. *See also* freedom
Rome attack, 70
Roosevelt, President Theodore, 19
Rousseau, Jean-Jacques, 32
Royal Ulster Constabulary (RUC), 117–18
rule of law, 3, 5–6, 10, 14, 17, 19, 23, 29–30, 35, 51–2, 102, 109, 126, 134–5, 138, 167
Russia, 16, 37, 65, 77

S
Saab, Hassan, 56
Said, Edward, 53
Saudi Arabia, 1, 18, 21, 27, 34
SDLP (Northern Ireland), 130, 133–4
Serbia, 37
shari'a (Islamic law) 30, 42–8, 50, 52–4, 56, 63
shari'atization, 44–5, 48, 52
Shi'i Islamists (Iraq), 43
Shiite minority (Iraq), 2, 33
"shoot to kill" policy (NI), 131
Sierra Leone, 37
Sikh terrorism, 71
silence (legal status in NI)
    inferences from, 102, 112–3, 122–3, 131, 138
    right to, 121–4
Sinn Féin, 132–3
Six Days War (1967), 45, 49
Slovakia, 22
"social capital" in civil society, 28
Society of Muslim Brotherhood. *See* Muslim Brothers
Somalia, 76
South Africa, 18, 71
South Korea, 6
Soviet Union, 16, 64–5, 74
Spain, 41, 46, 77, 91, 97
Special Criminal Courts (Republic of Ireland), 102–103, 127, 138
stiftungs (German political grants), 23
Stormont (NI parliament), 104–5
Sudan, 74, 76
suffrage in democracies, 14

Index

suicide bombers, 33, 67
Sunna (Mohammedan traditions), 63
Sunni Muslims (Iraq), 7, 43, 52
supergrasses (NI), 116, 118–20, 127, 131
Supreme Coucil for the Islamic Revolution in Iraq, 43, 55
surveillance, 20, 34, 53, 55
Swedish Institute (Istanbul), 67
Syria, 18, 48, 75, 81, 94, 166

T
Taiwan, 6
Taliban, 2, 67, 75, 82, 159
Taliban/al Qaeda network, 1–2, 75
Tamil terrorism, 71
technical assistance and incentives, 16, 72, 82–3
terrorism
    as threat to human rights, 71
    cost of defense against, 8–9
    definition, search for, 73, 83
    discouragement by democracies, 7
    export beyond national borders, 70
    financing of, 73, 157, 164
    Jewish, 69
    psychology of, 32
    radical Islamic, 17
    use to legitimize repression, 35
    where civil society weak, 32–3
Terrorism Act 1999 (UK), 133
Terrorism Act 2000 (UK), 131, 133–4
Terrorism Act 2006 (UK), 104
Terrorism (Northern Ireland) Bill 2005–6 (UK), 134
terrorists
    atrocities, 2, 107, 120, 132, 135
    internal cohesion, 93
    "nihilist" versus "traditional" 92
    negotiating with, 91–100
    state sponsored, 94
    view of violence, 93
Thatcher, Margaret (UK PM), 127
theocracy, 45–6, 68
Togo, 23
torture, 10, 34, 78–80, 117, 157–61, 166–7
totalitarianism, 31, 43, 47, 50
Treatise on Civil Government (Locke), 4

Troubles (Northern Ireland), 104, 109
Tuni meeting (1980), 53
Turkey, 6, 9, 34, 44, 46–7, 49, 65–7, 102, 138

U
Ukraine, 16, 22
Ulster Defense Association (UDA), 94, 120
Ulster Volunteer Force (UVF), 132, 134
Umma (perfect community), 63–4
Union de Transport Aériens (UTA) flight 772 attack, 74
Unionist control of Northern Ireland, 107
United Kingdom (UK)
    counter-terrorism legislation, 103, 158, 162
    derogation, 104
    erosion of human rights, 164
    interrogation techniques, 105, 138, 160
    Joint Declaration 2003, 133
    miscarriages of justice, 113, 118, 130, 135, 138
    mistreatment of detainees, 105, 113
    relationships with Republic of Ireland, 127–8, 133
    single-judge tribunals, 106, 114, 126–7, 130, 133, 137
    three-judge tribunals, 126–8, 136
    witness protection, 120–1. *See also* Northern Ireland
United Nations (UN), 2, 3, 14, 18, 164
    and terrorism, 69–86
United Nations General Assembly, 7, 14, 70–3, 75, 78, 80, 83–4
United Nations Democracy Fund, 22
United Nations Development Program (UNDP), 46, 48, 51
United Nations High Commission for Human Rights, 78–80
United Nations Office on Drugs and Crime (Terrorist Prevention Branch), 72, 80, 82–3, 85
United Nations Security Council, 7, 35, 72–3, 77, 79–80, 82–3, 85–6, 164–5
    Counter-Terrorism Committee (CTC), 76, 80–2, 83, 85

Counter-Terrorism Committee
Executive Directorate,
81–2
resoluteness of, 74–7
Resolution 1267 (1999), 75, 82
Resolution 1373 (2001), 73, 76,
80–1
Sanctions Committee, 82
United States pressure on, 157–8
United States (US)
abduction of Canadian subject, 166
charge of hypocrisy, 20
counter-productivity of measures, 5,
13, 17, 21, 159, 167
counter-terrorism measures, 101,
138
covert operations, 21
"disappearances", 10, 157, 165–6
financial blacklisting, 164
foreign policy, 13
human rights abuses, 20, 78–9, 159,
161
interference in Haiti/Venezuela, 20
leadership responsibilities, 22
national security interest, 17
national security policy, 20
opposition at United Nations, 18
pressure to collaborate with, 158
rendition of suspects, 158, 162, 166
secret designations, 164–5
secret reinterpretations, 160–2
target of jihad, 65
weakening of human rights, 157
witness protection in, 121
United States Congress, 23, 160–1, 166
United States Constitution, 101, 122,
160–2, 166
United States Department of Justice,
160–1
United States East Africa embassy
attack (1998), 72, 76
United States Supreme Court, 163,
165–6

Uruguay, 10
"us" versus "them", 18, 33–4
USAID, 20
Uzbekistan, 20

V
Venezuela, 16, 18, 20
victims of terrorism, 38, 51, 77, 84,
167
Vienna attack, 70
Vietnam, 20
voir dire (confessions in UK), 116–21

W
Waldheim, Kurt, Secretary-General, 70
war, conventional, 33
"war on terror", 10, 28, 32–4, 52, 78,
81, 157–9, 162, 165, 167
Wasat Party (Egypt), 55
Washington Post, 160, 165
"waterboarding", 159–60
"We are not Afraid" campaign (UK),
37
weapons of mass destruction, 36, 95
Whitelaw, William (UK minister), 105,
108
World Bank, 23
World Social Forum, 36
World Summit 2005, 14, 55, 77, 83–4
World Trade Center attack (1993), 71
World Trade Center and Pentagon
attacks (2001), 1, 3, 8–9,
17, 33, 37, 41, 50, 66, 72–4,
76–9, 80, 82, 102–103, 138,
157–9, 161–2, 164, 167
World Value Survey, 66
World War II, 70, 157

Y
Yemen, 21, 66

Z
Zimbabwe, 16, 18